D0103321

THE GLOBAL REFUGEE CRISIS

A Reference Handbook

THE GLOBAL REFUGEE CRISIS

A Reference Handbook

Gil Loescher
Ann Dull Loescher

CONTEMPORARY WORLD ISSUES

ABC-CLIO

Santa Barbara, California
Denver, Colorado
Oxford, England

Library of Congress Cataloging-in-Publication Data

Loescher, Gil.
The global refugee crisis : a reference handbook / Gil Loescher and Ann Dull Loescher.
p. cm. — (Contemporary world issues)
Includes bibliographical references and index.
1. Refugees. 2. Refugees—Services for. 3. Disaster relief. I. Loescher, Ann Dull. II. Title. III. Series.
HV640.L625 1994 362.87—dc20 94-25097

ISBN 0-87436-753-0

00 99 98 97 96 95 94 10 9 8 7 6 5 4 3 2 1

ABC-CLIO, Inc.
130 Cremona Drive, P.O. Box 1911
Santa Barbara, California 93116-1911

This book is printed on acid-free paper ♾.
Manufactured in the United States of America

This book is dedicated to refugees everywhere.
We must remember they are all individuals like ourselves.

Contents

Preface

IF ANYONE NEEDS TWO TERRIFYING EXAMPLES to illustrate the nature of today's refugee problem and the inadequacy of the current approach to dealing with this crisis, they can be found in Bosnia and Rwanda. In Bosnia, attempts by the United Nations to protect so-called safe areas call into question the very definition of the word *safe.* In Rwanda, the numbers alone tell the story: 2 million persons displaced, including over 1 million people who crossed into Zaire in one 48-hour period.

While those two examples happen to be the ones attracting the most headlines today, they are far from the only ones. Indeed, the 1990s represent a decade of displacement in which all regions of the world are experiencing forced population movements. Since the end of the Cold War, local wars and civil unrest in many regions of Africa, the Balkans, Southeast Asia, and the former Soviet Union have uprooted millions of people. International refugee issues are deeply embedded in the social, economic, and political conditions of our times and pose a range of difficult issues for the world community. The international community is ill-prepared to deal with the complexities of post–Cold War humanitarian issues. To be fully effective in managing these problems, the international system for protecting and assisting refugees will have to undertake major changes in its outlook, capabilities, and resource allocations, and the refugee issue will have to be factored into international political, economic, and security policies to a far greater extent than exists today.

As a result of rapid changes in international relations—in particular the end of the Cold War and the rise of internal conflicts, along with the merging of refugee issues with migration issues in the minds of both officials and the public—a consensus is emerging, internationally and nationally, on the need for giving more attention to forced population movements. Despite the growing recognition that refugee movements are a force for change and conflict in the post–Cold War era, there is little systematic thinking about the refugee issue and about what the implications of the new era are for assistance and protection of refugees both nationally and worldwide.

This book is designed to describe and discuss the current controversy concerning the handling of the global refugee problem by the United States government and the international community. It (1) discusses who refugees are and the transformation in the character and duration of refugee movements worldwide; (2) describes the international system that has developed a number of institutions, a body of international law, and a set of solutions to protect and assist those forced to flee their countries of origin; (3) analyzes the causes and consequences of refugee movements both for refugees and the countries involved; and (4) discusses the future challenges refugee movements pose and the evolving strategies of response to this rapidly growing global problem.

The text provides readers with sufficient background information about the global refugee issue to permit them to contribute to the debate about what needs to be done to respond to this complex problem. The first three chapters provide a historical account of the refugee issue, outlining the global dimensions of the problem and the political and economic strategies needed to deal with the issue in the future, as well as giving some biographical sketches of famous refugees, both past and present, and important activists for refugees' rights. Chapter 4 provides the principal statistics and legal documents regarding refugees. Chapters 5 through 7 offer resources for those who wish to pursue the study of refugees in more detail—a list of organizations already working on this issue and print and nonprint references on the topic. The book also includes a glossary of terms commonly used in the study of refugees and a listing of acronyms of the principal organizations and programs in the refugee field.

Acknowledgments

NUMEROUS ORGANIZATIONS AND INDIVIDUALS HAVE ASSISTED us and provided us the information necessary in the preparation of this book. We are particularly grateful to the United States Committee for Refugees (USCR) in Washington, D.C., which provided the information for the directory of organizations in chapter 5 and for many of the statistics that appear in chapter 4. Tom Argent and Ginny Hamilton of USCR were especially helpful in this regard. The Office of the United Nations High Commissioner for Refugees (UNHCR) in Geneva provided useful information on the chronology in chapter 2 and on electronic databases and videos in chapter 7. Both the UNHCR and the Secretariat for Inter-Governmental Consultations in Vienna also assisted with our compilation of statistics in chapter 4. We thank Robert DeVecchi of the International Rescue Committee, Philip Rudge of the European Council of Refugees, Arthur Helton of the Open Society Institute of the Soros Foundation, Beth Ferris of Church World Service, and Roger Winter of the USCR for providing biographical information for their entries in chapter 3. We gratefully acknowledge all of these organizations' and individuals' assistance and permission to reprint some of their material.

Finally, Joetta Schlabach of the Helen Kellogg Institute for International Studies at the University of Notre Dame typed two of these chapters and helped us a great deal with the handling of the statistical material. Linyu Sha of the Department of Government and International Studies at the University of Notre Dame provided some key research assistance.

1

Overview

ON EVERY CONTINENT PEOPLE ARE BEING FORCED from their homes, their communities, and their countries because of persecution or violence. Almost on a daily basis we see paraded across our television screens women and children forced out of their villages and deported to faraway places, while men are herded into detention centers where they are tortured and starved. Such images graphically illustrate the daily reality of millions of people, caught up in the crosscurrents of war, revolution, and famine, who have been forced into exile.

From the mid-1970s to 1994 there was an alarming increase in refugees. The total rose from 2.8 million in 1976 to 8.2 million in 1980. By August 1994, there were almost 20 million refugees. In addition, there were an estimated 25 million displaced people inside their own countries. Adding their numbers to those of refugees means that, in a world population of 5.5 billion, approximately 1 in every 130 people on earth has been forced into flight.

There are fears that many more people could become displaced, since ethnic and religious tensions previously suppressed by totalitarian regimes or East-West competition have been unleashed, potentially leading to violence.

In the 1990s, refugee emergencies have included the former Yugoslavia, where the number of displaced people rose from half a million in 1991 to more than 4 million in 1994; Somalia, where hundreds of thousands of people became refugees in neighboring Kenya, Ethiopia, and Yemen as a result of vicious interclan conflict; Armenia and Azerbaijan, where more than 1 million people have been displaced by the conflict over Nagorno-Karabakh; Tajikistan, where 60,000 people fled across borders and half a million have been uprooted by civil war between clans; Burma, where a quarter of a million Muslim refugees fled to poverty-stricken Bangladesh; Burundi and Rwanda, where well over 1 million refugees fled across borders because of intertribal war and mass slaughter; and Bhutan, where nearly 100,000 have fled ethnic strife.

It cannot be denied that a global refugee problem exists. In recent years, the international community has been confronted with one refugee emergency after another in rapid and sometimes overlapping succession. Refugee crises in Africa, Asia, the Middle East, the Balkans, and the former Soviet republics have strained the capacities of the United Nations almost to the breaking point. In particular, the Office of the United Nations High Commissioner for Refugees (UNHCR), the international community's principal institution for protecting and assisting refugees, has been stretched to the limit of its capacities.

Who Is a Refugee?

At a time when the numbers of refugees and asylum-seekers are growing rapidly, the question of precisely who is and who is not a refugee is one of considerable controversy. Presently, the principal international definition is the United Nations concept that was formulated in the immediate post–World War II period, largely in response to European refugee flows. According to the 1951 UN Convention Relating to the Status of Refugees, a refugee is "any person who, owing to a well-founded fear of being persecuted for reasons of race, religion, nationality, membership of a particular social group or political opinion, is outside the country of his nationality and is unable, or owing to such fear, is unwilling to avail himself of the protection of that country." Thus, the term *refugee* refers to a person who has fled across the physical borders of his homeland to seek refuge in another place and who, upon being granted refugee status, receives certain rights not available to other international migrants, including the right of resettlement and legal protection from deportation or forcible return to his country of origin (the so-called nonrefoulement protection). People requesting refugee status and seeking permanent settlement in a country to which they have fled are referred to as asylum-seekers. The UNHCR is mandated to oversee the implementation of the 1951 convention and offer protection to the world's 20 million refugees.

Apart from the narrow internationally agreed-upon definition, the term *refugee* has been widened in practice to cover a variety of people in diverse situations who need assistance and protection. The most notable of these expansions is found in the Convention on Refugee Problems in Africa, a regional instrument adopted by the Organization of African Unity in 1969. It includes people fleeing "external aggression, internal civil strife, or events seriously disturbing public order" in African countries. The Cartagena Declaration of 1984 covering Central American refugees also goes beyond the 1951 UN convention by including "persons who have fled their country because their lives, safety or freedom have been threatened by generalized violence, foreign aggression, internal conflicts, massive violation of human rights or other circumstances which have seriously disturbed public order."

These regional legal norms are in fact much more inclusive and in keeping with the actual causes of flight throughout the Third World than are the UN norms. Accordingly, over the past several decades UNHCR has interpreted its mandate to extend to people who have been forcibly displaced from their countries because of internal upheavals or armed conflicts. In recent years, however, there has been great resistance in the West to this pragmatic expansion of the refugee definition and of UNHCR's mandate. In most industrialized nations the 1951 definition is used for resettlement and asylum purposes, although groups of people at risk of death or grave harm from violence are often given temporary protection.

Although anyone uprooted because of exposure to violence and the denial of human rights is commonly referred to as a refugee, the definition of the 1951 UN convention is much more precise. By UN standards, the key criterion determining refugee status is persecution, which usually means a deliberate act of government against individuals. This excludes victims of general upheaval, insecurity, and oppression; victims of systemic economic deprivation; or people who have not crossed national frontiers to seek refuge. From the perspective of international law, a refugee is outside his home country and does not have the protection of his country of origin.

In addition to the variety of legal definitions for refugees, there are several other categories of uprooted people. For example, 2.4 million Palestinians are registered with the United Nations Relief and Works Agency for Palestine Refugees in the Near East (UNRWA), whose mandate is limited geographically to Syria, Lebanon, Jordan, and the Israeli-occupied territories. There are also large numbers of people who are displaced within their own countries because of armed conflict and ethnic strife or because of forcible relocation by their governments. Many of them are victims of the same civil wars that sent refugees out of Angola, Mozambique, Cambodia, Guatemala, or Afghanistan, or they are victims of ethnic strife in Rwanda, Liberia, Ethiopia, Somalia, or throughout the Balkans or the former Soviet Union. Because internally displaced persons remain within their own country and do not cross international boundaries, they cannot be protected as refugees. In addition, there are those who have been refugees who voluntarily return to their countries of origin. Sometimes returnees go home under the auspices of UNHCR, from whom they receive assistance for a limited time, but more often returnees go back on their own without international sponsorship because they do not want public recognition as former refugees. There are many constraints on providing protection and assistance to returnees, however, especially when the conditions that generated the exodus continue to exist in the countries of origin.

Finally, there are those who leave their countries because of economic factors and who are considered to be economic migrants. These people do not qualify for UNHCR protection or assistance; however, in developing countries that have few resources and weak government structures, economic hardships are generally exacerbated by political violence. Because of the close relationship between political conflict and economic and social problems, it is sometimes difficult to distinguish between refugees and migrants. While refugees flee to save their lives and migrants flee to improve their economic prospects, to distinguish between them becomes extremely difficult when people flee from countries where poverty and violence are direct consequences of the political system. Since the late 1950s, Haitian people have fled a country impoverished by the corrupt and violent Duvalier family, and until September 1994 they fled again from the military regime that overthrew Jean Bertrand Aristide, the elected president of Haiti. The influx of Albanians into Italy in 1990–1991 continued even after the election of a democratic government in their homeland, demonstrating anew the complexity of the problem.

While the definition contained in the 1951 UN convention remains important as a statement of legal responsibility and international commitment to protect refugees, increasingly large numbers of politically coerced and displaced people do not fall within its strict definition. As a result, migrants who flee threatening circumstances that do not involve individual persecution have not been widely accepted as refugees. There is a growing perception in the industrialized world that these movements of people can no longer be handled adequately by uncoordinated responses on the part of receiving countries.

The stark fact that must be faced is that the world is witnessing a huge growth in forcibly displaced people. In terms of sheer numbers, nonconvention refugees—those who flee civil wars, ethnic conflicts, and generalized violence in the Third World and Eastern Europe—are a bigger problem for the international community than those who fall within the 1951 UN definition. Nonconvention refugees are not adequately protected by present international norms—a situation that brings to question whether or not the current UN definition of *refugee* should be changed in order to respond to contemporary needs.

International Organizations

A number of international agencies exist to respond to refugee crises. Among these are the United Nations High Commissioner for Refugees (UNHCR); the International Committee for the Red Cross, which assists people caught in conflicts; the World Food Program, which coordinates food aid to refugees; and the United Nations Children's Fund (UNICEF), which aids women and children. The United Nations Relief and Works Administration for Palestinian Refugees (UNRWA) aids Palestinians in the Middle East, and the International Organization for Migration arranges for the transportation of refugees resettled overseas and for the safe and humane return home of refugees and migrants from countries unable or unwilling to absorb them.

The international community also relies on a vast network of nongovernmental organizations (NGOs), ranging from large international agencies to small organizations working in a single country, to offer assistance programs. As the implementing partners for the UNHCR, NGOs bear the brunt of delivering food and providing shelter, water, sanitation, and health care to refugees. Where funding is available, they also provide community outreach services and educational and skills programs.

Refugees and the UNHCR in a Changing World

Formally established in 1950 at the height of East-West confrontation, the United Nations High Commissioner for Refugees (UNHCR) was initially charged with protecting and assisting people displaced in the aftermath of World War II and those fleeing communist persecution in Europe. From the 1960s until recently, however, the focus shifted away from Europe to the Third World. During the last 30 years, the majority of UNHCR's budget has been allocated for operations in Africa, Asia, and Latin America. While the assistance contributed by the international community has at times been substantial, the pressures created by the presence of large refugee populations and sudden mass exoduses in recent years have been enormous.

More than two-thirds of all international assistance is channelled through UNHCR. With a staff of about 4,000 people in over 100 countries and annual expenditures of approximately $1.5 billion, the UNHCR protects and assists refugees and works toward one of three durable solutions: (1) voluntary repatriation, (2) local integration, or (3) third-country resettlement.

The growth in numbers and the complexity of refugee flows in recent years have presented enormous challenges to UNHCR to plan, manage, and fund its worldwide network of protection and relief programs. It is increasingly asked to bear more responsibility and leadership, but with diminishing resources. Despite its size and budget, the UNHCR is chronically underfunded and understaffed. It serves twice the number of refugees as it did a decade ago, but the financial support for basic care and maintenance for refugees worldwide has remained virtually the same. Thus, the UNHCR has been in many cases unable to fulfill its mandate in recent years because it lacks the necessary financial resources and personnel.

The Dimensions of the Refugee Problem

For many reasons—war, famine, poverty, environmental degradation, and persecution—a large portion of humanity is now on the move. Most of this movement occurs in the developing world, although larger numbers of people are migrating both from the Third World to the developed world and from Eastern Europe to the West. To a large extent, states have had great difficulty coping with these massive flows of migration, which are having disruptive effects within both the sending and the receiving countries.

The magnitude of refugee flows in recent years has generated urgent concern throughout the world. Widely perceived as an unprecedented crisis, these flows have produced a mixture of humanitarian concern for the millions of people forced into exile and fear for the potential threat to the social, economic, and political stability of host states caused by streams of unwanted newcomers. States are struggling to strike a proper balance between the need to maintain control over their borders and the need to protect refugees who seek asylum within their borders.

As alarming as current numbers are, there is nothing new in the phenomenon of forced displacement. Explosions of political and ethnic violence, persecution, and pogroms have produced large-scale movements of refugees throughout history. Some previous global migrations have been comparatively much larger in scope than contemporary population movements. For example, during the nineteenth and early twentieth centuries the intercontinental migrations from the Old World to the New World involved some 50 million people, many of whom were fleeing persecution and pogroms in Europe.

The growing recognition in the West of the refugee problem as a factor in international relations is, however, a phenomenon of only the last 70 years. This is because the twentieth century has produced the greatest number of refugees ever in history. Indeed, the twentieth century is, as the German novelist Heinrich Böll once remarked, "the century of refugees and prisoners." Millions of refugees were generated by World War I and the breakup of multinational empires in the early part of the century. World War II uprooted approximately 30 million civilians in Europe alone. The Cold War of the 1950s was marked by refugees fleeing the newly established communist regimes in Eastern Europe. The 1960s and 1970s witnessed new Third World refugee movements uprooted in the wake of anticolonial struggles and conflicts within newly independent states and by the economic migration of about 10 million guestworkers to Europe. The late 1970s and 1980s saw more massive refugee exoduses in the Third World with consequent spillover in the form of asylum-seekers in the industrialized world, and the 1990s have brought growing East-West migration and increasing South-North immigration pressures from regions on the southern peripheries of Europe and the United States. The refugee problem receives increasing international prominence due to the fact that policies affecting refugees are linked directly with the political and security interests of states.

Refugee Movements in the Post–Cold War Era

While violence and persecution have produced large-scale movements of refugees throughout history, there are many new and unique features to the contemporary refugee crisis.

Recent advances in communication and transportation have had a dramatic effect on the situation. Communications satellites transmit the reality of more prosperous and safer conditions in the West to the most impoverished and oppressive regions of the world, while making the West far more cognizant of worldwide suffering, the magnitude of the refugee problem, and its responsibility to the rest of humankind. The greater availability of long-range transportation facilitates transcontinental movements and makes it possible for people to reach distant countries where they can seek asylum and try to improve their situation.

The 1990s are years of fundamental political and economic changes in the international system. This fact is reflected by mass movements of people, which in turn affect political, economic, and strategic developments worldwide. Refugee movements played a key role in bringing down the Berlin Wall and in bringing about the unification of the two Germanies, thus generating the most significant transformation in international relations since World

War II. Early in the post–Cold War era, refugee movements precipitated external intervention in Iraqi affairs on behalf of the Kurds. In the early 1990s, maltreatment of minorities, forced displacement, famine, and environmental damage in the Middle East, the Horn of Africa, Southern Africa, Liberia, Burma, and most recently parts of the former Yugoslavia and the ex–Soviet Union have preoccupied international leaders.

The end of the Cold War has also revealed the scope and intensity of specific local tensions around the world. The most common form of warfare in the developing world and Eastern Europe in the 1990s is internal conflict, fueled by the increasing availability of modern weaponry, sharp socioeconomic inequalities, and human rights abuses. Contemporary refugee movements are likely to be the result of ethnic, communal, and religious conflicts. Ethnic antagonisms between Armenians and Azeris, Hutus and Tutsis, Tamils and Sinhalese, Serbs and Croatians and Muslims, and Palestinians and Israelis illustrate the local roots of many refugee exoduses.

Internal wars have been fought not only by military means but by preventing international aid from reaching people living in conflict areas. In such situations, the international community is frequently unable to assist or intervene, and the ability of governments or international organizations to influence the behavior of warring factions is limited or virtually nil. For example, in the former Yugoslavia, UNHCR staff not only distribute relief but also try to restrain ethnic cleansing and protect human rights. In the face of cynical manipulation by all the protagonists to the conflict, however, these humanitarian efforts have been stopgap measures only. One of the principal lessons of the conflict in Bosnia is that the humanitarian mandate of UNHCR cannot be viewed as a satisfactory substitute for wider-ranging political solutions.

While refugee flows frequently occur as the result of persecution at the hands of brutal rulers or because of indiscriminate violence and the collapse of civil authority, external powers can significantly influence the factors that generate them. By arming past and present dictators like Saddam Hussein of Iraq, Slobodan Milosevic of Serbia, Pol Pot of Cambodia, Mohammed Siad Barre of Somalia, and Mengistu Haile Mariam of Ethiopia, among others, outside powers help prolong instability, exacerbate nationality conflicts, divert scarce resources into militaristic activities, and increase repression, thereby multiplying the numbers of refugees. Only when governments and international organizations address the refugee issue in its international political context will the problem be given sufficient priority and resources by policymakers.

Challenges Confronting UNHCR and the International Community

The rapidly changing international context and the highly politicized nature of refugee problems are likely both to determine the humanitarian needs of the 1990s and to define the limitations under which UNHCR will have to operate.

Complex Emergencies

Refugee crises are complex emergencies, combining political instability, ethnic tensions, armed conflict, economic collapse, and the disintegration of civil society. Refugee movements frequently spill over borders and aggravate existing problems, such as environmental damage or severe food shortages. Rather than being confined to single countries, refugee emergencies often affect entire regions, such as the Horn of Africa or the Balkans. In recent years, few refugee crises have been fully resolved. Consequently, resources from one crisis often have not been made available for use in the next.

Assisting and Protecting Internally Displaced Persons

A critical weakness of the international humanitarian system is that at present there is no special international organization to protect and assist the world's 25 million internally displaced persons. While there is a clear mandate for the protection and the provision of humanitarian assistance to refugees, there is a lack of clarity within existing international instruments regarding the allocation of responsibilities and mechanisms for addressing the immediate needs of the internally displaced. There is no adequate body of international law to regulate their treatment by governments. Thus, internally displaced people are unprotected precisely because they do not become refugees, remaining instead within the boundaries of their own countries.

Nevertheless, in the post–Cold War period, the UNHCR is being asked to assume new roles within a de facto expanded mandate in an increasing number of internal conflicts. In the former Yugoslavia, it is the leading UN agency for humanitarian assistance both to displaced people and to besieged populations, and it is a partner with UN peacekeeping troops on the ground. In northern Kenya and Tajikistan, it has launched cross-border operations with the intention of stabilizing populations at home so refugee flight is unnecessary. In these cases, and in many others around the world, the responses demanded of UNHCR extend far beyond its traditional humanitarian role of working only with people who have crossed international borders to seek asylum. The challenge of assisting and protecting people within their own countries raises difficult questions concerning UNHCR's mandate and fundamental principles.

Repatriation and Reintegration

The immediate short-term issues of the refugee problem include dealing with the consequences of refugee exoduses and determining when and how repatriation and reintegration are most appropriate. Even as new refugee crises emerge, there remain numerous long-standing refugee populations in the Third World—some dating back 10 years, others 20 or more years. Unlike earlier forced migrations that were ultimately resolved by repatriation or overseas resettlement, during the 1980s Third World refugees found only temporary asylum in neighboring states. During most of the 1980s, the majority of Third World refugee populations languished in camps or survived illegally without any hope of a permanent place of settlement or eventual return home.

Although the international community is still dealing with immediate problems of handling sudden mass outflows of refugees and problems of reception in countries of asylum, there is much greater attention today on repatriation and even returns to situations of widespread conflict. About 2.5 million refugees returned home in 1993. If large numbers of refugees continue to repatriate in the coming years, the focus of concern must inevitably shift from repatriation to more long-standing reintegration and development. It is becoming increasingly evident that in countries such as Afghanistan, Cambodia, Ethiopia, and Mozambique one of the preconditions for successful returns is development aid and reintegration assistance aimed at alleviating poverty in countries of origin. Without careful reintegration and reconciliation, returning refugees will compete for scarce developmental resources, which, in turn, might result in fierce political and economic competition with local populations that did not flee.

Repatriation and reconstruction raise new, difficult questions for UNHCR. For how long should UNHCR seek to provide protection to returning refugees, particularly in situations of continuing conflict? Does UNHCR have the capacity to engage in human rights monitoring in countries of origin? How much and what kinds of assistance are required for returnees to reestablish themselves successfully? Should international economic development agencies such as the United Nations Development Programme (UNDP) provide refugee-targeted development assistance from the early stages of a repatriation? Should assistance be extended not only to returning refugees but also to needy local populations? Although answers to these questions have yet to be found, they are of critical importance if UNHCR is to respond effectively in the future.

Going beyond traditional refugee emergency assistance to facilitating reintegration of returnees requires the development of new or different competencies on the part of international agencies. A focus on reintegration will involve rethinking the roles and mandates of international organizations and NGOs; the shifting of their operational priorities from receiving countries to countries of return; and closer cooperation between development, human rights, and refugee agencies than has hitherto been the case.

Asylum Crises in the West

While in the Third World the contemporary situation is characterized by refugee-generating ethnic conflicts and repatriations, the numbers of asylum-seekers in the West rose from 90,000 in 1983 to about 825,000 in 1992. The attitudes of receiving countries, many of which have relied on migrants to fill a variety of labor needs in the past, have become increasingly negative and have spawned xenophobia, racism, and a deterioration in community relations. As a result, the advanced industrialized states are increasingly reluctant to let refugees enter their countries to apply for political asylum. To date, the political debate in the North concerning asylum-seekers and migrants has largely been informed by governmental concerns about border controls, not by human rights concerns. In Eastern and Central Europe, the collapse of communism has greatly increased the numbers of asylum-seekers and migrants and has opened up the possibility of mass migration from the East. Refugees have become an increasingly contentious issue in the post–Cold War era, particularly in Europe.

Confusions abound, both at the institutional level and in the minds of the general public, regarding definitions, standards of treatment of nonnationals, and methods for the management of the movement, reception, resettlement, or return of refugees. In shaping policy responses to the asylum crisis, many Western leaders have been prone to being influenced by extremists who seek to exploit anti-immigrant feelings and tensions. As a result, the refugee problem has reached such a critical point in some Western countries that the very institution of asylum is being threatened. What is required in today's situation is for political leaders to articulate and guide public opinion regarding the complex facets of the refugee problem and the short- and long-range measures that might help address its various aspects.

Migration of People Worldwide

It is important to recognize that the nature of migratory movements is changing worldwide. The refugee problem is a part of the emerging global crisis of mass migration, which is generated by economic, political, and social changes. The growing interdependence of the economies of nation states—including the creation of regional free-trade zones, the transnational impact of the world's communication, media, and transport systems, and the ever-increasing gap between poor and rich countries—has caused millions of people from less developed countries to seek opportunities in other parts of the world. The numbers of sending and receiving countries throughout the world continue to expand, and social networks, or bridgeheads, support migration flows once they have begun. The number of people seeking entry has increased not only in the advanced industrialized states of North America and Europe but also in the newly industrialized states of Asia and the oil-producing states of the Middle East. The contemporary global migration situation is considered by the United Nations to be one of the top five issues of the 1990s.

Organizational and Other Constraints Facing UNHCR

Extended Emergency Relief Care

Today, UNHCR is concerned primarily with meeting the immediate needs of refugees and internally displaced people who live under conditions that are precarious, difficult, and frequently dangerous. For example, UNHCR has committed approximately one-quarter of its staff and one-third of its total funds worldwide to providing assistance and protection to over 4 million people in the former Yugoslavia. UNHCR is increasingly concerned that it will be swamped by its involvement in chronic internal conflicts, such as in Bosnia, and that the political interest of donor governments to continue funding such protracted operations will eventually wane, leaving UNHCR with limited resources to assist dependent civilian populations.

The priority given to extended emergency relief aid in prolonged refugee situations has swallowed up most of UNHCR's resources, and it has also made it more difficult to achieve traditional solutions. Voluntary repatriation is not a realistic solution until political circumstances in the country of origin have changed. Local integration is virtually impossible in situations of mass influx where land and other resources are scarce and where ethnic or religious tensions exist. Resettlement in third countries is likewise a solution for only a very small percentage of the world's refugees—less than 1 percent of the world's refugees were resettled during 1993. Faced with economic difficulties and growing popular xenophobia, Western nations are much more reluctant to admit large numbers of people who are not easily assimilable. There is a need to go further than traditional solutions to improve conditions in countries of origin so the majority of refugees can either remain at home or repatriate in safety while at the same time preserving the most fundamental principle of refugee protection—the right of refugees to flee their countries, to seek asylum from persecution in other countries, and not to be returned into the hands of their persecutors.

Challenges of a Preventive Strategy

In the 1990s, the international community must place a greater emphasis on addressing the underlying causes of the refugee problem through a preventive policy that includes early warning, preventive diplomacy and on ensuring respect for human rights. Recently, UNHCR has adopted a comprehensive protection strategy designed both to address the root causes of refugee flows, with the aim of preventing the underlying conditions that force people to flee, and to reduce or contain refugee flows that have already begun, with the aim of providing immediate protection and assistance and obviating the need for further displacement.

This shift to a preventive strategy, however, cannot be accomplished easily or in a short time. Involvement in internal conflicts requires skills and competencies that many UNHCR staff do not now possess. In situations such as in Bosnia or Somalia, UNHCR is using techniques closely akin to the work of the International Committee of the Red Cross (ICRC), but without the special training, skills, and experience of ICRC staff. While in countries of asylum the UNHCR has a well-established history of providing protection and assistance to refugees, in countries undergoing civil war the internally displaced are often viewed as the enemy, and UNHCR staff are seen as sympathizers. The UNHCR finds itself working with opposition groups and guerrilla forces as well as with recognized governments. Under extremely stressful and dangerous conditions, UNHCR staff now engage in activities that include protecting civilians against reprisals and forced displacement, relocating and evacuating civilians from conflict areas, and assisting besieged populations who choose not to move from their homes. This is done without any firm institutional and legal basis. For many UNHCR officials and staff these are entirely new activities. If UNHCR is to respond effectively to these new situations of internal displacement, there is an urgent need both to reorganize its staffing, training, and operations to reflect the new roles and to give it the necessary resources and mandate to do the job.

Financial Constraints

One of the most significant weaknesses of UNHCR is its dependence on voluntary contributions to carry out new programs. Apart from a modest annual contribution from the UN Regular Budget toward administrative expenses, all of UNHCR's resources depend on voluntary contributions. Its assistance activities are divided broadly into General and Special Programs. Each year, UNHCR's Executive Committee approves a General Program budget, which comprises activities financed through the annual program as well as the Emergency Fund, and appeals to all UN members to provide the resources needed to cover the program year. The primary allocation of these resources goes to the traditional areas of the high commissioner's competence: emergency relief, voluntary repatriation, integration into host societies, and resettlement.

In addition to its General Program budget, UNHCR, at the request of the secretary-general or the United Nations General Assembly, undertakes Special Programs that include major new and unforeseen emergency operations (such as in Bosnia or Rwanda) and transportation and rehabilitation assistance to refugees and displaced people who have returned to their homes (such as in Mozambique). Special Programs are the subject of specific fund-raising appeals to interested governments and are financed from trust funds constructed with particular purposes and conditions. Thus, UNHCR must raise funds for each new refugee problem.

The 1990s have presented UNHCR with several new refugee emergencies, and its overall expenditures have therefore grown significantly. In 1991, as a result of emergency relief operations in northern Iraq and the Horn of Africa, total voluntary funds expenditure amounted to $862.5 million, an increase of almost 60 percent over 1990. In 1992 and 1993, new refugee and humanitarian crises in Bangladesh, Central Africa, the Horn of Africa, Southern Africa, and the former Yugoslavia, as well as continued responsibilities in northern Iraq and new repatriation programs in Cambodia, Ethiopia, and Mozambique, pushed UNHCR expenditures to about $1.5 billion annually. The sum for 1994 will be at least that high.

While the amounts for Special Programs have increased substantially, in recent years, contributions by donor countries to UNHCR's core activities (General Programs) have not kept pace with the ever-growing numbers of refugees. Indeed, the financial support levels for General Programs have remained virtually unchanged during the past decade. The lack of General Program funds has threatened to reduce or postpone repatriation programs, cancel needed improvements in refugee facilities, and force UNHCR to make cuts in certain nutrition and education programs.

The flow of assistance from donor governments is neither reliable nor always in the most appropriate form. Funding is often earmarked for particular uses; it is frequently provided late and does not allow sufficiently for operational flexibility. In addition, the funding of humanitarian operations has often been infused with a strong political element. During the Cold War, for example, Western donor governments often funded refugee programs to express condemnation of communist governments whose repressive policies forced their citizens to flee their countries. Today, however, refugee situations increasingly are seen as local or regional problems of little, if any, foreign policy or security concern to major donor governments. Without compelling strategic and ideological motivations, funding for refugee operations is in danger of being cut back in favor of the domestic priorities of industrialized states.

Challenges of Addressing Human Rights Violations

A final organizational constraint that makes preventive action difficult for UNHCR is that the root causes of contemporary refugee situations require political intervention against governments that violate human rights, preferably *before* people need to flee. For the most part, UN institutions have been unable or unwilling either to prevent human rights violations or to punish those responsible. In some measure, this is because prevention of human rights abuses depends on overcoming the barrier of national sovereignty, something no international organization has yet managed to accomplish consistently. As it is presently structured, UNHCR does not have the capability to politically intervene against governments that violate human rights. The UNHCR was designed to appear nonpolitical and strictly humanitarian in order to gain permission to work in host countries and secure funding from donor governments. UNHCR officials thus avoid raising political questions for fear of overstepping their mandate or damaging relations with sensitive governments, many of whom would consider such intervention as an interference in their internal affairs.

Hindered both by its dependence on voluntary contributions to carry out its programs and its need to obtain the acquiescence of host governments, UNHCR alone cannot resolve the global refugee problem. A comprehensive solution requires efforts going well beyond the scope of humanitarian organizations. International and regional peace, security, human rights, and economic structures must be strengthened with broader mandates and financial support to become more constructive interlocutors.

A Framework for Future Action

Refugee emergencies of the post–Cold War era have highlighted the fact that combating the causes of forced migration cannot proceed solely within the confines of international humanitarian organizations. There is a need for a better interface between relief agencies and political and security operations, on the one hand, and between emergency relief, development, and human rights mechanisms on the other. A multidimensional strategy to refugee crises must involve practically the entire UN system, as well as regional organizations and NGOs, and it requires enhancing these organizations' capacities to defuse, deter, and mediate incipient crises before they may need more serious and costly trans-sovereign intervention. The United Nations must be able to respond more quickly and effectively in order to address humanitarian needs in a growing number of emergency situations. Prevention is itself a form of intervention to stop a major crisis from expanding.

The end of the Cold War gives the international community a unique opportunity to lay the foundations of an action program that includes the elements outlined below.

Establishing and Utilizing More Effective Early Warning Systems

Early information on impending crises is critical not only for possible preventive action but also for effective and timely humanitarian responses and adequate preparedness. Establishing an effective monitoring body within the United Nations that would alert the secretary-general, the emergency relief coordinator, and the Security Council to potential conflicts and refugee emergencies could provide an early warning mechanism. The UN system should be broadly mobilized to provide timely warnings. Members of the monitoring body would include UN officials, NGO representatives, and governments.

For example, the capability and mandate of the United Nations Centre for Human Rights needs to be strengthened to enable it to monitor and collect accurate and up-to-date human rights information, identify situations that have the potential to produce mass refugee flows, and bring these to the attention of the international community. Furthermore, the United Nations Commission on Human Rights could assign its Sub-Commission on Prevention of Discrimination and Protection of Minorities to monitor the treatment of ethnic and religious minorities and to alert the secretary-general when action is needed. Similarly, the early warning capabilities of UNHCR and the United Nations Development Programme (UNDP) should be bolstered, and full support should be extended to initiatives aimed toward sharing such information at interagency levels.

Potentially among the most important new instruments added to the capacities of the United Nations is its ability to send fact-finding missions to defuse disputes and prevent major crises from expanding. Fact-finding missions are likely to play important roles at the early stages of conflict development and may prevent the misunderstandings that escalate conflict and result in more rigid positions. Observers in the field can also serve as a deterrent for those considering actions that cause forcible displacement. Nongovernmental organizations, such as Amnesty International or Helsinki Watch, may in some instances be more successful than UN monitors in collecting information and bringing human and minority rights abuses to the attention of the international community. It is not enough, however, for monitors to be in place and for information about potential refugee movements to be widely available—political obstacles frequently must be overcome to enable the relevant international and regional organizations to react in time to minimize suffering and problems of insecurity.

Early warning programs must be connected to decision-making and response strategies both in governments and in relief, development, and human rights organizations. Moreover, in many recent refugee crises, information about impending conflicts and mass migrations was available and well known in advance, but there was no willingness to act upon it. In ex-Yugoslavia and in Somalia, for instance, international agencies and analysts had accurately predicted what would happen well before the disasters unfolded, but there existed no mechanisms or institutions for averting conflicts or for dealing effectively and rapidly with these crises at a time when they were still manageable. Unless trigger mechanisms for prompt action regarding conflicts and refugee problems are established, and unless existing tools of diplomacy, human rights, and conflict resolution are reinforced, any measures that might be taken to prepare for future refugee flows are likely to be of limited use. The value of such measures depends largely on the willingness of states and international organizations to take the necessary concerted preventive action.

Interagency Cooperation

Interagency cooperation is the key to a more effective response to the problems of displacement. If UNHCR hopes to ensure cooperation in achieving a solution to displacement and phasing out the political source of such operations in the future, it must continue to work at improving coordination with other international, regional, and nongovernmental agencies, particularly in strategic planning and in making legal and institutional arrangements with other agencies charged with responding to refugees.

Improving Overall UN Coordination

Making the system work better requires a more effective division of labor among those responding to the humanitarian, political, and security dimensions of internal conflicts. The UN General Assembly took an important first step in December 1991 by creating the Office of Emergency Relief Coordinator, charged with providing a focal point—in government, intergovernmental, and nongovernmental organization communication—during UN emergency relief operations. In early 1992, Jan Eliasson, the emergency relief coordinator, became the first under secretary-general in the newly formed UN Department of Humanitarian Affairs (DHA). The creation of the DHA was an essential step in clarifying and assigning responsibilities to UN agencies in complex emergencies. This is particularly apparent in situations where mandates overlap or where no entity has a clear mandate to act; in making quick decisions on the best coordinating mechanisms to respond to humanitarian emergencies at the field level; and in negotiating access for these agencies without waiting for a formal government request. Donor states influential in creating the DHA envision it gathering data and managing information, mobilizing resources and orchestrating field activities, negotiating a framework of action with political authorities, and providing overall leadership to humanitarian aid efforts.

Unfortunately, in the past two years the vision has not been realized. Lack of adequate staff in the field, a rapid succession of humanitarian crises in the post–Cold War period, and incompletely established and largely untested mechanisms for interagency coordination have been problematic for DHA, leaving it wholly unprepared to assume its intended leadership role in most of the recent emergencies. Perhaps the greatest difficulty confronting DHA is that specialized agencies such as UNHCR possess a high degree of constitutional autonomy and consistently resist any attempt by DHA to impose strong authority over their actions in humanitarian emergencies. If DHA's presence is to lead to improvements in the response capacity of the United Nations, the significance of its coordinating role must be recognized by UNHCR and other agencies. DHA must also be equipped both politically and financially to undertake its assigned tasks effectively.

Coordinating Relief and Development

Closer coordination between UNDP and UNHCR represents a key solution to situations involving refugees, returnees, and the internally displaced. Cooperation between these agencies already takes place in joint projects aimed at assisting a variety of displaced groups in Central America, Mozambique, and Cambodia. In the early 1990s, UNHCR and UNDP also established joint management structures to create preventive zones and cross-mandate programs to prevent displacement and to stabilize border areas in the Horn of Africa.

Although there have been greater efforts at UNDP-UNHCR coordination in field operations, far more effective interagency planning, consultation, and implementation are required. Institutional constraints inhibit closer cooperation between the two agencies. The UNHCR is not a development agency, and although it can be a catalyst in initiating development-oriented assistance, the UNDP is more suited to the task. Unfortunately, in most countries humanitarian or emergency relief aid is administratively and programmatically divorced from developmental concerns. Thus a "development gap" exists between short-term humanitarian relief assistance and long-term development. UNHCR-UNDP joint projects have attempted to fill this gap in Central America, the Horn of Africa, and Indochina, where there are large returnee and displaced populations, but because these projects have been small in size and of a limited nature they have only partially filled the gap between immediate assistance and longer-term development. The task of the overall rehabilitation of these communities must be carried out by UNDP or other UN agencies that can more appropriately deal with reconstruction and development. This requires a full transfer of responsibility from UNHCR to UNDP after the immediate emergency relief phase is over—again, an idea that UNDP consistently resists because it views itself as having a development purpose without even a partial focus on emergency situations.

Increasing Human Rights Monitoring and Enforcement

Greater development assistance alone is not enough to create safe conditions for refugees; international cooperation must also ensure democratization and respect for human rights. Neither the enforcement of good governance or respect for human rights, however, fall within UNHCR's domain. The existing UN human rights machinery needs to be strengthened and applied more effectively to deal with refugees, returnees, and the internally displaced, because it is integral to the success of UN peacemaking.

In recent years, the UN human rights system has demonstrated its potential capabilities to respond quickly to a select number of human rights emergencies involving the internally displaced. In 1992, it called an unprecedented meeting of the UN Commission on Human Rights and appointed a special rapporteur to investigate human rights abuses of minority populations in Bosnia and to make recommendations to the Security Council. Similarly, an incriminating UN report on human rights violations in Iraq, including the alleged forced deportation and murder of the Shi'ite population by the Iraqi army, provided humanitarian justification for the establishment of an air exclusion zone over southern Iraq.

At the same time, the United Nations Centre for Human Rights, through its Advisory Services, has worked on a number of UN peacekeeping or peace-enforcement missions, providing significant technical assistance and cooperation to the UN human rights presence in the field in areas such as El Salvador, Somalia, and Cambodia. These actions underscore the potentially key role of the UN human rights machinery, the growing involvement of the Security Council in humanitarian matters, and the recognition that the promotion and protection of the human rights of refugees, returnees, and the internally displaced are an integral part of UN peacemaking.

At present the UN human rights program is grossly understaffed and underfunded. The Advisory Services section of the Centre for Human Rights, for example, has an annual budget of approximately $700,000. This is a minuscule sum in view of both the massive amounts being spent on relief and peacekeeping operations and the potential of the Advisory Services section to strengthen civil society, to promote democratic and pluralistic institutions and procedures, and thereby to prevent human rights abuses and mass displacements.

If the United Nations hopes to respond more effectively to the refugee crisis, it must strengthen its capacity to monitor developments in human rights issues. The creation of the post of UN High Commissioner for Human Rights in late 1993 was a step in this direction; however, a greater protection role in the field should be granted to UN human rights personnel. In the short term, the Centre for Human Rights can strengthen its coverage in the field by the continued expansion of its advisory services and technical cooperation. In addition, by offering services such as training judges, strengthening electoral commissions, establishing ombudsmen, training prison staff, and advising governments on constitutions and legislation regarding national minorities and human rights, the Centre for Human Rights is likely to be more successful in its activities and less threatening to governments than in more straightforward, fieldwork-oriented human rights monitoring.

In recent years, there has been much discussion about the creation of special human rights machinery for the internally displaced. At its 1993 session, the United Nations Commission on Human Rights reappointed the special representative on the internally displaced to monitor mass displacements of people, to collect information on violations of their human rights, and to help to sustain a positive dialogue toward achieving solutions with governments of the country of origin. The special representative must be given proper political support and funding, however, to carry out his tasks effectively. A General Assembly resolution confirming the role and mandate of the special representative is now required to institutionalize this office further. A significant first step toward trying to deal with the problem would be to designate a permanent representative for the internally displaced. This representative could undertake fact-finding missions, intercede with governments, embark on activities that strengthen institutions for sustaining democracy and civil society, publish reports, and bring violations to the attention of human rights bodies and the Security Council.

Recently, there have been attempts to create closer links between UNHCR and the human rights organs and activities of the UN system. In 1992, for example, the Centre for Human Rights and UNHCR drafted a memorandum of understanding so human rights information collected by UNHCR could be forwarded to the Centre for Human Rights. At the end of 1992, the two agencies established a joint working group to study mechanisms and approaches for enhanced and continuous collaboration. Such consultation should be strengthened to ensure that displacements emanating from human rights violations are brought to the attention of the Commission on Human Rights and that the work of the centre's Advisory Services section adequately addresses human rights issues associated with refugee movements and internal displacements.

Providing Asylum and Stability

The refugee crises in ex-Yugoslavia, Somalia, Haiti, and numerous other places and the reluctance of states to open their borders to people who are forcibly driven from their homes and subjected to murder, physical abuse, and starvation illustrate the vital importance of maintaining the principle of asylum. The major lesson we can learn from past efforts to deal with refugee problems is that building walls is no answer to those who feel compelled to move. The need to assure asylum to refugees is critical to maintaining human rights protection worldwide. The capacity of Western countries to improve prospects for granting asylum in the Third World depends on the fairness and generosity of their own policies in the heart of Europe and in the Caribbean and on the assistance they provide to others.

A generous commitment to asylum is not simply a matter of charity or burden-sharing; it is also a matter of regularizing and controlling large numbers of people whose irregular situation creates interstate tensions and regional instability. The success of economic liberalism and political pluralism in the new democracies of Africa, Latin America, Eastern Europe, and the former Soviet Union is of decisive importance, not only in averting future refugee and migrant flows but also in the political realm. Unduly restrictionist Western policies would lead to more isolation and deprivation in those countries forced to play host to rejected refugees and migrants.

Liberalizing domestic regimes and economic systems is scarcely possible without free movement of people, goods, and ideas. No single international development is likely to be more successful in improving economic growth in developing countries and Eastern Europe (thereby reducing economic incentives for emigration) than trade liberalization aimed at reducing economic disparities between countries in the South and North and the East and West. An angry, excluded world outside the West would inevitably give rise to conditions in which extremist and aggressive groups and governments can emerge and pose new political and security threats. Dealing effectively with refugee movements both at home and abroad through a combination of generous asylum policies and preventive programs in aid, trade, and human rights diplomacy is, therefore, in the interest of the industrialized states and coincides with their search for long-term global stability.

The Importance of American Leadership

Never before has it been so appropriate to launch a series of bold initiatives to deal with national and international policies and practices toward refugees. Although the leadership of the UNHCR is crucial, it is not enough. The president of the United States and other political leaders also hold key assets in any serious effort to strengthen the UN refugee system, and UN Secretary-General Boutros Boutros-Ghali must be prepared to proceed with imagination and political courage to invigorate multilateral mechanisms. These initiatives would draw attention to the serious deterioration in norms and proper conduct that has occurred in some states with respect to the treatment of citizens and refugees. They would attempt to deal with the *causes* of refugee flows rather than with the *consequences*.

The United Nations is still the only body capable of managing many of the complex global problems of the post–Cold War era. The international community needs to take advantage of both the structural and technical reforms that have occurred within the UN system and the higher expectations for the United Nations that now exist. Events in Iraq, in ex-Yugoslavia, and in Somalia, however, have demonstrated that the United Nations is not a separate entity capable of imposing order by itself, nor is it capable of achieving success in every endeavor. The United Nations is the sum of its member states, and U.S. and Western leadership in invigorating multilateral programs is a key factor if the United Nations is to achieve optimum results. The United States is still the only nation whose leadership most other nations are willing to follow, and it is the country most capable of setting up all sorts of measures to direct international efforts toward a constructive goal. Therefore, American leadership is vital in galvanizing collective efforts to resolve many of the complex humanitarian problems of the post–Cold War era. Without active U.S. involvement, the international community would be limited to reactive damage-control measures in the event of humanitarian crises. A failure by the United States and its allies to increase the capacities of the United Nations at this time would almost inevitably lead to a breakdown in international security, to costly military interventions to restore order, and to further needless drains on aid programs to deal with war-caused famines or refugee movements in the future. Not since 1945 has the United States and the international community been presented with such an opportunity to make substantial progress on many political and humanitarian issues. That opportunity should now be seized.

A Final Note

The time has come to broaden the scope of approach to the refugee problem to the larger agenda for peace and security in the post–Cold War world. Generosity and humanitarian action are still essential, but they alone are insufficient to deal with today's global refugee crisis. The time cannot be too distant when governments and people in the West will become profoundly tired of refugee emergencies, and the consequences of our compassion fatigue will be dehumanizing to us all. What is required is not only rededication to some fundamental values regarding asylum and human rights protection but also a reorientation of policy that more effectively addresses the abuses, violence, and social inequities that cause forced migration.

2

Chronology

REFUGEES HAVE EXISTED FOR AS LONG as humankind has lived in organized groups where intolerance and persecution have been prominent; however, refugees have only become an issue of international concern during the twentieth century. Organized international efforts to assist and protect refugees began in 1921 when the League of Nations appointed the first high commissioner for refugees. The following chronology provides a listing of the major events in the development of the global refugee problem and in the international community's response to the issue during the past 70 years.

1914–1919 Millions of people are displaced and made stateless in Europe and the Middle East as a result of World War I and the breakup of the Hapsburg, Romanov, Ottoman, and Hohenzollern empires.

1921 The League of Nations appoints Fridtjof Nansen, a Norwegian, as the first high commissioner for refugees.

Over 1 million Russians become refugees as a result of the collapse of czarist Russia, the Russian Civil War, the Russo-Polish War, and the Soviet famine.

1922 The Graeco-Turkish War of 1922 displaces more than 1 million people. Following the war, Nansen negotiates the exchange of populations between Greece and Turkey, and, later, between Greece and Bulgaria.

1931 After the death of Nansen, the International Nansen Office for Refugees is created.

1933 The Nazis come to power in Germany.

The office of the High Commissioner for Refugees Coming from Germany is established outside of the League of Nations framework. After Germany leaves, the High Commissioner for Refugees comes under the auspices of the League of Nations and remains so until 1938.

The Convention Relating to the International Status of Refugees (covering Russian, Armenian, Turkish, Assyrian, and Assyro-Chaldean refugees) is signed and ratified.

1935 The Nuremberg Laws, which discriminate against Jews, are passed in Germany.

1936 Conflict breaks out in Spain between Republicans and Fascists. During the next several years, over 400,000 Spanish Republicans take refuge in France.

1938 In a night of violence, *Kristallnacht,* Jews are attacked and murdered in Germany.

President Franklin D. Roosevelt calls together an international refugee conference at Evian-les-Bains concerning European Jews.

As a result of the conference at Evian-les-Bains, the Intergovernmental Committee on Refugees (IGCR) is established to discuss the fate of Jews with the German government.

The Convention Concerning the Status of Refugees Coming from Germany is signed and ratified.

1939 The High Commissioner for Refugees under the Protection of the League of Nations is created, merging the International Nansen Office with the High Commissioner for Refugees Coming from Germany.

World War II begins in Europe. Twenty to 30 million people will be displaced as a consequence of the war.

1940 Nazis begin deporting German Jews to Poland.

1941 Nazis adopt the "Final Solution" (extermination of the Jewish population) as state policy. As a result, approximately 6 million Jews are murdered as well as huge numbers of Gypsies, other minorities, and political dissidents.

1943 The United Nations Relief and Rehabilitation Administration (UNRRA) is created to provide postwar reconstruction, but it becomes involved with relief for displaced persons and war victims and their repatriation. UNRRA repatriates millions of East Europeans and Soviet citizens, many of them forcibly.

The American Council for Voluntary Agencies in Foreign Service (ACVA) is established as the main umbrella organization for refugee voluntary agencies in the United States (now called InterAction).

1946 The International Refugee Organization (IRO) is established. IRO resettles well over 1 million displaced persons overseas between 1946 and 1952.

1947 The partition of India unleashes the outflow of 14 million Hindus and Muslims from India and Pakistan.

1948 Conflict in Palestine and the creation of the state of Israel result in the expulsion and flight of some 700,000 Palestinians from their homelands.

The United Nations Relief and Works Agency for Palestine Refugees in the Near East (UNRWA) is created to provide assistance to displaced Palestinians.

The Universal Declaration of Human Rights is approved by the United Nations.

1950 Conflict breaks out in Korea, where millions of people are displaced. The United Nations Korean Reconstruction Agency (UNKRA) is established to assist Korean refugees.

On 14 December, Resolution 428 (V) of the United Nations General Assembly provides for the creation of the United

1950 *cont.* Nations High Commissioner for Refugees (UNHCR). Resolution 429 (V) calls for a conference of plenipotentiaries to draw up a convention on refugees.

1951 On 1 January, UNHCR starts operations. At the time there are roughly 1.5 million refugees in the world—mainly in Europe, but also in Asia (Hong Kong and Macau) and in Latin America.

On 28 July, the Convention Relating to the Status of Refugees is adopted in Geneva.

The Intergovernmental Committee for European Migration is established (now called International Organization for Migration).

1954 UNHCR is awarded the Nobel Peace Prize.

1956 Due to crisis in Hungary, 200,000 refugees flee to Austria and Yugoslavia.

An independence war in Algeria triggers an outward flow into Tunisia and Morocco.

1957 UNHCR intervenes to assist Algerian refugees in Morocco and Tunisia.

1958 Additional refugee flows take place in Africa, with Uganda receiving people from Sudan and Rwanda.

1959 World Refugee Year is celebrated throughout the world.

1960 The Government of the Federal Republic of Germany institutes an indemnification fund for victims of Nazism and entrusts its administration to UNHCR.

1962 Burundi witnesses a mass influx of ethnic Tutsi from Rwanda.

The International Council of Voluntary Agencies (ICVA) is created as the umbrella organization for many international and regional voluntary agencies working for refugees.

UNHCR helps to repatriate 260,000 Algerians from Morocco and Tunisia.

1965 Ethnic Hutu of Burundi migrate to Rwanda. This will occur again twice before 1994.

1966 Refugees from Mozambique, fighting for independence, migrate to neighboring countries. Many will repatriate in 1975, when Mozambique becomes independent.

1967 On 31 January, the Protocol to the 1951 Convention Relating to the Status of Refugees is adopted in New York.

The United Nations makes its Declaration on Territorial Asylum.

1968 After repression of the Prague Spring, 42,000 Czechs abroad do not return to their country.

1969 On 10 September, the Organization of African Unity (OAU) Convention governing the specific aspects of refugee problems in Africa is adopted in Addis Ababa.

1971 Nearly 10 million Bengalis from Eastern Pakistan take refuge in India.

1972 UNHCR launches special operations to repatriate and reintegrate over 200,000 refugees in southern Sudan as well as to assist hundreds of thousands of displaced persons.

The Bengalis taking refuge in India return home to the newly created state of Bangladesh.

Thousands of Asians expelled from Uganda are resettled abroad within a very short time.

Ethnic Hutu of Burundi migrate to Rwanda.

1973 Following political repression after the military coup that overthrew Salvadore Allende in Chile, a refugee movement begins, resulting in some 200,000 Chileans taking flight abroad.

A military take-over in Uruguay generates the flight of about 200,000 Uruguayan refugees.

1973 *cont.* Approximately 160,000 Biharis are transferred from Bangladesh to Pakistan. (Between 1977 and 1982 another 37,000 are moved.)

1974–1976 Independence in Guinea-Bissau, Mozambique, and Angola allows repatriation of hundreds of thousands of refugees from neighboring countries.

1974 In Cyprus, UNHCR launches a humanitarian program in favor of those who have sought refuge on the other side of the demarcation line. This includes 164,000 Greek Cypriots from the North and 34,000 Turkish Cypriots from the South.

1975–1980 About 350,000 Cambodians seek asylum in Thailand, of which 310,000 are resettled in third countries. (In 1993, as designated lead agency, UNHCR repatriates approximately 370,000 border Khmers and Cambodian refugees from Thailand, in the context of an overall political settlement in their country.)

1975 Tens of thousands of Saharawi move from Western Sahara into Algeria.

In Argentina a military dictatorship emerges, which drives 600,000 Argentine citizens into flight abroad.

The fall of Vietnam and Laos provokes the flight of 1.5 million Indochinese refugees into other countries in Southeast Asia. More than 1.3 million of these people are eventually resettled in North America, Europe, and Oceania.

1977 Approximately 90,000 Muslim Filipinos seek refuge in Malaysia.

Angola receives 200,000 Zairians from the province of Katanga (now Shaba).

An outward flow of refugees from Equatorial Guinea move to Cameroon and Gabon. They will repatriate after a change of regime in their country.

About 200,000 Burmese of Bengali origin take refuge in Bangladesh.

1977 *cont.* The Conference to Review Draft Convention on Territorial Asylum fails.

1978–1979 Movement from Laos to Thailand becomes a mass exodus. A number of Laotians also seek refuge in Vietnam.

The exodus of the so-called boat people, who have been leaving Vietnam by sea since 1975, assumes dramatic dimensions. Many drown or become victims of piracy.

1978 The 200,000 Bengali Burmese displaced the previous year repatriate to Burma.

Afghan refugees begin to arrive in Pakistan and Iran. By 1990, 5 million Afghans leave their home country.

Approximately 130,000 Vietnamese of Chinese origin take refuge in China. In 1990 they will total 286,000.

Zairians, who in previous years sought refuge in neighboring countries, start returning to their home country.

Émigrés from all over the world rejected at European borders begin to ask for asylum, in addition to those arriving in Europe because of the political crises prevailing in Africa, in the Middle East, and in Latin America.

Central America begins to register outflows of population from Nicaragua, El Salvador, and Guatemala, and there are also many displaced persons within the countries themselves. In the Caribbean area, many Haitians have already sought asylum in Santo Domingo, Venezuela, nearby islands, and the United States.

UNHCR launches an assistance program in the Horn of Africa for hundreds of thousands of Ethiopian refugees in the Sudan, Somalia, and Djibouti, as well as 500,000 internally displaced people in Ogaden.

1979 A change of regime in Nicaragua brings about the repatriation of 100,000 Nicaraguans.

Thousands of Chadians flee to the Sudan, Cameroon, and other neighboring countries.

1979 *cont.* An exodus of Ugandans moves into the Sudan.

Following the Iranian Islamic Revolution, large numbers of Iranian asylum-seekers cross into neighboring countries. About 25,000 approach UNHCR in Pakistan and Turkey, requesting asylum, and the majority of those accepted are eventually resettled in Western countries.

The Conference on Indochinese Refugees meets in Geneva, and countries make pledges to resettle Vietnamese boat people.

The Pan-African Refugee Conference meets in Arusha, Tanzania, to determine ways to better assist and protect refugees.

1980 In repatriation efforts in Africa, 200,000 refugees return to Zimbabwe following independence, 190,000 to Zaire, and 50,000 to Angola.

Civil war in Chad again forces hundreds of thousands of people to take refuge in neighboring countries. They will repatriate in 1981–1982.

In March, the U.S. Congress passes the 1980 Refugee Act, the first comprehensive American legislation on refugee admission.

From April to September, 130,000 Cuban boat people arrive in Florida, causing a refugee emergency.

1981 UNHCR is awarded the Nobel Peace Prize for the second time.

The International Conference on Assistance to Refugees in Africa (ICARA I) is held in Geneva to encourage donor states to increase their assistance to African host countries.

1982 The number of refugees in Central America, Mexico, and Panama increases considerably.

The United Nations Border Relief Operation (UNBRO) is established to assist refugees on the Thai-Cambodian border until 1991.

1983 Civil war in Sri Lanka causes an exodus of Tamils. By 1992, the numbers of Tamil refugees worldwide rises to half a million—200,000 asylum-seekers in Europe and 230,000 in the Tamil-populated regions of southern India.

A mass influx from southern Sudan into Ethiopia begins; by 1990, this movement will have involved 400,000 Sudanese refugees.

A limited repatriation operation starts from Somalia to Ethiopia, and about 12,000 refugees return by 1990. A 1990 crisis in Somalia will, however, force many more Ethiopian refugees to repatriate or to take refuge into Kenya.

1984 Papua-New Guinea begins receiving refugees from the Indonesian province of Irian Jaya.

Salvadoran refugees—in limited numbers—begin to return home, mainly from Honduras. In 1990, almost all of them will have repatriated under the auspices of UNHCR.

On 22 November the Cartagena Declaration on International Protection of Refugees in Central America, Mexico, and Panama is adopted.

The second International Conference on Assistance to Refugees in Africa (ICARA II) meets in Geneva.

1985 The Sudan is in crisis as it receives an influx of tens of thousands of Ethiopians whose lives are menaced by war and famine.

1986–1989 Approximately 320,000 Ugandans repatriate from the Sudan and Zaire.

1986 Europe registers a considerable increase in asylum-seekers, with a growing percentage being non-European.

A mass exodus from Mozambique into neighboring countries begins. More than 900,000 of the 1 million refugees seek asylum in Malawi, an amount equaling 10 percent of its population.

1987 Tens of thousands of Poles arrive in various countries of Western Europe.

A Peace Plan for Central America (Esquipulas II) offers new opportunities for repatriation.

1988 About 60,000 Burundese take refuge in Rwanda. They will be able to repatriate a few months later.

Ethiopia receives a mass influx of Somali refugees following armed conflict in Northwestern Somalia.

The International Conference on the Plight of Refugees, Returnees and Displaced Persons in Southern Africa (SARRED) meets in Oslo to effect a plan of action for the region.

1989 Masses of East Germans flee to neighboring countries, particularly West Germany. In November, when it is clear that refugee flows cannot be contained, the Berlin Wall collapses and the post–Cold War era begins.

Hungary, which has received refugees from Romania, signs the 1951 Convention Relating to the Status of Refugees. Other East-European countries, such as Poland, begin to receive asylum-seekers and to consider adhesion to the convention.

Following incidents in border areas, 75,000 refugees and displaced persons arrive in Senegal and Mauritania from Liberia.

In Geneva, the Conference on Southeast Asia adopts a Comprehensive Plan of Action to provide solutions—including refugee status determination and voluntary repatriation—for Vietnamese and Laotian refugees.

In Guatemala, the International Conference on Central American Refugees (CIREFCA) adopts a Plan of Action for Central American refugees, returnees, and displaced persons.

After many years in exile, 43,000 Namibians return to their home country from Angola and other countries.

1990–1994 Some 300,000 Colombians are forcibly displaced within their country during the early 1990s as a result of guerrilla war, counterinsurgency, and violence related to drug trafficking.

1990–1994 *cont.* At least 500,000 Peruvians are displaced in the early 1990s as a result of continuing political violence between the military and the Shining Path guerrillas.

1990 As a consequence of civil war in Somalia the number of Somali refugees in Ethiopia reaches 375,000.

Due to civil war, 750,000 Liberians (32 percent of the entire population) take refuge in Guinea, the Ivory Coast, and Sierra Leone.

Approximately 30,000 Salvadorans from Honduras and 50,000 Nicaraguans from Honduras and Costa Rica return to their countries under UNHCR auspices.

Approximately 4 million people are displaced in the 12 months following Iraq's August invasion of Kuwait. Between August and September, more than 1 million migrant workers and other foreign nationals flee from Iraq and Kuwait into Jordan and other neighboring countries, while 850,000 Yemenis living in Saudi Arabia return home.

1991 President Siad Barre of Somalia is ousted, and fighting breaks out between rival clans. Increasing numbers of Somalis flee into Kenya, Ethiopia, or the interior of Somalia.

Shortly after the Gulf War, armed conflict between the Iraqi government and Iraqi Kurds and Shi'ites provokes one of the largest and fastest refugee movements in recent history. About 1.4 million people take refuge either in Iran or along the eastern border of Iraq. A huge international relief effort, Operation Provide Comfort, is mounted to aid the Kurds.

As fighting breaks out in Croatia, UNHCR begins to aid people displaced by war.

A military coup overthrows the first democratically elected president of Haiti, Jean-Bertrand Aristide. As repression spreads throughout the country over the next few months, more than 38,000 Haitians risk their lives at sea in an attempt to reach the United States.

1991 *cont.* The United Nations General Assembly creates the post of emergency relief coordinator to ensure more rapid and effective international responses to humanitarian emergencies.

1992 As conflict spreads to Bosnia-Herzegovina, UNHCR begins to distribute food aid to war victims. During the war, UNHCR assumes the lead role in organizing the UN relief effort in the former Yugoslavia.

The secretary-general creates the Department of Humanitarian Affairs, to be led by a new under secretary-general for humanitarian affairs.

Kenya is struck by one of the world's fastest-growing refugee emergencies, with an average of 900 refugees, mostly from Somalia, entering the country each day. By the end of the year, more than 400,000 refugees are in Kenya. In September, UNHCR launches a cross-border operation with the aim of stabilizing population movements inside Somalia.

During the first half of the year, nearly 100,000 Nepalese from Bhutan flee ethnic persecution and enter Nepal.

In a war between the government and opposition forces, up to half a million Tajiks are driven from their homes. About 356,000 of these remain in the southern part of the country of Tajikistan, while 60,000 refugees enter Afghanistan.

At the end of the year, the first of 28,000 U.S. troops arrive in Somalia in Operation Restore Hope to establish a more secure environment for humanitarian relief operations.

1993 In Togo, political unrest and government repression force more than 200,000 Togolese into Ghana and Benin.

In Rwanda, peace negotiations between rebels and the government fail, leading to renewed fighting that displaces about 600,000 persons.

In Zaire, an outbreak of politically instigated ethnic violence forces an estimated 300,000 people from their homes by mid-year.

1993 *cont.*

In Mozambique, UNHCR begins a three-year repatriation program for about 1.5 million Mozambican refugees. The repatriation is the largest in the history of Africa.

In Germany, the parliament passes a comprehensive asylum law that significantly restricts the previous unqualified right to apply for asylum in Germany.

In the United States, the Supreme Court rules that international law prohibiting the forced return of refugees does not apply to a country that goes outside its borders to apprehend and return refugees, upholding the U.S. policy of summarily returning all Haitian asylum-seekers seized by the U.S. Coast Guard on the high seas.

The conflict over Nagorno-Karabakh, a region inside Azerbaijan populated mainly by Armenians, causes the largest refugee movement in the former Soviet Union. By June, almost 200,000 Azeris have fled from Armenia to Azerbaijan, while some 300,000 Armenians have escaped in the opposite direction. Within Azerbaijan, an additional 300,000 people have been uprooted.

In Georgia, secessionist struggles in Abkhazia and Ossetia cause large-scale population displacement.

In Burundi, 800,000 people are displaced as a result of an attempted coup d'etat in October.

1994

UNHCR assists 4 million people displaced by the conflict in the former Yugoslavia.

Israel and the Palestine Liberation Organization (PLO) sign a Declaration of Principles, establishing the basis for a peace accord, which includes a provision for the return of the Palestinian refugees who fled from Gaza and the West Bank in 1967. The accord delays discussion of the return of Palestinian refugees who fled in 1948.

In Burma, the military government and UNHCR sign an agreement on repatriation of Burmese Rohingya refugees from Bangladesh.

After massive bloodletting in Rwanda, over 250,000 Rwandese, mostly Tutsis, flee to Tanzania in a 24-hour period in April.

1994 *cont.*

As the Tutsi-led Rwanda Patriotic Front sweeps to victory in Rwanda, over 1 million Rwandese, mostly Hutus, take refuge in neighboring Zaire over a 48-hour period in July, causing a huge humanitarian crisis.

The United States rescinds its program of automatically returning all Haitian boat people to Haiti without an asylum hearing. Instead, the U.S. Coast Guard ships all Haitian asylum applicants it picks up at sea to the U.S. base at Guantanamo on Cuba for asylum processing.

Alarmed by a sudden surge in the number of Cubans reaching Florida in August, the Clinton Administration dramatically changes its policy of open entry for all Cubans arriving in the United States. About 30,000 Cubans are picked up at sea and are taken to Guantanamo for processing. The Clinton Administration agrees to admit more than 20,000 Cubans a year as part of a deal in which it won Fidel Castro's promise to stop the huge exodus of Cuban boat people.

3

Biographical Sketches

THIS BIOGRAPHICAL SELECTION IS ONLY A PARTIAL LIST of men and women who are important in the area of refugees, either because they were refugees themselves or because they actively sought to find solutions to the refugee problem. The chapter is divided into two sections: distinguished refugees and activists for refugees.

Distinguished Refugees

Many more people should be included in a list of famous refugees, but space does not permit it. Every year there will be more people who earn recognition. Each influx of refugees brings with it people who will go on to distinguish themselves in their new homelands. They will become some of the poets and writers, scientists and doctors, politicians, educators, and philosophers of future generations. The schools and universities of receiving countries are now graduating refugee children, many of whom have distinguished themselves in their studies. Since refugees often need a great deal of help, it is easy for receiving countries sometimes to forget that refugees themselves have a great deal to give. In the future, lists like this one will also include people with Chinese, Cambodian, Ethiopian, Sudanese, Spanish, Croat, Serb, and Bosnian names.

Yasir Arafat (1929–)

Yasir Arafat was born in Jerusalem in 1929, before the establishment of the state of Israel left the Palestinians without a country. Both his father and his older brother were committed anti-Zionists. It was in the local secondary school that Arafat first began to develop an interest in politics. Arafat went to Cairo to study engineering and continued his political activities there. He was elected president of the League of Palestinian Students in 1952 and served in the Egyptian army during the Suez Crisis in 1956. He then worked as an engineer in Kuwait from 1957 to 1965. In 1956, he helped establish the Arab guerrilla movement called Al Fatah. This organization developed into the Palestinian Liberation Organization (PLO), and Arafat became leader of the PLO in 1968. The PLO was, at that time, the government of the stateless, displaced Palestinian people who were living in refugee camps in what had been Palestine. As leader of the PLO, Arafat finally recognized Israel and denounced terrorist methods in 1989, and in 1990 he announced the existence of the Palestinian state. His reputation with the West was damaged when he supported Saddam Hussein's regime during the Gulf War. Palestine is still not recognized by all countries, and the struggle of Palestinians to establish their own state continues with Arafat at the forefront of the effort. In 1993, Arafat signed an agreement with Israel regarding the future autonomy of the West Bank and Gaza Strip.

Dietrich Bonhoeffer (1906–1943)

Dietrich Bonhoeffer was born in 1906 in Breslau. He was the son of a professor at Berlin University, and he and his twin sister enjoyed a happy childhood in pre–Second World War Germany. Bonhoeffer studied theology at Berlin and Thubingin universities and Union Theological Seminary in New York. He became a Lutheran minister and took up a professorship at Berlin University in 1931. From the outset of Hitler's rise to power, Bonhoeffer was an outspoken adversary of Nazism and was a central figure in the church's opposition to Hitler. Bonhoeffer became a refugee when his position put him in danger. He went to New York in 1939, but remained a refugee for only two weeks. He realized he had to "share the trials of this time" with the German people. It was after considerable soul searching that Bonhoeffer concluded it was right to kill someone as evil as Hitler. Bonhoeffer took part in a plot to plant a bomb in an aircraft that was to carry the führer. The bomb failed to detonate, the plotters were arrested, and Bonhoeffer was tortured and imprisoned. He was hanged in prison at Flossenberg in 1943 at age 39. Since then his writings, published postmortem, have made him a renowned and respected contemporary theologian.

Willy Brandt (1913–1993)

Willy Brandt was born Herbert Ernst Karl Frahm in 1913 in Lubeck, Germany. He left school in 1932 to become an apprentice shipbuilder. An outspoken anti-Nazi and a socialist worker, he held dangerous opinions in the changing political climate of Germany in the 1930s. He emigrated from Germany to Norway, became a Norwegian citizen, and changed his name to Willy Brandt. He then attended the University of Oslo and became a journalist. During World War II Brandt was active in the Norwegian and German resistance movements. He was able to return to Germany in 1945 and regained his German citizenship in 1947. Brandt was elected to the German parliament in 1949 as the member for Berlin. In 1957, he was elected mayor of Berlin and served in that capacity until 1966. In 1964, he became chairman of the Social Democratic Party (SPD). He was minister of foreign affairs and vice chancellor, and then, in 1969, he became chancellor of West Germany. Brandt resigned after a 1974 scandal named his personal aide as an East German spy. He continued to work in international politics, however, including four years as a member of the European parliament. Willy Brandt worked tirelessly for reconciliation between East and West Germany during the Cold War. This policy was known as Ostpolitik. For his efforts he was awarded the Nobel Peace Prize in 1971. He received numerous other awards, including the Reinhold Neibuhr Award in 1972 and the B'nai B'rith Gold Medal in 1981.

Bertolt Brecht (1898–1956)

Bertolt Brecht was first a refugee from Nazism in Germany and then from McCarthyism in the United States. Born in Germany in 1898, he would become one of the most influential dramatists of the twentieth century. His work in Germany before World War II included the wildly successful *Three Penny Opera,* which he wrote with Kurt Weill in 1928. Brecht's work was despised by Hitler, and he found it necessary to leave Germany in 1933. Joined by his wife and son, he went first to Denmark and then to Sweden. As the Nazis closed in, the family decided to go to the United States, hoping to get aboard a boat in Finland to make the crossing. Their visas were delayed, however, and by the time they could leave there was no escape by sea. They went instead via the trans-Siberian railway and crossed the Pacific from Vladivostok. Once settled in the United States, Brecht continued to write plays, producing such theatrical classics as *Mother Courage* (1939), *The Good Woman of Szechuan* (1941), and *The Caucasian Chalk Circle* (1945). With the rise of McCarthyism in the United States, however, a number of creative minds were being censured. Brecht was among those suspected of communist leanings, and he was investigated by the House Committee on UnAmerican Activities. He came away vindicated but decided to leave the United States. In the meantime, the East German government had invited him to create a state theater there, and he and his family went to Berlin. He remained in Germany, working with his new company, producing imaginative versions of classics, and staging his own works.

Marc Chagall (1887–1985)

Marc Chagall was born in Vitebsk, Russia, in 1887 of a poor Jewish family. From an early age, he was determined to be famous and finally decided to become a painter. His mother believed in his remarkable abilities, and he was fortunate to be taken on as a student with a well-known local artist. As a Jew, there were restrictions on his movement, but in spite of this, Chagall managed to go to Petersburg, the capital of imperial Russia. There he further developed his style of painting, combining realism and fantasy. He received a stipend to go to Paris, which was then the hub of artistic creativity in Europe. He was invited to show some of his work in Berlin in 1914. He went, and intending to return to Paris after a short absence, left a number of canvases behind. The war and the Russian Revolution kept Chagall from returning for nine years, by which time his friends had sold his canvases. After the revolution, he returned to his homeland and enjoyed a short period as an art teacher. When famine gripped Russia, however, artists became viewed first as unnecessary and then as reactionary. Chagall was forced to flee back to Paris in 1919. His reputation grew, and he enjoyed several years of familial happiness. As a Jew living in France, he was forced once again into exile by the Nazi invasion.

He went to the United States, where he lived and worked, returning to Europe after the war. He died in France.

Albert Einstein (1879–1955)

A slightly wistful-looking, white-haired man looks out of a UNHCR poster under the words, "A bundle of belongings isn't the only thing a refugee brings to his new country." The face is unmistakably that of Albert Einstein, probably the most famous of all refugees. His valuable mathematical and scientific works guaranteed him a welcome in his new home, the United States. Born in Germany of Jewish parents in 1879, Einstein was destined to become a refugee. He showed little promise during his formal education, but in 1905, left to his own insightful thinking, he came up with theories that would revolutionize twentieth-century physics. Because he was Jewish and a pacifist, the Nazis denounced his work as worthless, and Einstein left Germany when Hitler came to power. He went first to Belgium, where he stayed until fear of the Nazi invasion drove him to seek refuge in Britain and finally in the United States. Knowing he was fortunate to have escaped Nazism, Einstein worked to help others like himself leave Germany and settle in the United States. He was attached to Princeton University, where he lived quietly and worked on the theoretical aspects of nuclear physics, his knowledge adding greatly to the collective genius that led to the development of the atom bomb. He was awarded the Nobel Prize for Physics. After seeing what the atom bomb could do, he campaigned for peace until his death in 1955.

Enrico Fermi (1901–1954)

Born in Italy in 1901, Enrico Fermi earned his Ph.D. from the University of Pisa in physics in 1924. He then worked at the University of Florence, where he made his first important contribution to physics—working out the statistics of particles (fermions) that would later be named after him. In 1927, he was appointed professor of physics at the University of Rome. After the discovery of the neutron in 1932, Fermi focused his genius on investigating the structure of nuclei. He was to discover over 40 isotopes. Because he was an outspoken anti-Fascist with a Jewish wife, he began to fear the rising Fascist movement in Italy. When he was invited to Stockholm in 1938 to receive the Nobel Prize for Physics, he saw it as an opportunity to escape to safety. He and his wife sailed to Sweden, and, after the prize-giving, they continued on to New York, where Fermi worked first at Columbia University. During World War II, when the drive was on to create nuclear weapons, he worked at the University of Chicago and helped build the first atomic reactor, or pile, in a unused squash court. He was present at Los Alamos when the first nuclear bomb was detonated. After the war he continued to serve the United States as an advisor to the government and to the Atomic Energy Commission. Fermi defended the reputation of his fellow scientist, Robert Oppenheimer, when he was accused of being a communist sympathizer during the McCarthy era. Enrico Fermi died of cancer in 1954.

Sigmund Freud (1856–1939)

Sigmund Freud was born in Austria in 1856. By the 1920s, his theories and work in the field of psychoanalysis were world famous. He excited controversy as his ideas spread. When Austria was absorbed into the Third Reich in the Anschluss, Freud, aged 80, was still working in Vienna. Hitler despised Freud and very possibly feared the man who could shed light on his deeply disturbed and vindictive personality. When Freud's books were burned in Vienna, he is reported to have commented that mankind had progressed from burning people only to burning their books. Freud's children, Anna and Martin, were arrested but released. This experience, coupled with the insistence of his friends, convinced Freud that he should leave Austria and seek refuge outside Nazi-occupied areas. Until then he had steadfastly refused to leave Vienna. Due to his reputation, he had no difficulty getting a visa to enter Britain, but exit visas from Austria for himself and his family had to be bought with bribes and diplomatic pressure. Freud and his immediate family members relocated in London, where he was able to continue his valuable work until his death in 1939.

Lenin (1870–1924)

Born Vladimir Ilyich Ulyanov in 1870, Lenin became known to the world by his pen name. The name excited and enraged people, depending upon their reception of his views on Marxist socialism. Young Ulyanov was a lawyer in Russia at the turn of the century, when political activity against the czar was growing. His brother was hanged for attempting to assassinate the czar, another brother and a sister were imprisoned for circulating revolutionary propaganda, and Ulyanov and his wife spent time in exile in Siberia. In 1900, Ulyanov found himself under observation by the political police, and leaving Russia seemed a good idea. He went first to Geneva, where he attempted to publish a propagandist newspaper called *The Spark.* Quarrels with fellow revolutionaries forced him to move to Munich, where he took the pen name that was to be his label for the rest of his life. Lenin wrote, spoke, and raged against a political system he saw as profoundly unfair. He gathered around him other Russian refugees who agreed with his views, and they spent long hours debating how to change the world. During this time Lenin developed the qualities of certainty and leadership that would put him in good stead when the revolution finally took place. Lenin left Munich and made his way to London—the beginning of the somewhat frantic wanderings back and forth across Europe that characterized Lenin's life until he could finally return to Russia to lead the Revolution of 1917.

Golda Meir (1898–1978)

Golda Meir was born in Kiev, Russia, in 1898. Anti-Semitism was rife there, and although her family was very poor, they managed to leave Russia illegally and flee to Canada. They eventually settled in Milwaukee, Wisconsin, where Golda grew up. By the age of 18, she had become a committed Zionist and was travelling around the United States to gather support for the establishment of a Jewish homeland in Palestine. In 1917, she married Morris Myerson. They moved to Palestine after the World War I and eventually hebraicized Myerson to Meir in response to an appeal from Ben-Gurion that all Jews have Hebrew names. In Israel, Meir continued her work toward a Jewish homeland and held various positions of leadership. She was a member of the Histradut party, and when the party leader was arrested in 1946, Golda took his place in negotiations with the British. In 1947, when war with the surrounding Arab states looked inevitable, Golda went to the United States to raise $50 million for arms for the Jews. In 1956, she became an Israeli foreign minister. When she was 67 years old, she was asked to form a coalition government, and at age 70 she became the prime minister of Israel. She resigned in 1974, four years before her death.

Rudolf Nureyev (1938–1993)

Most refugees are driven from their home countries by war, oppression, or natural disaster. Some, however, such as Rudolf Nureyev, leave home to find a country where they are free to express themselves. Born in Ufa in the USSR's Bashkir province, Nureyev was a ballet dancer of some renown in his country. His artistic expression, however, was proscribed by government preferences on the nature of ballet. For that reason, he defected to the West in 1961, when the Kirov ballet company with which he was travelling was about to leave Paris and return to Moscow. He lived and worked in Paris, gaining a reputation as both dancer and choreographer. He later worked with a number of major dance companies in the West. His dynamism brought the male dancer to the center of the ballet stage and drew wider audiences to ballet than the discipline had previously enjoyed. He worked until his death in 1993. Nureyev will remain an important influence in the field of dance for years to come.

Alexander Solzhenitsyn (1918–)

Alexander Solzhenitsyn was born in 1918 in Rostov, Russia. He studied physics and mathematics at the university level and served in the Soviet army during World War II as an artillery commander. In 1945, he was arrested, charged with anti-Soviet behavior, and imprisoned for eight years. He spent an additional three years in internal exile in Siberia. Solzhenitsyn was rehabilitated in 1956, and he took up a teaching post. In 1962, he published *One Day in the Life of Ivan Denisovich,* a novel about life in Stalin's prison camps. This caused him further trouble with the authorities, and in 1969 he was forbidden to publish both inside and outside the Soviet Union. He ignored the order, publishing *The First Circle* (1968) and *Cancer Ward* (1969). Solzhenitsyn was awarded the Nobel Prize for Literature in 1970, but he could not travel to Sweden to receive it, nor would his government allow a member of the Swedish Academy to present it to him in the Soviet Union. Following the publication of *The Gulag Archipelago* in 1973, Solzhenitsyn was expelled from the Soviet Union and went to live in Switzerland. He moved from there to the United States, where he continued to write and speak out about Soviet denial of human rights. He also spoke out against the decadence and materialism of the West. With the end of the Cold War and the dissolution of the

USSR, Solzhenitsyn's Russian citizenship was restored, and he returned home to Russia in mid-1994.

Sun Yat-sen (1866–1925)

Sun Yat-sen was born in Kwantung, China, to a peasant family in 1866. He lived most of his young life in Hawaii, where he went to school and was brought up in the Christian tradition. He returned to China to study medicine in Canton and Hong Kong, graduating in 1895. In 1894, he founded the Revive China Society. As a result of his participation in an unsuccessful uprising in Canton in 1895, he was forced into exile. He went first to the United States and then to Britain, where he achieved some notoriety by being briefly imprisoned at the Chinese Legation in London in 1896. In 1905, Sun Yat-sen founded the Alliance Society and began to develop his notion of the three principles to which everyone is entitled—nationalism, democracy, and livelihood. After an absence of 16 years, Sun returned to China when the 1911 revolution overthrew the Manchu dynasty. He was elected president of the provisional government, but resigned in 1912 in the face of conservative opposition. He then led an unsuccessful revolt in 1913 and was once again forced to leave his country. The Soviet Union helped him regain power in 1923, and he was again elected president, this time of the republican government in Canton. Using what he had learned in the Soviet Union, he founded the Chinese nationalist party called the Kuomintang and formed an early alliance with the Chinese Communist party. When he died in 1925, he was respected by both the Kuomintang and the communists. The reconciliation of the two parties, however, was to be short-lived.

Tenzin Gyatso (1935–)

Tenzin Gyatso was born Lhamo Dhondrub in Tibet in 1935. An expedition of Tibetan Buddhist lamas searching for the child who was the reincarnation of the late Dalai Lama decided two-year-old Lhamo Dhondrub was that child. His name was changed to Tenzin Gyatso, and he began the long period of training needed to become the spiritual leader of the Tibetan people. He was enthroned as the fourteenth Dalai Lama—the Tibetan God King—in Lhasa in 1940. After Tibet was invaded by the Chinese in 1950, the Chinese allowed the Tibetans to continue their traditional way of life for a short time, but more and more pressure was put on them to become more like the Chinese. The Dalai Lama tried to negotiate with the Chinese to reach compromises that would allow the continuation of Tibetan cultural and religious traditions. The Chinese would not compromise, however, and they seriously mistreated the Tibetans in their own land. The Tibetans began to stage revolts that were cruelly put down. After an uprising in Lhasa in 1959, many Tibetans fled across the Himalayas to safety in India. The Dalai Lama was among them. He has been forced to remain in exile since then, but he has worked tirelessly for a solution to his country's difficulty. He has travelled extensively and made many overtures for peace with the Chinese. He continues to lead and inspire the Tibetan people—those in exile and those still in Tibet. He was awarded the Nobel Peace Prize in 1989 in recognition for his continued efforts to preserve his people's cultural heritage through nonviolent struggle.

Activists for Refugees

The people whose names appear on this list are those for whom biographical information was readily available. There are many activists in the refugee field, both in the United States and abroad, whose names do not appear in this section. Lack of time and space prohibits mentioning them all. In the United states, for instance, Charles Sternberg and Leo Cherne of the International Rescue Committee, the late Charles McCarthy of the U.S. Catholic Conference/Migration Service, Julia Taft of InterAction, Wells Klein of the American Council for Nationalities Service, and many others have worked tirelessly and against great odds to succeed at what appears to be an almost hopeless task.

Robert P. DeVecchi (1930–)

Robert DeVecchi was born in New York City in 1930 into a family with a tradition of public and social service. His parents devoted much time to volunteer work, and his paternal grandfather, Paolo DeVecchi, was on the first International Red Cross field surgical team in the Franco-Prussian War in 1870. Robert DeVecchi was educated at Yale and Harvard. He became a foreign service officer for the U.S. Department of State, serving from 1956 to 1966 in Washington, D.C., Warsaw, Rome, and in Paris with NATO. From

1972 to 1975 he was the New York director for Save the Children Federation. In 1975, DeVecchi decided to make a change. He volunteered to work with the International Rescue Committee (IRC) in Fort Chaffee, Arkansas, helping to resettle Vietnamese refugees who had been evacuated from Saigon and brought to the United States. He subsequently became IRC Indochina program director, then IRC program director, and executive director. During those years he visited many areas where refugees needed the help of the International Rescue Committee, including Malaysia, Thailand, Kurdistan, Mogadishu (Somalia), and Sarajevo (ex-Yugoslavia). DeVecchi is currently president of the International Rescue Committee. During the years he has been with the organization, its role has shifted from being mainly concerned with resettlement to devoting much of its effort and budget to relief and assistance to refugees and internally displaced peoples. Of his involvement with the IRC, DeVecchi says: "The work has called upon every possible talent or energy I may have, and represents the coming together in a single focus, of every interest and passion of my life. I feel truly blessed."

Elizabeth G. Ferris (1950–)

Elizabeth (Beth) Ferris's interest in the world beyond U.S. borders began when she was a high school exchange student to Manaus, Brazil. She continued to travel during her university years, including a year in the Andean countries researching her dissertation. Ferris received her B.A. in history from Duke University and an M.A. in Latin American studies and Ph.D. in political science from the University of Florida. After finishing her degrees in 1975, she taught at Miami University of Ohio and Lafayette College, among others. During 1981–1982, she was a Fulbright Professor at Universidad Autonoma de Mexico. She was then based in Geneva with the Refugee Service of the World Council of Churches from 1985 to 1991. From 1991 to 1993, she was research director for the Life and Peace Institute in Uppsala, Sweden, where she coordinated the work of researchers around the world working on peace issues and the nonviolent resolution of conflict. Beth Ferris is a Quaker, and this has been central to shaping her commitment to justice issues and refugees. She is currently director of the Immigration and Refugee Program of Church World Service in New York City, where she is involved not only with refugee resettlement and asylum work in the United

States but also with mobilizing U.S. church support for international refugee work. Ferris says that work in the field of refugees is "special because individual human beings are at the center of concern. [It is] about relieving suffering, offering hope for lasting solutions, and working to make it possible for people to return [home]."

Arthur Cleveland Helton (1949–)

Arthur Helton was born in 1949 in St. Louis, Missouri, where he attended local schools. In 1971 he graduated from Columbia College in New York City, and in 1976 he graduated from New York University School of Law, where he currently teaches immigration and refugee law. After becoming a lawyer, Helton worked in private practice, providing legal assistance to the underprivileged. His first work in the field of refugees was in 1981, when he represented Haitian boat people who were transferred to New York from detention in Florida. In 1982, he joined the Lawyers Committee for Human Rights and directed its Refugee Project for 12 years. During Helton's time with the Lawyers Committee, it was one of the leading voices on asylum and refugee protection. He trained over 1,000 lawyers around the country in techniques of representing Haitians and established the country's largest volunteer lawyer program assisting refugees. He worked on the creation of a corps of government asylum adjudicators, a program to release detainees who would not abscond, and the granting of temporary permission to remain in the United States to Bosnians, Liberians, and Somalis until it was safe for them to return home. Helton's work has been recognized worldwide, and he has investigated the plights of refugees and displaced persons wherever emergencies have arisen. In 1991, he received the Ninoy Aquino Refugee Recognition Award from the president of the Republic of the Philippines. In 1994, Helton was appointed director of migration programs at the Open Society Institute in New York, where his first task was to establish an organization to ameliorate forced population movements in the countries of the former Soviet Union. When asked why he became involved with refugees, Helton explained: "I have great sympathy for innocent victims."

Gaynor Jacobson (1912–)

Gaynor Jacobson's father, Morris, was a member of a Jewish socialist organization in Latvia and had been arrested and sentenced to life in a Siberian labor camp. After serving five years, he was able to bribe his way to freedom, and he and his wife Rose emigrated to the United States in 1907. Gaynor Jacobson was born Israel Gaynor Jacobson in Buffalo, New York, in 1912. When he was about three years old, he experienced his first taste of racism. His was the only Jewish family in the small New York town of Angola, and other young children taunted him about being Jewish. He graduated from high school with very good grades and went on to attend Columbia University in New York City. Unfortunately, family funds ran out during the Depression, and Gaynor was forced to leave before he finished. Eventually he was able to complete his degree in social work at the University of Buffalo. He went to work for the Jewish Welfare Society of Buffalo in 1937 and for the Jewish Family Agency in Rochester, New York, in 1938. While in Rochester he became executive secretary of the Jewish Community Council and executive director of the Jewish Family and Children's Agency. He also became the first vice president of the local branch of the National Association for the Advancement of Colored People (NAACP). He was very much involved in social and political activities, doing weekly radio talks to counteract pro-Nazi, racist broadcasts. Jacobson's refugee work began with the American Jewish Joint Distribution Committee in 1944. He was given the job of helping Jews who were coming out of concentration camps at the end of World War II. He was determined that the only solution to problems facing Jews in Europe was the establishment of the state of Israel. For many years up to the present, Jacobson has been involved in helping refugees and immigrants through the Hebrew Sheltering and Immigrant Aid Society. He divides his time between his homes in New York and Arizona.

James G. McDonald (1886–1955)

James McDonald was born in Ohio in 1886. He did his graduate work at Harvard University, began his career as a professor of politics and history, and went on to become a journalist. From 1919 to 1933, he was chairman of the Foreign Policy Association and was keenly interested and well informed about all international issues. In 1933, the flood of refugees from Germany required the international community to urgently address the problem, and McDonald was appointed the high commissioner for refugees coming from Germany. He felt the rise of Hitler was a tragedy for Germany as well as for Jews, and he tried to counteract prejudice against all things German. He was a devout Christian and believed Christians had a special responsibility to fight Nazism. During his short tenure of office, many countries were becoming less disposed to receive Jewish refugees, and McDonald took a great interest in Palestine as a place of refuge for them. In 1935, as it became apparent that more and more refugees would be forced to flee Germany, McDonald decided to resign his post in a manner that would bring the impending horrors of Nazism to world attention. He wrote a letter of resignation, which was widely published, denouncing Hitler and the Third Reich. It was an outspoken condemnation of Nazi policies that endangered the Jews of Europe. McDonald continued to work in the field of refugees, becoming chairman of the President's Advisory Committee on Political Refugees. He later became the first U.S. ambassador to Israel.

Rigoberta Menchu (1959–)

Rigoberta Menchu is a Guatemalan human rights activist. A Mayan Indian, she was born in 1959 to Vincente and Juana Menchu. As a teenager, she became concerned about the plight of indigenous peoples and began to campaign for their rights. (Guatemala has a particularly bad record of repression and violence against its indigenous peoples.) Because of Rigoberta's political involvement, her mother, father, and brother were murdered by Guatemalan security forces in 1980. She continued to oppose her government's repressive policies toward the indigenous and, fearing for her own life, was forced to flee Guatemala and seek refuge in Mexico. Since then she has continued to fight for social justice and the rights of indigenous peoples. In 1992, in San Marcos, Guatemala, she coordinated protests against the celebrations of the 500th anniversary of the landing of Columbus in the New World. She became internationally well known when she was awarded the Nobel Peace Prize in 1992 for her work on behalf of the indigenous peoples of Central America.

Fridtjof Nansen (1861–1930)

Fridtjof Nansen, a Norwegian born in 1861, first achieved notoriety as an arctic explorer. He was a member of the first expedition to cross Greenland in 1888 and was part of a team that tried to reach the North Pole between 1893 and 1895. Being in the public eye, he later went on to become the Norwegian minister in London. Nansen was very enthusiastic about the idea of a League of Nations, and he worked hard toward its inception. He became leader of the Norwegian delegation to the League and argued that it had a humanitarian role to play in the world. He worked against difficult odds to convince other member countries to give humanitarian aid where it was needed. Europe was in chaos after World War I, and hundreds of thousands of people were displaced and starving. After the war, Nansen was put in charge of the repatriation of 500,000 prisoners of war, becoming in 1921 the first high commissioner for refugees for the League of Nations. That same year he headed the Red Cross mission to relieve famine in Russia. In 1922, Nansen instituted the Nansen Passport, an identification document for stateless persons without which they were unable to move around or find employment. Nansen was awarded the Nobel Peace Prize in 1922 for his humanitarian work on behalf of casualties of World War I. His efforts to help the impoverished and displaced peoples of Europe did not confine themselves to politics. He used imagination and understanding to develop meaningful aid programs. At his urging, the League of Nations loaned £10 million to exiles living in Greece so they could develop fallow farmland. This was the first economic development project funded by an international organization. Nansen's work to establish a homeland for displaced Armenian people displaced by Turkey was never realized.

Sadako Ogata (1927–)

Sadako Ogata became the United Nations high commissioner for refugees in 1991. She was born Sadako Nakamura in Tokyo, Japan, in 1927 and was the daughter and granddaughter of diplomats. She was educated at Georgetown University in Washington, D.C., and at the University of California at Berkeley. She is married to Shijiro Ogata, a Tokyo banker. She was a professor and director and dean of the Institute of International Relations at Sophia University in Tokyo, where she worked until 1990. She was a senior member of the Japanese delegation to the United Nations from 1976 to 1979 and a minister of the Japanese mission to the United Nations from 1978 to 1979. From 1982 to 1985, Ogata was the Japanese representative to the United Nations Commission on Human Rights in Geneva. She has served as chairperson to the Executive Board of the United Nations Children's Fund (UNICEF). She led the Human Rights Mission in Myanmar (formerly Burma) in 1990 and was a member of the Trilateral Commission in 1984. Ogata was the UN special emissary investigating problems of Cambodian refugees on the Thai-Cambodian border and has, since becoming high commissioner, shown particular interest in instituting programs of repatriation for refugees and developing preventive strategies for dealing with refugee movements. Ogata is the first female high commissioner and one of the few women in the senior leadership of the United Nations, where she has earned a reputation as an energetic and determined advocate for the human rights of refugees, asylum-seekers, and the internally displaced. In 1994, she was the recipient of the International Human Rights Law Group's annual award.

Joyce Pearce (1915–1985)

Born in 1915, Joyce Pearce took a degree in modern history at Oxford University and taught secondary school for a short time. She was one of those rare individuals who believed that one person could make a difference, and she worked to do just that. In 1951, Pearce started the Ockenden Venture when five displaced teenage girls from Eastern Europe were invited to her home in Surrey, England, for "health, home and education." Even Pearce did not realize that from this small beginning the Ockenden Venture would go on to help thousands of refugees. In the beginning, it concentrated its efforts on helping refugee children, but it has branched out to help refugees of all ages as well as disabled and disadvantaged people all over the world. Wherever there was a need, the Ockenden Venture was ready to help. In 1956, it went to the aid of Hungarian refugees. In 1963, Pearce's attention was turned to Tibetan refugees, and she became a close friend of the Dalai Lama. In 1971, Pearce went to Vietnam, set up an orphanage in Saigon, and arranged for seriously ill children to be treated in Britain. She helped refugees from places as far apart as Chile, Ethiopia, and Southeast Asia. The Ockenden Venture encourages refugees to take an active part in the projects it establishes to help them. It now has a number of centers around the world, all funded by charitable donations. Although Pearce died in 1985, the work of the Ockenden Venture continues.

Philip Rudge (1945–)

Philip Rudge was born in Cheltenham, England, in 1945. He attended London University from 1963 to 1971, earning degrees in English Language and Literature, Philosophy, Economics, Sociology, and Comparative Education in Developing Countries. He was a lecturer at the University of Tuebingen, Germany, from 1969 to 1970. Rudge's life changed direction and his interest in refugee issues grew as a result of his experiences in Laos in the mid-1970s, a time of great upheaval in Southeast Asia. Rudge was then working in Laos as a development aid officer under the Colombo Plan, a project sponsored jointly by the British Council/ Ministry of Overseas Development and the government of Laos. He stayed on in Laos to help with postwar reconstruction. In 1983, Rudge became Reorientation Adviser with World University Service. He was responsible for coordinating programs for Latin American refugees at British universities. Since 1983, Rudge has been general secretary of the London-based European Council on Refugees and Exiles (ECRE), a pan-European network concerned with the treatment of refugees and asylum-seekers in Europe and the development of European governmental refugee policies. During the past decade, Rudge has been a key contributor to the development of this organization. He views work in the refugee field as challenging to head and heart, and says that anyone pursuing refugee work will "need to think about internationalism and solidarity; they will be able to see how the way we live (in the West) all too often depends on the economic and political suppression of others. They will also have the chance to meet some of the most extraordinary human beings."

Raoul Wallenberg (1912–?)

Raoul Wallenberg was born in Sweden in 1912. His mother had been widowed before his birth, and she and his grandparents brought him up. His grandfather was a banker, and the family was one of the most privileged in Sweden. Wallenberg's education took him to Europe to learn languages and to the United States to study architecture. His early career in banking led him to South Africa and Haifa. When President Franklin Roosevelt set up the War Refugee Board and a person from a neutral country was needed to negotiate in Hungary on behalf of the Hungarian Jews,

Raoul Wallenberg was asked to go. He was given diplomatic status, but the tactics he employed to save Hungarian Jews from the gas chambers at Auschwitz-Birkenau were not all diplomacy. He resorted to bribery and extortion and many times risked his own life to save others. He had thousands of false documents made that declared the holders to be Swedish citizens. He distributed the documents in the ghettoes and even at stations where trains were being loaded for the death camps. He set up safe houses that flew the flag of neutral Sweden, and thousands of Jews sheltered in them. When the Russians liberated Budapest, Wallenberg apparently made the mistake of trusting them. He went off to negotiate with General Malinovsky in 1945 and was never seen again. No one is certain what happened to Raoul Wallenberg.

Elie Wiesel (1928–)

Elie Wiesel was born in 1928 in Sighet, Romania, to Shlomo and Sarah Wiesel. In 1944, when Elie was still a teenager, he and the rest of his family were sent to Auschwitz concentration camp. Wiesel went from Auschwitz to Buchenwald and became the only member of his family to survive the camps. Like so many others after the war, Wiesel was a refugee and went to the United States. Since then, he has taught, written, and lectured about the Holocaust. His unforgettable message is that such horror must never happen again. Wiesel has received numerous awards for his important work. Among them are the Jewish Heritage Award (1965), the Ellis Island Medal of Honor (1992), and the President's Medal of Freedom (1993). In 1986, Wiesel was awarded the Nobel Peace Prize for his tireless work in the area of human rights. Upon receiving the prize he said, "Sometimes we must interfere. When human lives are endangered, when human dignity is in jeopardy, international borders and sensitivities become irrelevant. Wherever men and women are persecuted because of their race, religion or political views, that place must, for the moment, become the center of the universe. This is awareness in action." Wiesel continues to be a prolific writer and vociferous lecturer against violence, repression, and racism.

Roger Paul Winter (1942–)

Roger Winter was born in Hartford, Connecticut, in 1942. He did his undergraduate work in psychology at Wheaton College in Illinois and his graduate work in urban sociology at the University of Connecticut. He went on to do antipoverty and social welfare work in Hartford, Chicago, Boston, and New Britain, Connecticut. From 1970 to 1979, Winter worked for the state of Maryland as assistant secretary of human resources and assistant secretary for budget and fiscal planning. In 1980, he became the director of the Office of Refugee Resettlement (ORR) under the Carter administration, and in that capacity was instrumental in implementing the Refugee Act of 1980. Shortly thereafter, he became director of the U.S. Committee for Refugees (USCR), and he helped make it the country's principal refugee advocacy agency. USCR operates like a human rights agency for refugees, publishes the influential *World Refugee Survey,* and has had a significant impact over the years in matters such as pirate attacks on boat people, humanitarian assistance in southern Sudan, and the setting up of a legal framework for uprooted people in the former Soviet Union. In January 1994, Winter was made executive director of Immigration and Refugee Services of America, the parent organization of USCR, and, as such, is involved in issues of immigration and diversity. He currently serves as director of USCR. Winter holds that "the worth of individuals [is] paramount [and that] the promotion of justice is a prerequisite for true peaceful relations among people. . . ." Moreover, as an American, he believes that he is "accountable for assisting those who are less well-positioned in life."

4

Facts, Statistics, and Legal Documents

THIS CHAPTER PROVIDES SOME OF THE MOST IMPORTANT statistics, data, and legal documentation relating to refugees.

Refugee Statistics

Counting refugees is at best an approximate undertaking. Not only is the collection of accurate statistical data on refugees and asylum-seekers extremely problematic, but the figures provided by the Office of the United Nations High Commissioner for Refugees (UNHCR), governments, nongovernmental organizations (NGOs), and journalists frequently conflict with each other.

There are several reasons for these differences. The term *refugee* means different things to different organizations. For the United Nations, refugees are people who have left their country because they have a well-founded fear of persecution or because their safety is threatened by events seriously disturbing public order. Governments will describe refugees as either those people whom they have accepted as recognized refugees or those people who have applied for political asylum. The media and many NGOs, on the other hand, often use a much broader approach, considering a refugee to be anyone who has been forced to leave their usual place of residence by circumstances beyond their control. These differing interpretations lead to widely varying refugee statistics.

Apart from definitional problems, there are many practical and political obstacles to the collection of accurate refugee statistics. Contemporary refugee movements are often sudden mass exoduses in which as many as a million people can flee their countries within weeks or even days. In such situations, it is impossible to register all the refugees. Moreover, in many parts of the world refugees do not live in organized camps, but settle with family relatives or among ethnically related local people. Because local populations may themselves register as refugees to receive international assistance, it is often difficult to establish how many refugees actually live in an area. In addition, refugees are highly mobile populations, moving between refugee camps and local communities, frequently registering more than once in order to gain higher levels of assistance, and sometimes even moving back and forth between countries. It is very difficult for agencies to keep track of such movements. It is also the case that governments will at times either deliberately exaggerate the numbers of refugees in order to gain more international assistance or deliberately downplay the numbers in order to not embarrass the country from which the refugees fled. Given these conceptual, practical, and political factors, the statistics can at best be considered approximate figures.

Table 1 lists the total numbers of refugees and asylum-seekers who are unwilling to repatriate due to fear of persecution and violence in their homelands as of 31 December 1993. This table does not include refugees permanently settled in other countries. In some cases, refugees listed in Table 1 may no longer require assistance, but they still need international protection. Host countries are printed in bold type.

The global number of refugees has been growing rapidly in the past decade. There are nearly twice as many refugees now as there were in 1984. Most of the growth in recent years has occurred in the developing world, the Middle East, South Asia, and Africa, and as Table 1 illustrates, it is in these regions where most of the world's refugees originated and stayed during the year 1993. Countries such as Tanzania, Iran, and Croatia saw the refugee population that they host swell by hundreds of thousands.

Table 2 lists selected populations in refugee-like situations as of 31 December 1993. Many people who fear persecution or harm if returned to their home countries, and thus who may be refugees, are not recognized by governments as refugees or asylum-seekers. Some are given temporary refuge or allowed to remain on humanitarian grounds; others remain undocumented. Because information on such groups is fragmentary, this table presents only reported estimates, and no total is provided.

Table 3 identifies selected countries in which substantial numbers of people have been displaced within their homeland as a result of human conflict or forced relocations. Practically every country that generates refugees also creates internally displaced persons. In recent years, Angola, Mozambique, Afghanistan, Sudan, Peru, Colombia, Armenia, Azerbaijan and Tajikistan have been among many countries whose numbers of internally displaced are in the millions. Although the internally displaced share many characteristics with refugees who cross international borders, they are generally not eligible for protection under international refugee law. Because information on internal displacement is fragmentary, this table presents only reported estimates, and no total is provided. It is important to note, however, that even this selected list includes more than 25 million people, and that the number of internally displaced is undoubtedly much higher.

Table 4 identifies countries that have generated the greatest number of the world's refugees in recent years. The majority of contemporary refugee movements are caused by war, ethnic strife, and persecution. The countries involved in the most destructive wars of the last decade—Afghanistan, Angola, Armenia, Azerbaijan, Burundi, Cambodia, Georgia, Iran, Iraq, Liberia, Mozambique, Rwanda, Somalia, Sudan, Vietnam, and the former Yugoslavia—have also been the main sources of refugees. It is also true that the principal sources of the current world refugee problem—Angola, Burma, Iran, Iraq and Sudan—are among the world's most repressive societies.

Counts may understate the total number of refugees from a given country, as asylum states do not always specify refugees' countries of origin. This table does not include populations considered to be in the refugee-like circumstances listed in Table 2, many of whom are also refugees. It also does not include refugees or people in refugee-like circumstances who have been offered permanent resettlement and status in another country. Examples of such refugees include 42,775 Vietnamese who were resettled in the United States and nearly 105,000 members of religious minorities who departed the former Soviet Union for Israel and the United States in 1993.

Table 5 reflects estimated numbers of refugees who participated in formal voluntary repatriation programs administered by UNHCR, as well as those who spontaneously returned to their homelands during 1993. The largest repatriations occurred in Afghanistan and Mozambique, and in total, some 2.5 million refugees returned home during 1993.

Repatriations generally occur under difficult conditions. Nevertheless, in recent years the international community has begun to give much greater attention to repatriation and even to returning refugees to countries that continue to experience widespread conflict. There is hope that millions of refugees may be able to return safely to their homes in Africa, South Asia, the Middle East, Europe, and elsewhere in the next few years. Accordingly, UNHCR has declared the 1990s as the "decade of repatriation" and has committed a high proportion of its resources to repatriation programs. Much will depend on continued progress toward peace in countries still undergoing civil conflict and on the willingness of the international community to encourage and support repatriation and reconstruction.

Table 6 lists some instances of involuntary returns and expulsions that occurred during 1993. The United Nations Refugee Convention and Protocol prohibits the forced repatriation of refugees (refoulement), and governments rarely force the repatriation of persons they acknowledge to be refugees. More often, however, they forcibly repatriate persons who are either denied access to refugee determination procedures or who are subjected to unfair procedures. Not all the persons listed on this table are bona fide refugees; instead, they were expelled under questionable procedures, which could result in refoulement of genuine refugees among those returned. As this is not a comprehensive list, no total is given.

Table 7 lists refugees in relation to total population and per capita gross national product (GNP) of the asylum country in 1993. The table demonstrates that the greatest burden of refugee flows is borne by the world's poorest countries. The sheer size of refugee populations and their rapid growth seriously strain host countries. For example, in the aftermath of the Gulf War, Jordan played host to 1 million refugees—one for every four of its citizens! Malawi, one of Africa's poorest and most densely populated countries, gave refuge to nearly 1 million Mozambican refugees—equivalent to about one-tenth of its population. The Iranian government granted asylum and assistance to more than 1 million Kurdish and Shi'ite Muslim refugees from Iraq on top of an existing refugee population of more than 2 million Afghans and another 400,000 Iraqis who had fled Iraq during the previous decade. Mass refugee influxes can endanger social and economic security, particularly in countries already suffering from economic underdevelopment, unstable political systems, and ethnic and other social cleavages.

Donor governments assist refugees through direct assistance to host governments, usually in the form of food aid, and by supporting international agencies and nongovernmental organizations. Donor governments support the international refugee agencies through annual contributions to their budgets.

Table 8 lists the top 20 countries that contributed to international refugee aid agencies during 1993. The table ranks countries by the financial contribution of their governments per capita. The United States was the largerst single donor in 1993. However, the U.S. contribution per capita ranks only number eight among donor countries. The most generous countries on a per capita basis are the Nordic states.

U.S. contributions have not grown nearly as quickly as the number of refugees, nor as quickly as the contributions of other donors. Up until the mid-1980s, U.S. contributions for humanitarian assistance generally kept pace with the explosive growth in refugee numbers. Then, during 1985–1989, U.S. financial support declined consistently. For example, its share of the UNHCR's total expenditures dropped from 30 percent in 1982 to 22 percent in 1989, during a period when the number of refugees under UNHCR care increased by 50 percent. American financial support for the International Committee of the Red Cross, another important refugee agency, dropped from 30 percent to 15 percent of the agency's total expenditures, from 1985 to 1988. One reason for the decline in U.S. aid for overseas refugees is the increase in spending on refugee admissions, primarily for those refugees from the former Soviet Union and Southeast Asia. Recent American administrations have done little to rectify the situation. Since the end of the Cold War, the major donor governments have lost interest in the now much less strategic regions where many refugees are located. As a result, the Western powers, including the United States, are not investing the resources that countries experiencing refugee flows or just emerging from conflict need to make the transition to peace, development, and economic stability.

The generosity of the industrialized states can also be measured by the number of refugees resettled and granted asylum in relation to domestic population.

Table 9 details the numbers of refugees resettled and persons granted asylum in relation to total population in the major resettlement countries of North America, Europe, and Australia from 1975 to 1992. The most generous countries are Sweden, Canada, and Australia, with the United States ranked fourth out of 14 countries.

Overall, in terms of both financial aid and resettlement of refugees, the Scandanavian countries are the most generous of the industrialized nations; southern European countries are the least generous; and the traditional resettlement countries—the United States, Canada, and Australia—are in the middle. Although Japan has substantially increased its financial contributions in recent years, it stands out as a rich country that provides mid-level assistance but admits practically no refugees—a record that could clearly stand continued improvement.

Table 10 lists the numbers of asylum applications in Western Europe, North America, and Australia from 1983 to 1992. The annual totals for those countries covered in the table have increased from 90,400 in 1983 to 825,200 in 1992. Over 3 million applications have been made in Europe during the past decade. Governments are skeptical of the claims of political persecution made by the majority of asylum applicants, and, as a result, the acceptance rate for asylum applicants in Europe in 1993 was less than 5 percent. Nevertheless, governments permitted most of the more than 1 million rejected asylum applicants over the past decade to stay under temporary statuses. The numbers of asylum applications make heavy demands on asylum adjudication systems and have caused great expense. Care for asylum applicants in industrial countries and adjudication of their claims are estimated to cost from $8 billion to $10 billion annually. This contrasts with a 1993 budget for the UNHCR of approximately $1.5 billion.

Table 11 details the numbers of emigrants from Eastern Europe and the former Soviet Union to the West from 1984 to 1992. With the disintegration of communist regimes at the end of the 1980s, citizens from former Eastern Bloc countries arriving in

Western Europe represented the biggest population movement the continent had seen since the late 1940s. In 1989, over 1.2 million people left Eastern Europe and the Soviet Union for the West. During the next two years, the East-to-West flow moderated, with 923,000 moving westward in 1990 and 800,000 in 1991. Most of the emigrants have been members of ethnic minority or religious groups with close links to receiving countries such as Germany, Hungary, Turkey, the United States, Israel, and Greece. But there have also been unanticipated outflows of war refugees from the former republics of Yugoslavia, of boat people from Albania, and of Gypsies and other minorities from Romania.

In the early 1990s, emigration from Croatia, Serbia, Bosnia-Herzegovinia, and Kosovo to other European countries increased dramatically as a result of ethnically motivated violence and prolonged and brutal civil war among Yugoslavia's erstwhile republics. By 1994, more than 2.5 million had been displaced in the former Yugoslavia, and several hundred thousand had taken refuge in Germany, Hungary, Austria, Italy, and Sweden. Any extension of the war into Macedonia or Kosovo, with an attendant and massive spillover of ethnic conationals into Albania, Greece, Turkey, or Bulgaria, could internationalize the conflict and increase the likelihood of further refugee outflows.

Table 12 gives the ceilings for U.S. refugee admissions by region from fiscal years (FY) 1986 to 1993. The refugee resettlement program in the United States has, in recent years, increasingly resettled persons leaving their home countries through direct departure programs rather than refugees who have fled to countries of asylum. This table demonstrates that the great majority of refugees admitted to the United States over the past eight years have originated from Asia (mostly Vietnamese, Laotians, and Cambodians) and from the former Soviet Union (mainly Jews, Armenians, and Pentacostal Christians). In addition, increasing proportions of those resettled have weak claims to refugee status. U.S. resettlement slots for refugees in regions with the largest refugee concentrations (Africa and countries hosting Muslim refugees) are comparatively few. For example, the United States has always had a low ceiling for the number of African refugees to be resettled here. Although the number has been raised in recent years, the allocation for Africa still represents a small percentage of the overall number of persons admitted to the United States as refugees each year. The resettlement priorities of the United States have always been strongly biased by foreign policy and ideological considerations. Even though the number of refugees worldwide continues to grow, the U.S. resettlement program will probably shrink over the next few years, and it is unlikely that any reduction in U.S. resettlement will be compensated by increases in the resettlement programs of Canada and Australia, the other principal resettlement countries.

Table 13 lists the numbers of asylum cases filed with immigration and naturalization service asylum officers and those cases approved or denied, by selected nationalities, from April 1991 to September 1993 in the United States. Persecution of individuals is supposed to be the criteria upon which asylum decisions are made, but foreign policy and ideological considerations continue to influence these decisions. Throughout the 1980s, asylum adjudications clearly showed that an applicant's country of origin and the relationship of that country to the U.S. government were the primary factors determining the granting of asylum. For example, a 1987 U.S. General Accounting Office (GAO) study of asylum compared the treatment of four different nationalities—Salvadorans, Nicaraguans, Poles, and Iranians. The study found that "aliens who stated on their application forms that they were arrested, imprisoned, had their life threatened, or were tortured had much lower approval rates if they were from El Salvador and Nicaragua than if they were from Poland or Iran." Among asylum-seekers making such claims, the approval rates were: Iranians, 64 percent; Poles, 55 percent; Nicaraguans, 7 percent; and Salvadorans, 3 percent. Only Haitians (1.8 percent) and Guatemalans (0.9 percent) fared worse. Moreover, of the four groups examined in the GAO study, only Salvadorans were deported to their home country after having been denied asylum.

In 1992 and 1993, most asylum applicants came from the Western Hemisphere. Salvadorans and Nicaraguans were arriving in smaller numbers, only to be replaced by Guatemalans who accounted for some 40 percent of the total applications in 1992. The island nations of Haiti and Cuba present the greatest risk of mass, uncontrolled refugee movement to the United States in the near future.

Table 14 details the budget of the Office of the United Nations High Commissioner for Refugees by region for 1991 and 1992. The table indicates that Africa and Asia consume the largest resources, but that in recent years refugee emergencies in Europe have required larger financial attention. In general, UNHCR expenditures have tracked the shifts in geographic distribution of refugees around the world, and they continue to grow as refugee numbers increase.

The most significant institutional weakness of the UNHCR is its dependence on voluntary contributions to carry out its programs. Less than 5 percent of the UNHCR's annual expenditures are covered by the UN regular budget; the remainder of UNHCR's funding and resources comes from national governments. Its assistance programs are divided broadly into general and special programs. Each year the High Commissioner's Executive Committee approves a General Program budget, which comprises activities financed through the annual program as well as the Emergency Fund, and appeals to all UN members to provide the resources needed to cover the program year. The primary allocation of these resources goes to the traditional areas of the High Commissioner's competence: emergency relief, voluntary repatriation, integration into host societies, and resettlement.

In addition to its General Program budget, UNHCR, at the request of the secretary-general or the UN General Assembly, undertakes Special Programs, which include major new and unforeseen emergency operations and transportation and rehabilitation assistance to refugees and displaced people who have returned to their homes. Special Programs are the subject of specific fund-raising appeals to interested governments and are financed from trust funds constricted with particular purposes and conditions. Thus, the UNHCR must raise funds for each new refugee problem.

The level of annual UNHCR expenditures has increased progressively over the years. Until the mid-1970s, the UNHCR spent only modest sums, the annual average remaining less than $10 million during the 1960s and just exceeding $20 million during the early 1970s. Annual expenditures rose from $9 million in 1971 to $135 million in 1978, and from $270 million in 1979 to nearly $500 million in 1980. The dramatic leaps in expenditures were in response to major refugee emergencies in Indochina, Africa, and Afghanistan. During the 1980s, the annual spending of UNHCR remained over $400 million, and, even allowing for inflation, the level of expenditures amounted to a fifteenfold increase over the early 1970s.

The 1990s have presented UNHCR with several new refugee emergencies and its overall expenditures have therefore continued to grow. In 1991, as a result of emergency relief operations in northern Iraq and in the Horn of Africa, total voluntary funds expenditure amounted to $882.9 million, an increase of almost 60 percent over 1990. In 1992, new refugee and humanitarian crises in the former Yugoslavia, Bangladesh, the Horn of Africa, and Southern Africa, as well as continued responsibilities in northern Iraq and new repatriation programs in Cambodia, Ethiopia, and Angola, pushed UNHCR expenditures over $1 billion.

TABLE 1
Refugees and Asylum-Seekers in Need of Protection and/or Assistance (as of 31 December 1993)

AFRICA	TOTAL–5,825,000
Algeria	121,000*
West Sahara	80,000*
Mali	35,000
Niger	6,000
Angola	11,000
Zaire	11,000
Benin	120,000
Togo	120,000
Botswana	500
Burkina Faso	6,000
Mali	6,000
Burundi	110,000*
Rwanda	85,000*
Zaire	25,000
Cameroon	2,500
Chad	2,000
Other	500
Central African Republic	41,000
Sudan	23,000
Chad	18,000
Congo	13,000
Angola	10,000
Chad	2,000
Other	1,000
Côte d'Ivoire	250,000
Liberia	250,000
Djibouti	60,000
Somalia	40,000
Ethiopia	20,000
Egypt	11,000
Somalia	6,000
Palestinians	4,300
Ethiopia	400
Other	300
Ethiopia	156,000*
Somalia	100,000*
Sudan	43,000
Djibouti	7,000

TABLE 1 *(continued)*

Kenya	6,000
Gabon	200
Gambia	2,000
Senegal	2,000
Ghana	133,000
Togo	120,000
Liberia	13,000
Guinea	570,000*
Liberia	420,000*
Sierra Leone	150,000*
Guinea-Bissau	16,000
Senegal	16,000
Kenya	332,000*
Somalia	280,000*
Sudan	37,000
Ethiopia	10,000
Other	5,000
Lesotho	100
South Africa	100
Liberia	110,000
Sierra Leone	110,000
Malawi	700,000
Mozambique	700,000
Mali	13,000
Mauritania	13,000
Mauritania	46,000
Mali	46,000
Namibia	5,000
Niger	3,000
Chad	3,000
Nigeria	4,400
Liberia	3,000
Chad	1,400
Rwanda	370,000
Burundi	370,000
Senegal	66,000
Mauritania	66,000
Sierra Leone	15,000
Liberia	15,000
South Africa	300,000*
Mozambique	300,000*
Sudan	633,000*
Eritrea	420,000*
Ethiopia	200,000*
Chad	7,000*
Other	6,000
Swaziland	57,000
Mozambique	50,000
South Africa	7,000
Tanzania	479,500
Burundi	350,000
Mozambique	60,000

TABLE 1 (*continued*)

Rwanda	50,000
Zaire	15,000
South Africa	3,000
Somalia	1,200
Other	300
Uganda	257,000*
Sudan	150,000
Rwanda	90,000*
Zaire	15,000
Other	2,000
Zaire	452,000
Angola	200,000
Sudan	120,000
Burundi	60,000
Rwanda	50,000
Uganda	20,000
Other	2,000
Zambia	158,500
Angola	120,000
Mozambique	22,000
Zaire	13,000
South Africa	500
Other	3,000
Zimbabwe	200,000
Mozambique	200,000
EUROPE AND NORTH AMERICA†	**TOTAL–2,785,000**
Armenia	290,000*
Azerbaijan	290,000*
Austria	77,700
Former Yugoslavia	74,300
Other	3,400
Azerbaijan	251,000*
Armenia	200,000*
Uzbekistan	51,000
Belarus	10,400
Belgium	32,900
Former Yugoslavia	6,000
Other	26,900
Bosnia and Herzegovina	70,000*
Former Yugoslavia	70,000*
Canada	20,500
Croatia	280,000*
Former Yugoslavia	280,000*
Czech Republic	6,300
Former Yugoslavia	4,100
Other	2,200
Denmark	23,300
Former Yugoslavia	17,300
Other	6,000
Finland	3,700
Former Yugoslavia	2,200
Other	1,500

TABLE 1 (*continued*)

France	30,900
Former Yugoslavia	7,000
Other	23,900
Germany	529,100*
Former Yugoslavia	300,000*
Other	299,100
Greece	800
Hungary	10,000
Former Yugoslavia	10,000
Italy	33,550*
Former Yugoslavia	32,000*
Other	1,500
Luxembourg	1,500
Former Yugoslavia	1,300
Other	200
Macedonia	12,100
Former Yugoslavia	12,000
Other	100
Netherlands	35,400
Norway	14,200
Former Yugoslavia	12,500
Other	1,700
Poland	600
Portugal	2,250
Former Yugoslavia	150
Other	2,100
Romania	1,000
Russian Federation	347,500*
Georgia	143,000*
Tajikistan	108,000*
Armenia/Azerbaijan	52,000*
Afghanistan	25,000
Somalia	6,500
Iraq	6,000
Other	7,000
Slovak Republic	1,900
Former Yugoslavia	1,900
Slovenia	38,000*
Former Yugoslavia	38,000*
Spain	14,000
Former Yugoslavia	2,200
Other	11,800
Sweden	58,800*
Former Yugoslavia	50,000*
Other	8,800
Switzerland	27,000
Former Yugoslavia	14,500
Other	12,500
Turkey	24,600*
Former Yugoslavia	20,000*
Iraq	4,000
Iran	500
Other	100

TABLE 1 (*continued*)

United Kingdom	28,100
Former Yugoslavia	6,600
Other	21,500
United States	150,400
Yugoslavia (Serbia/Montenegro)	357,000*
Former Yugoslavia	357,000*
LATIN AMERICA AND THE CARIBBEAN	**TOTAL–102,000**
Belize	8,900
El Salvador	6,100
Guatemala	2,200
Nicaragua	300
Honduras	200
Other	100
Bolivia	600
Colombia	350
Other	250
Brazil	1,000
Chile	100
Peru	100
Colombia	400
Costa Rica	24,800
Nicaragua	20,000
El Salvador	4,300
Other	500
Dominican Republic	1,300
Haiti	1,300
Ecuador	100
Colombia	100
El Salvador	150
Nicaragua	150
Guatemala	4,700
El Salvador	2,400
Nicaragua	2,200
Other	100
Honduras	100
Mexico	52,000
Guatemala	47,000
El Salvador	4,000
Other	1,000
Nicaragua	4,750
El Salvador	4,700
Other	50
Panama	950
El Salvador	400
Nicaragua	300
Other	250
Peru	400
Cuba	400
Venezuela	1,300
Cuba	1,000
Haiti	200
Nicaragua	100

TABLE 1 (*continued*)

EAST ASIA AND THE PACIFIC	**TOTAL—468,000**
Australia	2,950
China	296,900*
Vietnam	285,500
Burma	10,000*
Laos	1,400
Hong Kong	3,500
Vietnam	3,550
Indonesia	2,400
Vietnam	1,900
Cambodia	500
Japan	950
Vietnam	900
Other	50
Malaysia	8,150
Burma	5,100
Indonesia	1,700
Vietnam	1,150
Former Yugoslavia	200
Papua New Guinea	7,700
Indonesia	7,700
Philippines	1,700
Vietnam	1,700
Thailand	108,300
Burma	74,000
Laos	25,100
Vietnam	8,800
Sri Lanka	250
Other	150
Vietnam	35,000
Cambodia	35,000
MIDDLE EAST	**TOTAL–4,924,000**
Gaza Strip	603,000
Palestinians	603,000
Iran	1,995,000*
Afghanistan	1,900,000*
Iraq	95,000
Iraq	39,500
Iran	38,500
Other	1,000
Jordan	1,073,600
Palestinians	1,073,000
Former Yugoslavia	400
Other	200
Lebanon	329,000
Palestinians	328,000
Other	1,000
Saudi Arabia	25,000
Iraq	25,000
Syria	319,200
Palestinians	314,000
Iraq	4,700

TABLE 1 (*continued*)

Somalia	500
West Bank	479,000
Palestinians	479,000
Yemen	60,500
Somalia	57,000
Ethiopia	1,800
Eritrea	1,500
Other	200
SOUTH AND CENTRAL ASIA	**TOTAL–2,151,000**
Afghanistan	35,000
Tajikistan	35,000
Bangladesh	199,000
Burma	198,800
Other	200
India	325,600*
China (Tibet)	119,000
Sri Lanka	106,400*
Bangladesh	53,500
Afghanistan	24,400
Bhutan	20,000*
Burma	1,600
Other	700
Kazakhstan	6,500
Tajikistan	6,500
Kyrgyzstan	3,500
Tajikistan	3,500
Nepal	99,100
Bhutan	85,100
China (Tibet)	14,000
Pakistan	1,482,300
Afghanistan	1,480,000
Other	2,300
Tajikistan	400
Afghanistan	400
GRAND TOTAL	**16,255,000**

* Indicates that sources vary significantlly in the number reported.
† Figures for Europe and North America are generally those for individuals who applied for asylum in 1993, except for countries such as Armenia, Croatia, and others that do not use individualized asylum procedures. U.S. Committee for Refugees considers Bosnians and Croatians as having a prima facie claim to refugee status within the parameters of the Refugee Convention and has therefore attempted to include all such persons who have received temporary legal status, applied for asylum in 1993, or have been excluded from applying for status. Because many countries do not report the republic or origin of "former Yugoslavs," this table may include under that heading other asylum-seekers from the former Yugoslavia.
Source: U.S. Committee for Refugees, 1994.

TABLE 2
Selected Populations in Refugee-Like Situations (as of 31 December 1993)

Host Country	Origin	Number
Jordan	Palestinians	750,000
Iran	Iraq	500,000
Russia	Former USSR	460,000
Pakistan	Afghanistan	400,000
Thailand	Burma	350,000
Bangladesh	Pakistan (Biharis)	238,000
Burundi	Rwanda	170,000
Saudi Arabia	Somalia	150,000
Iraq	Kuwait (Bidoon)	130,000
Lebanon	Palestinians	125,000
Kuwait	Bidoon	120,000
Uganda	Rwanda	120,000
Egypt	Palestinians	100,000
Mexico	Guatemala	100,000
Iraq	Palestinians	70,000
Turkey	Iran	50,000
Cameroon	Chad	40,000
Syria	Palestinians	40,000
Ecuador	Colombia	30,000
Honduras	Central Americans	30,000
Jordan	Iraq	30,000
Uzbekistan	Tajikistan	30,000
Venezuela	Colombia	30,000
Hong Kong	Vietnam	27,560
Kuwait	Palestinians	25,000
Dominican Republic	Haiti	25,000
Mauritania	Senegal	22,000
Hungary	Former Yugoslavia	20,000
Namibia	Angola	20,000
Southeast Asia	Vietnam	19,600

Source: U.S. Committee for Refugees, 1994.

TABLE 3
Selected List of Countries with Significant Populations of Internally Displaced Civilians (as of 31 December 1993)

Country	Number
Sudan	4,000,000
South Africa	4,000,000
Mozambique	2,000,000
Angola	2,000,000
Bosnia	1,300,000
Liberia	1,000,000
Iraq	1,000,000
Lebanon	700,000
Somalia	700,000
Zaire	700,000
Azerbaijan	600,000
Sri Lanka	600,000
Peru	600,000
Burma	500,000–1,000,000
Burundi	500,000
Ethiopia	500,000
Sierra Leone	400,000
Croatia	350,000
Colombia	300,000–600,000
Haiti	300,000
Kenya	300,000
Rwanda	300,000
Cyprus	265,000
Iran	260,000
Georgia	250,000
India	250,000
Philippines	200,000–1,000,000
Eritrea	200,000
Guatemala	200,000
Togo	150,000
Djibouti	140,000
Cambodia	95,000

Source: U.S. Committee for Refugees, 1993.

TABLE 4
Principal Sources of the World's Refugees and Asylum-Seekers (as of 31 December 1993)

Afghanistan	3,429,800*
Palestinians	2,801,300
Mozambique	1,332,000*
Former Yugoslavia	1,319,650*
Burundi	780,000
Liberia	701,000*
Somalia	491,200*
Eritrea	421,500*
Sudan	373,000
Angola	335,000
Vietnam	303,500
Azerbaijan	290,000*
Burma	289,500
Rwanda	275,000*
Sierra Leone	260,000*
Togo	240,000
Ethiopia	232,200
Armenia	200,000*
Tajikistan	153,000*
Georgia	143,000*
Iraq	134,700
China	133,000
Sri Lanka	106,650*
Bhutan	105,100*
Mali	87,000
Western Sahara	80,000*
Zaire	79,000
Mauritania	79,000
Bangladesh	53,500
Uzbekistan	51,000
Guatemala	49,200
Iran	39,000
Cambodia	35,500
Chad	33,400
Laos	26,500
Nicaragua	23,050
El Salvador	21,900
Uganda	20,000
Senegal	18,000
South Africa	10,600

* Indicates that sources vary widely in number reported.
Source: U.S. Committee for Refugees, 1993.

TABLE 5
Significant Voluntary Repatriations—1993

To	From	Number
Afghanistan	Iran	337,500
Afghanistan	Pakistan	358,800
Burma	Bangladesh	36,100
Cambodia	Thailand	128,500
Chad	Sudan	11,000
El Salvador	Belize and Costa Rica	250
Eritrea	Sudan	10,000
Ethiopia	Kenya	56,000
Ethiopia	Sudan	13,000
Guatemala	Mexico	5,100
Haiti	Bahamas	350
Haiti	Cuba	1,400
Indonesia	Papua New Guinea	200
Laos	China	2,600
Laos	Thailand	3,900
Liberia	Ghana	7,000
Liberia	Guinea and Côte d'Ivoire	70,000
Mali	Algeria, Burkina Faso, Mauritania	5,000
Mozambique	Malawi and others	500,000
Nicaragua	Costa Rica and Guatemala	300
Somalia	Kenya	50,000
Sri Lanka	India	6,900
Tajikistan	Afghanistan	25,000
Uganda	Kenya	1,000
Vietnam	Hong Kong and others	19,200

Source: U.S. Committee for Refugees, 1993.

TABLE 6
Involuntary Returns and Expulsions—1993

From	To	Number
Bangladesh	Burma	16,000
Croatia	Bosnia	300
Dominican Republic	Haiti	600
Hong Kong	Vietnam	450
Kenya	Somalia	1,300
Mexico	Guatemala	130,000
South Africa	Mozambique	65,000
Sudan	Ethiopia	22
Thailand	Burma	1,400
Thailand	Cambodia	576
Turkey	Iraq	19
United States	Haiti	2,329

Source: U.S. Committee for Refugees, 1993.

TABLE 7
Refugees in Relation to Total Population and Per Capita GNP of the Asylum Country—1993

Country	Ratio of Refugee Population to Total Population	Number of Refugees	Total Population (in millions)	Per Capita GNP (in US$)
Gaza Strip*	1:1	603,000	0.7	N/A
West Bank*	1:3	479,000	1.6	N/A
Jordan	1:4	1,073,600	3.8	1,120
Djibouti	1:8	60,000	0.5	N/A
Guinea	1:11	570,000	6.2	450
Lebanon	1:11	329,000	3.6	N/A
Armenia	1:12	300,000	3.6	2,150
Swaziland	1:14	57,000	0.8	1,060
Malawi	1:14	700,000	10.0	230
Croatia	1:16	280,000	4.4	N/A
Rwanda	1:20	370,000	7.4	260
Belize	1:22	8,900	0.2	2,050
Liberia	1:25	110,000	2.8	N/A
Yugoslavia (Serbia/ Montenegro)	1:27	357,000	9.8	N/A
Azerbaijan	1:29	251,000	7.2	1,670
Iran	1:31	1,995,000	62.8	2,320
Syria	1:42	319,200	13.5	1,110
Benin	1:43	120,000	5.1	380
Sudan	1:43	633,000	27.4	400
Mauritania	1:48	46,000	2.2	510
Slovenia	1:53	38,000	2.0	N/A
Burundi	1:53	110,000	5.8	210
Zimbabwe	1:54	200,000	10.7	620
Côte d'Ivoire	1:54	250,000	13.4	690
Zambia	1:54	158,500	8.6	420

* Territories, not sovereign states.
Source: U.S. Committee for Refugees, 1993. Primary source for total population and GNP data: Population Reference Bureau, Inc.

TABLE 8
1993 Government Contributions to International Refugee Aid Agencies Top 20 Countries
(Ranked by contribution per capita)

Country	Contribution Per Capita (in US$)	Population (in millions)	Contribution (in millions) of US $)	Per Capita GNP (in US$)
Norway	14.12	4.3	60.71	24,160
Sweden	11.31	8.7	98.43	25,490
Denmark	8.14	5.2	42.31	23,660
Netherlands	6.46	15.2	98.20	18,560
Switzerland	5.56	7.0	38.95	33,510
Luxembourg	2.95	0.4	1.18	31,080
Finland	2.50	5.1	12.72	24,400
United States	1.74	258.3	451.99	22,560
Canada	1.68	28.1	47.10	21,260
United Kingdom	1.48	58.0	85.62	16,750
Kuwait	1.15	1.7	1.95	N/A
Japan	1.14	124.8	141.99	26,920
France	0.95	57.7	54.55	20,600
Belgium	0.92	10.1	9.26	19,300
Australia	0.68	17.8	12.04	16,590
Germany	0.66	81.1	53.36	23,650*
Austria	0.50	7.9	3.95	20,380
Italy	0.50	57.8	28.93	18,580
Ireland	0.43	3.6	1.53	10,780
New Zealand	0.25	3.4	0.86	12,140

* GNP data include former West Germany only.
Source: U.S. Committee for Refugees, 1993. Primary source for population and GNP data: Population Reference Bureau, Inc.

TABLE 9

Refugees Resettled and Persons Granted Asylum in Relation to Total Population (In order of refugees/asylees to total population ratio)

Resettlement Country	1975–1992 Cumulative	1992 Only	Total Population (in millions)	Ratio of Refugees/Asylees to Total Population
Sweden	152,608	12,791	8.7	1:57
Canada	407,379	36,409	28.1	1:69
Australia	205,862	9,758	17.8	1:86
United States	1,731,090	137,395	258.3	1:149
Denmark	34,089	4,100	5.2	1:153
Norway	27,410*	2,830	4.3	1:157
Switzerland	32,297	8,839	7.0	1:217
France	227,085	10,943	57.7	1:254
New Zealand	13,028	800	3.4	1:261
Austria	29,007	2,289	7.9	1:272
Netherlands	30,300	4,553	15.2	1:502
Germany	112,264†	9,189	81.1	1:722
Spain	39,166	296	39.1	1:998
United Kingdom	35,032*	16,435	58.0	1:1,656

Note: The primary source for numbers on refugees resettled or granted asylum was the U.S. State Department. Countries that have established resettlement programs generally provide particularly precise data, but data were not available for all countries for all years. Israel is not included because it does not differentiate between resettled refugees and immigrants. The primary source for total population was the Population Reference Bureau, Inc.

* Statistics were unavailable for 1975–1981.

† Does not include ethnic Germans from the former Soviet Union, Poland, and Romania.

Source: U.S. Committee for Refugees, 1993.

TABLE 10

Asylum Applications in Western Europe, North America, and Australia, 1983–1992

	1983	1984	1985	1986	1987	1988	1989	1990	1991	1992	Cumulative 1983–1992
Australia	—	—	—	—	—	—	500	3,600	16,000	4,100	24,200
Austria	5,900	7,200	6,700	8,700	11,400	15,800	21,900	22,800	27,300	16,200	143,900
Belgium	2,900	3,700	5,300	7,700	6,000	5,100	8,100	13,000	15,200	17,800	84,800
Canada	5,000	7,100	8,400	23,000	35,000	45,000	22,000	36,000	30,500	37,700	249,700
Denmark	800	4,300	8,700	9,300	2,800	4,700	4,600	5,300	4,600	13,900	59,000
Finland	—	—	—	—	50	50	200	2,500	2,100	3,600	8,500
France	14,300	15,900	25,800	23,400	24,800	31,600	60,000	56,000	46,500	27,500	325,800
Germany	19,700	35,300	73,900	99,700	57,400	103,100	121,000	193,000	256,100	438,200	1,397,400
Italy	3,000	4,500	5,400	6,500	11,000	1,300	2,200	4,700	31,700	2,500	72,800
Netherlands	2,000	2,600	5,700	5,900	13,500	7,500	14,000	21,200	21,600	17,500	111,500
Norway	200	300	900	2,700	8,600	6,600	4,400	4,000	4,600	5,200	37,500
Spain	1,400	1,100	2,300	2,300	2,500	3,300	4,000	8,600	8,100	11,700	45,300
Sweden	3,000	12,000	14,500	14,600	18,100	19,600	32,000	29,000	27,300	83,200	253,300
Switzerland	7,900	7,500	9,700	8,600	10,900	16,700	24,500	36,000	41,600	18,100	181,500
UK	4,300	3,900	5,500	4,800	5,200	5,100	10,000	30,000	57,700	24,600*	151,100
USA	20,000	24,300	20,000	18,900	26,100	57,000	100,000	73,600	70,000	103,400	513,300
Total	90,400	129,700	192,800	236,100	233,350	322,450	429,400	539,300	660,900	825,200	3,659,600

* Excluding dependents.
Source: UN High Commissioner for Refugees, 1994.

TABLE 11

Emigration from East Europe and the Former USSR to the West, 1984–1992

	1984	1985	1986	1987	1988	1989	1990	1991	1992
Asylum-Seekers	25,000	30,000	41,000	48,000	91,000	127,000	156,000	245,000	170,600
Jews from USSR	1,000	1,000	4,000	6,000	30,000	71,000	220,000	173,000	115,000*
German Settlers	77,000	64,000	69,000	98,000	240,000	720,000	397,000	222,000	230,500
Former Yugoslav Asylum-Seekers	—	—	—	—	—	—	—	—	250,000
Former Yugoslav Temporarily Protected	—	—	—	—	—	—	—	—	350,000
Others (estimate)	6,000	6,000	10,000	25,000	50,000	300,000	150,000	160,000	700,000†
Total	109,000	101,000	124,000	177,000	411,000	1,218,000	923,000	800,000	1,816,100

* Former USSR.
† Albanians, Baltics, Bulgarians, Pontian Greeks, Romanians, Russians, and some other groups.
Source: Secretariat for Inter-Governmental Consultations, Vienna, 1993.

TABLE 12

Ceilings for U.S. Refugee Admissions by Region, Fiscal Years (FY) 1986–1993

Region	FY 86	FY 87	FY 88	FY 89	FY 90	FY 91	FY 92	FY 93
Africa	3,500	2,000	3,000	2,000	3,000	4,900	6,000	7,000
Asia	45,500	40,500	38,000	50,000	51,500	52,000	52,000	52,000
Near East & South Asia	6,000	10,200	9,000	7,000	6,500	5,000	6,000	7,000
Latin America	3,000	1,000	3,500	3,500	3,500	3,100	3,000	3,500
Eastern Europe	0	0	0	0	0	5,000	3,000	1,500
Soviet Union	9,500	12,300	30,000	50,000	50,000	50,000	61,000	50,000
Unallocated Reserve		4,000	4,000	4,000	4,000	1,000	1,000*	1,000*
Total	67,500	70,000	87,500	116,500	118,500	131,000*	142,000*	132,000*

* In addition, there are 10,000 unallocated numbers funded through the Private Sector Initiative (PSI).
Source: U.S. Committee for Refugees, 1993. Interpreter Releases, Vol. 67, No. 38, 5 Oct. 1991, Vol. 68, No. 40, 21 Oct. 1991, pp. 1493–1494, and Vol. 69, No. 41, 26 Oct. 1992, pp. 1377–1378.

TABLE 13

Asylum Cases Filed with Immigration and Naturalization Service Asylum Officers Approved and Denied, by Selected Nationalities, April 1991–September 1993

	April 1991–September 1993			Fiscal Year 93 (Preliminary)				
Country	Approval Rate for Cases Decided	Cases Granted	Cases Denied	Applications Filed	Approval Rate for Cases Decided	Cases Granted	Cases Denied	Pending as of 9/30/93
Total*	27.3%	9,436	25,061	150,386	22.0%	5,105	18,110	329,817
Somalia	85.4%	217	37	178	76.0%	92	29	584
Sudan	79.3%	157	41	254	76.6%	98	30	620
Syria	67.6%	244	117	872	73.5%	230	83	1,314
Iran	64.3%	421	234	728	58.7%	229	161	2,523
Iraq	64.3%	117	65	228	62.4%	68	41	530
China	63.6%	525	301	14,354	49.4%	250	256	17,509
Ethiopia	59.1%	655	454	1,383	46.3%	296	343	3,533
Afghanistan	54.9%	101	83	278	38.9%	42	66	794
Former Yugoslavia†	49.3%	351	361	2,425	50.4%	303	298	5,024
Cuba	49.2%	414	427	3,010	50.0%	249	249	5,433
Liberia	43.6%	323	417	1,192	37.0%	166	283	4,590
Former USSR†	40.9%	957	1,381	5,913	37.1%	621	1,055	12,804
Peru	28.8%	199	491	3,244	26.3%	142	398	4,036
Ghana	26.8%	22	60	1,572	21.2%	14	52	2,086
India	25.8%	372	1,068	5,902	23.8%	306	981	7,427
Lebanon	24.7%	94	287	690	19.3%	39	163	1,743
Haiti	23.7%	608	1,959	11,377	22.8%	525	1,776	13,596
Laos	22.6%	122	418	825	16.2%	66	342	1,756
Romania	20.8%	301	1,147	1,591	18.1%	174	789	4,825
Bangladesh	15.7%	24	129	3,759	15.1%	22	124	4,614

Pakistan	14.9%	167	952	4,653	12.2%	127	911	6,588
Bulgaria	13.8%	85	530	584	12.2%	47	339	1,672
Colombia	13.8%	27	168	1,315	11.3%	18	142	1,780
Fiji	11.9%	42	312	312	12.8%	33	224	1,004
Nicaragua	10.7%	388	3,251	4,286	7.8%	178	2,097	22,602
El Salvador	9.5%	165	1,574	15,362	4.6%	65	1,345	57,998
Sierra Leone	8.8%	22	229	547	8.1%	20	225	929
Guatemala	8.7%	209	2,194	34,681	6.5%	135	1,952	99,928
Honduras	8.3%	45	491	2,836	6.3%	27	402	4,356
Philippines	4.8%	52	1,037	4,107	4.4%	41	891	7,442
Poland	1.3%	5	374	1,059	0.9%	2	221	2,888
Mexico	0.0%	0	504	6,192	0.0%	0	491	5,633

* The total includes all nationalities, not just those listed here. Country-specific fiscal year 1993 data supplied by Immigration and Naturalization Service include only nationalities for which more than 500 cases are pending.

† Figures include all former republics.

Source: U.S. Department of Justice, Immigration and Naturalization Service. Tabulated by the U.S. Committee for Refugees, 1993.

TABLE 14
UNHCR Budget by Region for 1991 and 1992—All Sources of Funds (In thousands of U.S. dollars)

Region	1991	1992
Africa	303,338.9	298,169.9
Asia	425,310.0	327,463.9
Europe	26,845.0	327,998.3
Latin America	43,744.6	46,983.5
North America	2,711.4	2,823.7
Oceania	2,624.8	1,078.1
Headquarters/Global projects	78,363.4	88,541.3
TOTAL	882,938.1	1,093,058.7

Source: UN High Commissioner for Refugees, 1993.

UNHCR Commissioners, Executive Committee Members, and Signatories

Table 15 lists the past and present United Nations high commissioners for refugees. There have been eight high commissioners since UNHCR was established in 1950. The high commissioner for refugees is elected by the UN General Assembly on the nomination of the secretary-general. The current incumbant, Mrs. Sadako Ogata of Japan, took up office on 1 January 1991. The high commissioner acts under the authority of the UN General Assembly and reports to UNHCR's Executive Committee.

Table 16 lists the composition of the Executive Committee (governing body) of UNHCR. Following the election of Spain, at present there are forty-seven governments who are members of the Executive Committee. It is the governing body of UNHCR. It oversees UNHCR assistance budgets and advises on refugee protection. The Executive Committee has its principal meetings each year in early October in Geneva.

Table 17 lists governments according to whether they have signed the 1951 United Nations Convention and/or the 1967 Protocol relating to the Status of Refugees, as of 1 March 1994. Despite the fact that over 120 governments are signatories to the Convention, many major asylum countries have not yet signed the basic instruments. As of 1994, the only Asian signatories were Japan, the Republic of Korea, the People's Republic of China, Fiji,

Papua New Guinea, and the Philippines; and the only Middle East signatories were Israel, Iran, and Yemen. Many of the world's largest and most urgent refugee situations have arisen in these regions. While many of these nonsignatories have offered asylum-seekers at least temporary refuge, they have done so on the basis of their own policy decisions rather than from an incurred responsibility to international legal instruments.

TABLE 15
High Commissioners

Mr. Gerrit J. van Heuven Goedhart (Netherlands) December 1950–July 1956	Mr. Poul Hartling (Denmark) January 1978–December 1985
Mr. Auguste R. Lindt (Switzerland) December 1956–December 1960	Mr. Jean-Pierre Hocké (Switzerland) January 1986–November 1989
Mr. Felix Schnyder (Switzerland) December 1960–December 1965	Mr. Thorvald Stoltenberg (Norway) January 1990–November 1990
Sadruddin Aga Khan (Iran) December 1965–December 1977	Mrs. Sadako Ogata (Japan) January 1991–present

Source: UN High Commissioner for Refugees, 1993.

TABLE 16
Composition of UNHCR's Executive Committee

The Executive Committee is composed of the following 46 member states:

Algeria, Argentina, Australia, Austria, Belgium, Brazil, Canada, China, Colombia, Denmark, Ethiopia, Finland, France, Germany, Greece, Holy See, Hungary, the Islamic Republic of Iran, Israel, Italy, Japan, Lebanon, Lesotho, Madagascar, Morocco, Namibia, Netherlands, Nicaragua, Nigeria, Norway, Pakistan, Philippines, Somalia, Sudan, Sweden, Switzerland, Thailand, Tunisia, Turkey, Uganda, United Kingdom, United Republic of Tanzania, United States of America, Venezuela, Yugoslavia, and Zaire.

In 1993, Spain made a formal application to become the 47th member of the committee.

Source: UN High Commissioner for Refugees, 1993.

TABLE 17

United Nations Member States: Signatories and Nonsignatories to the United Nations Convention and Protocol Relating to the Status of Refugees

Signatories

Albania	China	Guinea-Bissau	Nicaragua	Suriname
Algeria	Colombia	Haiti	Niger	Swaziland (P)
Angola	Congo	Honduras	Nigeria	Sweden
Argentina	Costa Rica	Hungary	Norway	Tajikistan
Armenia	Cote d'Ivoire	Iceland	Panama	Tanzania
Australia	Croatia	Iran	Papua New Guinea	Togo
Austria	Cyprus	Ireland	Paraguay	Tunisia
Azerbaijan	Czech Republic	Israel	Peru	Turkey
Bahamas	Denmark	Italy	Philippines	Uganda
Belgium	Djibouti	Jamaica	Poland	United Kingdom
Belize	Dominican Republic	Japan	Portugal	United States (P)
Benin	Ecuador	Kenya	Romania	Uruguay
Bolivia	Egypt	Korea (South)	Russian Federation	Venezuela (P)
Bosnia and Herzegovina	El Salvador	Lesotho	Rwanda	Yemen
Botswana	Equatorial Guinea	Liberia	Samoa (C)	Yugoslavia
Brazil	Ethiopia	Liechtenstein	Sao Tome and Principe	Zaire
Bulgaria	Fiji	Luxembourg	Senegal	Zambia
Burkina Faso	Finland	Madagascar (C)	Seychelles	Zimbabwe
Burundi	France	Malawi	Sierra Leone	
Cambodia	Gabon	Mali	Slovak Republic	
Cameroon	Gambia	Malta	Slovenia	
Canada	Germany	Mauritania	Somalia	
Cape Verde (P)	Ghana	Morocco	Spain	
Central African Republic	Greece	Mozambique	St. Vincent and the Grenadines	
Chad	Guatemala	Netherlands	Sudan	
Chile	Guinea	New Zealand		

Nonsignatories

Afghanistan	Federated States of Micronesia	Laos	Namibia	Syria
Antigua and Barbuda	Georgia	Latvia	Nepal	Thailand
Bahrain	Grenada	Lebanon	Oman	Trinidad and Tobago
Bangladesh	Guyana	Libya	Pakistan	Turkmenistan
Barbados	India	Lithuania	Qatar	Ukraine
Belarus	Indonesia	Macedonia	St. Kitts & Nevis	United Arab Emirates
Bhutan	Iraq	Malaysia	St. Lucia	Uzbekistan
Bruni	Jordan	Maldives	San Marino	Vanuatu
Burma (Myammar)	Kazakhstan	Marshall Islands	Saudi Arabia	Vietnam
Comoros	Korea (North)	Mauritius	Singapore	
Cuba	Kuwait	Mexico	Solomon Islands	
Dominica	Kyrgyzstan	Moldova	South Africa	
Estonia		Mongolia	Sri Lanka	

(C) Signatories to the convention only.
(P) Signatories to the protocol only.
Note: Non-UN members Switzerland, Tuvalu, and the Holy See have also signed the UN convention and protocol; Monaco has signed the convention only.
Source: U.S. Committee for Refugees, 1994.

International Refugee Law

International refugee law mainly comprises international instruments that define basic standards for the treatment of refugees. The texts of the major international and regional refugee instruments are presented in this section.

The Statute of the Office of the United Nations High Commissioner for Refugees (UNHCR) of 1950 sets out the functions of UNHCR, the principal international institution with the mandate to protect and assist refugees. Its functions include "providing international protection" and "seeking permanent solutions" to the problems of refugees by way of voluntary repatriation or assimilation in new national communities. Of these, the provision of international protection is of primary importance, for without protection, lasting solutions cannot possibly be found. The UNHCR statute also prescribes the relationship of the high commissioner with the United Nations General Assembly and the United Nations Economic and Social Council, makes provision for organization and finance, and lists the ways in which the high commissioner is to provide for protection.

The Statute of the Office of the United Nations High Commissioner for Refugees

GENERAL ASSEMBLY RESOLUTION 428 (V)
of 14 December 1950

The General Assembly,
In view of its resolution 319 A (IV) of 3 December 1949,Y.

1. Adopts the annex to the present resolution, being the Statute of the Office of the United Nations High Commissioner for Refugees;

2. Calls upon Governments to co-operate with the United Nations High Commissioner for Refugees in the performance of his functions concerning refugees falling under the competence of his Office, especially by:

(a) Becoming parties to international conventions providing for the protection of refugees, and taking the necessary steps of implementation under such conventions;
(b) Entering into special agreements with the High Commissioner for the execution of measures calculated to improve the situation of refugees and to reduce the number requiring protection;

(c) Admitting refugees to their territories, not excluding those in the most destitute categories;
(d) Assisting the High Commissioner in his efforts to promote the voluntary repatriation of refugees;
(e) Promoting the assimilation of refugees, especially by facilitating their naturalization;
(f) Providing refugees with travel and other documents such as would normally be provided to other aliens by their national authorities, especially documents which would facilitate their resettlement;
(g) Permitting refugees to transfer their assets and especially those necessary for their resettlement;
(h) Providing the High Commissioner with information concerning the number and condition of refugees, and laws and regulations concerning them.

3. Requests the Secretary-General to transmit the present resolution, together with the annex attached thereto, also to States nonmembers of the United Nations, with a view to obtaining their co-operation in its implementation.

ANNEX
STATUTE OF THE OFFICE OF THE UNITED NATIONS HIGH COMMISSIONER FOR REFUGEES

CHAPTER I
General Provisions

1. The United Nations High Commissioner for Refugees, acting under the authority of the General Assembly, shall assume the function of providing international protection, under the auspices of the United Nations to refugees who fall within the scope of the present Statute and of seeking permanent solutions for the problem of refugees by assisting Governments and, subject to the approval of the Governments concerned, private organizations to facilitate the voluntary repatriation of such refugees, or their assimilation within new national communities. In the exercise of his functions, more particularly when difficulties arise, and for instance with regard to any controversy concerning the international status of these persons, the High Commissioner shall request the opinion of the advisory committee on refugees if it is created.

2. The work of the High Commissioner shall be of an entirely nonpolitical character; it shall be humanitarian and social and shall relate, as a rule, to groups and categories of refugees.

3. The High Commissioner shall follow policy directives given him by the General Assembly or the Economic and Social Council.

4. The Economic and Social Council may decide, after hearing the views of the High Commissioner on the subject, to establish an advisory committee on refugees, which shall consist of representatives of States Members and States nonmembers of the United Nations, to be selected by the Council on the basis of their demonstrated interest in and devotion to the solution of the refugee problem.

5. The General Assembly shall review, not later than at its eighth regular session, the arrangements for the Office of the High Commissioner with a view to determining whether the Office should be continued beyond 31 December 1953.

CHAPTER II
Functions of the High Commissioner

6. The competence of the High Commissioner shall extend to:

A. (i) Any person who has been considered a refugee under the Arrangements of 12 May 1926 and of 30 June 1928 or under the Conventions of 28 October 1933 and 10 February 1938, the Protocol of 14 September 1939 or the Constitution of the International Refugee Organization.

(ii) Any person who, as a result of events occurring before 1 January 1951 and owing to well-founded fear of being persecuted for reasons of race, religion, nationality or political opinion, is outside the country of his nationality and is unable or, owing to such fear or for reasons other than personal convenience, is unwilling to avail himself of the protection of that country; or who, not having a nationality and being outside the country of his former habitual residence, is unable or, owing to such fear or for reasons other than personal convenience, is unwilling to return to it.

Decisions as to eligibility taken by the International Refugee Organization during the period of its activities shall not prevent the status of refugee being accorded to persons who fulfill the conditions of the present paragraph;

The competence of the High Commissioner shall cease to apply to any person defined in section A above if:

(a) He has voluntarily re-availed himself of the protection of the country of his nationality; or

(b) Having lost his nationality, he has voluntarily re-acquired it; or

(c) He has acquired a new nationality, and enjoys the protection of the country of his new nationality; or

(d) He has voluntarily re-established himself in the country which he left or outside which he remained owing to fear of persecution; or

(e) He can no longer, because the circumstances in connexion with which he has been recognized as a refugee have ceased to exist claim grounds other than those of personal convenience for continuing to refuse to avail himself of the protection of the country of his nationality. Reasons of a purely economic character may not be invoked; or

(f) Being a person who has no nationality, he can no longer, because the circumstances in connexion with which he has been recognized as a refugee have ceased to exist and he is able to return to the country of his former habitual residence, claim grounds other than those of personal convenience for continuing to refuse to return to that country;

B. Any other person who is outside the country of his nationality, or if he has no nationality, the country of his former habitual residence, because he has or had well-founded fear of persecution by reason of his race, religion, nationality or political opinion and is unable or, because of such fear, is unwilling to avail himself of the protection of the government of the country of his nationality, or, if he has no nationality, to return to the country of his former habitual residence.

7. Provided that the competence of the High Commissioner as defined in paragraph 6 above shall not extend to a person:

(a) Who is a national of more than one country unless he satisfies the provisions of the preceding paragraph in relation to each of the countries of which he is a national; or

(b) Who is recognized by the competent authorities of the country in which he has taken residence as having the rights and obligations which are attached to the possession of the nationality of that country; or

(c) Who continues to receive from other organs or agencies of the United Nations protection or assistance; or

(d) In respect of whom there are serious reasons for considering that he has committed a crime covered by the provisions of treaties of extradition or a crime mentioned in article Vl of the London Charter of the International Military Tribunal or by the provisions of article 14, paragraph 2, of the Universal Declaration of Human Rights.

8. The High Commissioner shall provide for the protection of refugees falling under the competence of his Office by:

(a) Promoting the conclusion and ratification of international conventions for the protection of refugees, supervising their application and proposing amendments thereto;
(b) Promoting through special agreements with Governments the execution of any measures calculated to improve the situation of refugees and to reduce the number requiring protection;
(c) Assisting governmental and private efforts to promote voluntary repatriation or assimilation within new national communities;
(d) Promoting the admission of refugees, not excluding those in the most destitute categories, to the territories of States;
(e) Endeavouring to obtain permission for refugees to transfer their assets and especially those necessary for their resettlement;
(f) Obtaining from Governments information concerning the number and conditions of refugees in their territories and the laws and regulations concerning them;
(g) Keeping in close touch with the Governments and inter-governmental organizations concerned;
(h) Establishing contact in such manner as he may think best with private organizations dealing with refugee questions;
(i) Facilitating the co-ordination of the efforts of private organizations concerned with the welfare of refugees.

9. The High Commissioner shall engage in such additional activities, including repatriation and resettlement, as the General Assembly may determine, within the limits of the resources placed at his disposal.

10. The High Commissioner shall administer any funds, public or private, which he receives for assistance to refugees, and shall distribute them among the private and, as appropriate, public agencies which he deems best qualified to administer such assistance. The High Commissioner may reject any offers which he does not consider appropriate or which cannot be utilized. The High Commissioner shall not appeal to Governments for funds or make a general appeal, without the prior approval of the General Assembly. The High Commissioner shall include in his annual report a statement of his activities in this field.

11. The High Commissioner shall be entitled to present his views before the General Assembly, the Economic and Social Council and their subsidiary bodies. The High Commissioner shall report annually to the General Assembly through the Economic and Social Council;

his report shall be considered as a separate item on the agenda of the General Assembly.

12. The High Commissioner may invite the co-operation of the various specialized agencies.

CHAPTER III
Organization and Finances

13. The High Commissioner shall be elected by the General Assembly on the nomination of the Secretary-General. The terms of appointment of the High Commissioner shall be proposed by the Secretary-General and approved by the General Assembly. The High Commissioner shall be elected for a term of three years, from 1 January 1951.

14. The High Commissioner shall appoint, for the same term, a Deputy High Commissioner of a nationality other than his own.

15.

(a) Within the limits of the budgetary appropriations provided, the staff of the Office of the High Commissioner shall be appointed by the High Commissioner and shall be responsible to him in the exercise of their functions.
(b) Such staff shall be chosen from persons devoted to the purposes of the Office of the High Commissioner.
(c) Their conditions of employment shall be those provided under the staff regulations adopted by the General Assembly and the rules promulgated thereunder by the Secretary-General.
(d) Provision may also be made to permit the employment of personnel without compensation.

16. The High Commissioner shall consult the Government of the countries of residence of refugees as to the need for appointing representatives therein. In any country recognizing such need, there may be appointed a representative approved by the Government of that country. Subject to the foregoing, the same representative may serve in more than one country.

17. The High Commissioner and the Secretary-General shall make appropriate arrangements for liaison and consultation on matters of mutual interest.

18. The Secretary-General shall provide the High Commissioner with all necessary facilities within budgetary limitations.

19. The Office of the High Commissioner shall be located in Geneva, Switzerland.

20. The Office of the High Commissioner shall be financed under the budget of the United Nations. Unless the General Assembly subsequently decides otherwise, no expenditure other than

administrative expenditures relating to the functioning of the Office of the High Commissioner shall be borne on the budget of the United Nations and all other expenditures relating to the activities of the High Commissioner shall be financed by voluntary contributions.

21. The administration of the Office of the High Commissioner shall be subject to the Financial Regulations of the United Nations and to the financial rules promulgated thereunder by the Secretary-General.

22. Transactions relating to the High Commissioner's funds shall be subject to audit by the United Nations Board of Auditors, provided that the Board may accept audited accounts from the agencies to which funds have been allocated. Administrative arrangements for the custody of such funds and their allocation shall be agreed between the High Commissioner and the Secretary-General in accordance with the Financial Regulations of the United Nations and rules promulgated thereunder by the Secretary-General.

1951 Convention Relating to the Status of Refugees Done at Geneva on 28 July 1951

The 1951 Convention Relating to the Status of Refugees is the major document in international refugee law since it:

contains a general definition of the term *refugee* (Article 1);

embodies the principle of nonrefoulement (Article 33) according to which no person may be returned to a territory where he or she may be exposed to persecution;

sets the minimum standard of treatment of refugees, including the basic rights to be granted, and the duties of refugees vis-a-vis their country of refuge;

contains provisions that concern refugees' judicial status, gainful employment, and welfare;

contains provisions regarding the issue of identity and travel documents, naturalization, and other administrative matters;

requires states to cooperate with UNHCR in the exercise of its functions and to facilitate the task of supervising the application of the convention.

At the time the convention was adopted, governments were anxious to focus on the existing refugee problems, and not to assume obligations for the future, the extent of which could not be foreseen. This resulted in two major limitations:

1. The benefits of the convention were not to apply to persons who corresponded to the definition, but who became refugees as a result of events occurring after 1 January 1951 (Article 1);
2. When becoming a party to the convention, states had the possibility of making a declaration, limiting their obligations under the convention to European refugees.

Entry into force: 22 April 1954, in accordance with Article 43

Text: United Nations Treaty Series No. 2545, Vol. 189, p. 137

PREAMBLE

The High Contracting Parties

Considering that the Charter of the United Nations and the Universal Declaration of Human Rights approved on 10 December 1948 by the General Assembly have affirmed the principle that human beings shall enjoy fundamental rights and freedoms without discrimination,

Considering that the United Nations has, on various occasions, manifested its profound concern for refugees and endeavoured to assure refugees the widest possible exercise of these fundamental rights and freedoms,

Considering that it is desirable to revise and consolidate previous international agreements relating to the status of refugees and to extend the scope of and the protection accorded by such instruments by means of a new agreement,

Considering that the grant of asylum may place unduly heavy burdens on certain countries, and that a satisfactory solution of a problem of which the United Nations has recognized the international scope and nature cannot therefore be achieved without international co-operation,

Expressing the wish that all States, recognizing the social and humanitarian nature of the problem of refugees, will do everything within their power to prevent this problem from becoming a cause of tension between States,

Noting that the United Nations High Commissioner for Refugees is charged with the task of supervising international conventions providing for the protection of refugees, and recognizing that the effective co-ordination of measures taken to deal with this problem will depend upon the cooperation of States with the High Commissioner,

Have agreed as follows:

CHAPTER I
GENERAL PROVISIONS

ARTICLE 1
Definition of the term "REFUGEE"

A. For the purposes of the present Convention, the term "refugee" shall apply to any person who:

(1) Has been considered a refugee under the Arrangements of 12 May 1926 and 30 June 1928 or under the Conventions of 28 October 1933 and 10 February 1938, the Protocol of 14 September 1939 or the Constitution of the International Refugee Organization;

Decisions of non-eligibility taken by the International Refugee Organization during the period of its activities shall not prevent the status of refugee being accorded to persons who fulfil the conditions of paragraph 2 of this section;

(2) As a result of events occuring before 1 January 1951 and owing to well-founded fear of being persecuted for reasons of race, religion, nationality, membership of a particular social group or political opinion, is outside the country of his nationality and is unable or, owing to such fear, is unwilling to avail himself of the protection of that country; or who, not having a nationality and being outside the country of his former habitual residence as a result of such events, is unable or, owing to such fear, is unwilling to return to it.

In the case of a person who has more than one nationality, the term "the country of his nationality" shall mean each of the countries of which he is a national, and a person shall not be deemed to be lacking the protection of the country of his nationality if, without any valid reason based on well-founded fear, he has not availed himself of the protection of one of the countries of which he is a national.

B. (1) For the purposes of this Convention, the words "events occurring before 1 January 1951" in Article 1, Section A, shall be understood to mean either

(a) "events occurring in Europe before 1 January 1951"; or

(b) "events occurring in Europe or elsewhere before 1 January 1951" and each Contracting State shall make

a declaration at the time of signature, ratification or accession, specifying which of these meanings it applies for the purpose of its obligations under this Convention.

(2) Any Contracting State which has adopted alternative (a) may at any time extend its obligations by adopting alternative (b) by means of a notification addressed to the Secretary-General of the United Nations.

C. This Convention shall cease to apply to any person falling under the terms of section A if:

(1) He has voluntarily re-availed himself of the protection of the country of his nationality; or
(2) Having lost his nationality, he has voluntarily re-acquired it, or
(3) He has acquired a new nationality, and enjoys the protection of the country of his new nationality; or
(4) He has voluntarily re-established himself in the country which he left or outside which he remained owing to fear of persecution; or
(5) He can no longer, because the circumstances in connexion with which he has been recognized as a refugee have ceased to exist, continue to refuse to avail himself of the protection of the country of his nationality;

Provided that this paragraph shall not apply to a refugee falling under section A(l) of this Article who is able to invoke compelling reasons arising out of previous persecution for refusing to avail himself of the protection of the country of nationality;
(6) Being a person who has no nationality he is, because the circumstances in connexion with which he has been recognized as a refugee have ceased to exist, able to return to the country of his former habitual residence;

Provided that this paragraph shall not apply to a refugee falling under section A(l) of this Article who is able to invoke compelling reasons arising out of previous persecution for refusing to return to the country of his former habitual residence.

D. This Convention shall not apply to persons who are at present receiving from organs or agencies of the United Nations other than the United Nations High Commissioner for Refugees protection or assistance.

When such protection or assistance has ceased for any reason, without the position of such persons being definitively settled in accordance with the relevant resolutions adopted by the General Assembly of the United Nations, these persons shall *ipso facto* be entitled to the benefits of this Convention.

E. This Convention shall not apply to a person who is recognized by the competent authorities of the country in which he has taken residence as having the rights and obligations which are attached to the possession of the nationality of that country.

F. The provisions of this Convention shall not apply to any person with respect to whom there are serious reasons for considering that:

(a) he has committed a crime against peace, a war crime, or a crime against humanity, as defined in the international instruments drawn up to make provision in respect of such crimes;
(b) he has committed a serious non-political crime outside the country of refuge prior to his admission to that country as a refugee;
(c) he has been guilty of acts contrary to the purposes and principles of the United Nations.

ARTICLE 2
GENERAL OBLIGATIONS

Every refugee has duties to the country in which he finds himself, which require in particular that he conform to its laws and regulations as well as to measures taken for the maintenance of public order.

ARTICLE 3
NON-DISCRIMINATION

The Contracting States shall apply the provisions of this Convention to refugees without discrimination as to race, religion or country of origin.

ARTICLE 4
RELIGION

The Contracting States shall accord to refugees within their territories treatment at least as favourable as that accorded to their nationals with respect to freedom to practise their religion and freedom as regards the religious education of their children.

ARTICLE 5
RIGHTS GRANTED APART FROM THIS CONVENTION

Nothing in this Convention shall be deemed to impair any rights and benefits granted by a Contracting State to refugees apart from this Convention.

ARTICLE 6
THE TERM "IN THE SAME CIRCUMSTANCES"

For the purpose of this Convention, the term "in the same circumstances" implies that any requirements (including requirements as to length and conditions of sojourn or residence) which the particular individual would have to fulfil for the enjoyment of the right in question, if he were not a refugee, must be fulfilled by him, with the exception of requirements which by their nature a refugee is incapable of fulfilling.

ARTICLE 7
EXEMPTION FROM RECIPROCITY

1. Except where this Convention contains more favourable provisions, a Contracting State shall accord to refugees the same treatment as is accorded to aliens generally.

2. After a period of three years' residence, all refugees shall enjoy exemption from legislative reciprocity in the territory of the Contracting States.

3. Each Contracting State shall continue to accord to refugees the rights and benefits to which they were already entitled, in the absence of reciprocity, at the date of entry into force of this Convention for that State.

4. The Contracting States shall consider favourably the possibility of according to refugees, in the absence of reciprocity, rights and benefits beyond those to which they are entitled according to paragraphs 2 and 3, and to extending exemption from reciprocity to refugees who do not fulfil the conditions provided for in paragraphs 2 and 3.

5. The provisions of paragraphs 2 and 3 apply both to the rights and benefits referred to in Articles 13, 18, 19, 21 and 22 of this Convention and to rights and benefits for which this Convention does not provide.

ARTICLE 8
EXEMPTION FROM EXCEPTIONAL MEASURES

With regard to exceptional measures which may be taken against the person, property or interests of nationals of a foreign State, the Contracting States shall not apply such measures to a refugee who is formally a national of the said State solely on account of such nationality. Contracting States which, under their legislation, are prevented from applying the general principle expressed in this Article, shall, in appropriate cases, grant exemptions in favour of such refugees.

ARTICLE 9
PROVISIONAL MEASURES

Nothing in this Convention shall prevent a Contracting State, in time of war or other grave and exceptional circumstances, from taking provisionally measures which it considers to be essential to the national security in the case of a particular person, pending a determination by the Contracting State that that person is in fact a refugee and that the continuance of such measures is necessary in his case in the interests of national security.

ARTICLE 10
CONTINUITY OF RESIDENCE

1. Where a refugee has been forcibly displaced during the Second World War and removed to the territory of a Contracting State, and is resident there, the period of such enforced sojourn shall be considered to have been lawful residence within that territory.

2. Where a refugee has been forcibly displaced during the Second World War from the territory of a Contracting State and has, prior to the date of entry into force of this Convention, returned there for the purpose of taking up residence, the period of residence before and after such enforced displacement shall be regarded as one uninterrupted period for any purposes for which uninterrupted residence is required.

ARTICLE 11
REFUGEE SEAMEN

In the case of refugees regularly serving as crew members on board a ship flying the flag of a Contracting State, that State shall give sympathetic consideration to their establishment on its territory and the issue of travel documents to them or their temporary admission to its territory particularly with a view to facilitating their establishment in another country.

CHAPTER II
JURIDICAL STATUS

ARTICLE 12
PERSONAL STATUS

1. The personal status of a refugee shall be governed by the law of the country of his domicile or, if he has no domicile, by the law of the country of his residence.

2. Rights previously acquired by a refugee and dependent on personal status, more particularly rights attaching to marriage, shall be

respected by a Contracting State, subject to compliance, if this be necessary, with the formalities required by the law of that State, provided that the right in question is one which would have been recognized by the law of that State had he not become a refugee.

ARTICLE 13
MOVABLE AND IMMOVABLE PROPERTY

The Contracting States shall accord to a refugee treatment as favourable as possible and, in any event, not less favourable than that accorded to aliens generally in the same circumstances, as regards the acquisition of movable and immovable property and other rights pertaining thereto, and to leases and other contracts relating to movable and immovable property.

ARTICLE 14
ARTISTIC RIGHTS AND INDUSTRIAL PROPERTY

In respect of the protection of industrial property, such as inventions, designs or models, trade marks, trade names, and of rights in literary, artistic and scientific works, a refugee shall be accorded in the country in which he has his habitual residence the same protection as is accorded to nationals of that country. In the territory of any other Contracting State, he shall be accorded the same protection as is accorded in that territory to nationals of the country in which he has his habitual residence.

ARTICLE 15
RIGHT OF ASSOCIATION

As regards non-political and non-profit-making associations and trade unions the Contracting States shall accord to refugees lawfully staying in their territory the most favourable treatment accorded to nationals of a foreign country, in the same circumstances.

ARTICLE 16
ACCESS TO COURTS

1. A refugee shall have free access to the courts of law on the territory of all Contracting States.

2. A refugee shall enjoy in the Contracting State in which he has his habitual residence the same treatment as a national in matters pertaining to access to the Courts, including legal assistance and exemption from *cautio judicatum solvi*.

3. A refugee shall be accorded in the matters referred to in paragraph 2 in countries other than that in which he has his habitual residence the treatment granted to a national of the country of his habitual residence.

CHAPTER III
GAINFUL EMPLOYMENT

Article 17
Wage-earning employment

1. The Contracting State shall accord to refugees lawfully staying in their territory the most favourable treatment accorded to nationals of a foreign country in the same circumstances, as regards the right to engage in wage-earning employment.

2. In any case, restrictive measures imposed on aliens or the employment of aliens for the protection of the national labour market shall not be applied to a refugee who was already exempt from them at the date of entry into force of this Convention for the Contracting State concerned, or who fulfils one of the following conditions:

(a) He has completed three years' residence in the country,
(b) He has a spouse possessing the nationality of the country of residence. A refugee may not invoke the benefits of this provision if he has abandoned his spouse,
(c) He has one or more children possessing the nationality of the country of residence.

3. The Contracting States shall give sympathetic consideration to assimilating the rights of all refugees with regard to wage-earning employment to those of nationals, and in particular of those refugees who have entered their territory pursuant to programmes of labour recruitment or under immigration schemes.

Article 18
Self-employment

The Contracting States shall accord to a refugee lawfully in their territory treatment as favourable as possible and, in any event, not less favourable than that accorded to aliens generally in the same circumstances, as regards the right to engage on his own account in agriculture, industry, handicrafts and commerce and to establish commercial and industrial companies.

Article 19
Liberal professions

1. Each Contracting State shall accord to refugees lawfully staying in their territory who hold diplomas recognized by the competent authorities of that State, and who are desirous of practising a liberal profession, treatment as favourable as possible and, in any event, not less favourable than that accorded to aliens generally in the same circumstances.

2. The Contracting States shall use their best endeavours consistently with their laws and constitutions to secure the settlement of such refugees in the territories, other than the metropolitan territory, for whose international relations they are responsible.

CHAPTER IV
WELFARE

Article 20
Rationing

Where a rationing system exists, which applies to the population at large and regulates the general distribution of products in short supply, refugees shall be accorded the same treatment as nationals.

Article 21
Housing

As regards housing, the Contracting States, in so far as the matter is regulated by laws or regulations or is subject to the control of public authorities, shall accord to refugees lawfully staying in their territory treatment as favourable as possible and, in any event, not less favourable than that accorded to aliens generally in the same circumstances.

Article 22
Public education

1. The Contracting States shall accord to refugees the same treatment as is accorded to nationals with respect to elementary education.

2. The Contracting States shall accord to refugees treatment as favourable as possible, and, in any event, not less favourable than that accorded to aliens generally in the same circumstances, with respect to education other than elementary education and, in particular, as regards access to studies, the recognition of foreign school certificates, diplomas and degrees, the remission of fees and charges and the award of scholarships.

Article 23
Public relief

The Contracting States shall accord to refugees lawfully staying in their territory the same treatment with respect to public relief and assistance as is accorded to their nationals.

Article 24
Labour legislation and social security

1. The Contracting States shall accord to refugees lawfully staying in their territory the same treatment as is accorded to nationals in respect of the following matters:

(a) In so far as such matters are governed by laws or regulations or are subject to the control of administrative authorities: remuneration, including family allowances where these form part of remuneration, hours of work, overtime arrangements, holidays with pay, restrictions on home work, minimum age of employment, apprenticeship and training, women's work and the work of young persons, and the enjoyment of the benefits of collective bargaining;

(b) Social security (legal provisions in respect of employment injury, occupational diseases, maternity, sickness, disability, old age, death, unemployment, family responsibilities and any other contingency which, according to national laws or regulations, is covered by a social security scheme), subject to the following limitations:

(i) There may be appropriate arrangements for the maintenance of acquired rights and rights in course of acquisition;

(ii) National laws or regulations of the country of residence may prescribe special arrangements concerning benefits or portions of benefits which are payable wholly out of public funds, and concerning allowances paid to persons who do not fulfil the contribution conditions prescribed for the award of a normal pension.

2. The right to compensation for the death of a refugee resulting from employment injury or from occupational disease shall not be affected by the fact that the residence of the beneficiary is outside the territory of the Contracting State.

3. The Contracting States shall extend to refugees the benefits of agreements concluded between them, or which may be concluded between them in the future, concerning the maintenance of acquired rights and rights in the process of acquisition in regard to social security, subject only to the Conditions which apply to nationals of the States signatory to the agreements in question.

4. The Contracting States will give sympathetic consideration to extending to refugees so far as possible the benefits of similar agreements which may at any time be in force between such Contracting States and non-contracting States.

CHAPTER V
ADMINISTRATIVE MEASURES

Article 25
Administrative assistance

1. When the exercise of a right by a refugee would normally require the assistance of authorities of a foreign country to whom he cannot

have recourse, the Contracting States in whose territory he is residing shall arrange that such assistance be afforded to him by their own authorities or by an international authority.

2. The authority or authorities mentioned in paragraph 1 shall deliver or cause to be delivered under their supervision to refugees such documents or certifications as would normally be delivered to aliens by or through their national authorities.

3. Documents or certifications so delivered shall stand in the stead of the official instruments delivered to aliens by or through their national authorities, and shall be given credence in the absence of proof to the contrary.

4. Subject to such exceptional treatment as may be granted to indigent persons, fees may be charged for the services mentioned herein, but such fees shall be moderate and commensurate with those charged to nationals for similar services.

5. The provisions of this Article shall be without prejudice to Articles 27 and 28.

ARTICLE 26
FREEDOM OF MOVEMENT

Each Contracting State shall accord to refugees lawfully in its territory the right to choose their place of residence and to move freely within its territory, subject to any regulations applicable to aliens generally in the same circumstances.

ARTICLE 27
IDENTITY PAPERS

The Contracting States shall issue identity papers to any refugee in the territory who does not possess a valid travel document.

ARTICLE 28
TRAVEL DOCUMENTS

1. The Contracting States shall issue to refugees lawfully staying in the territory travel documents for the purpose of travel outside their territory unless compelling reasons of national security or public order otherwise require, and the provisions of the Schedule to this Convention shall apply with respect to such documents. The Contracting States may issue such travel document to any other refugee in their territory, they shall in particular give sympathetic consideration to the issue of such a travel document to refugees in their territory who are unable to obtain a travel document from the country of their lawful residence.

2. Travel documents issued to refugees under previous international agreements by parties thereto shall be recognized and

treated by the Contracting States in the same way as if they had been issued pursuant to this article.

ARTICLE 29
FISCAL CHARGES

1. The Contracting States shall not impose upon refugees duties charges or taxes, of any description whatsoever, other or higher than those which are or may be levied on their nationals in similar situations.

2. Nothing in the above paragraph shall prevent the application to refugees of the laws and regulations concerning charges in respect of the issue to aliens of administrative documents including identity papers.

ARTICLE 30
TRANSFER OF ASSETS

1. A Contracting State shall, in conformity with its laws and regulation permit refugees to transfer assets which they have brought into its territory to another country where they have been admitted for the purposes of resettlement.

2. A Contracting State shall give sympathetic consideration to the application of refugees for permission to transfer assets wherever they may be and which are necessary for their resettlement in another country to which they have been admitted.

ARTICLE 31
REFUGEES UNLAWFULLY IN THE COUNTRY OF REFUGE

1. The Contracting States shall not impose penalties, on account of their illegal entry or presence, on refugees who, coming directly from a territory where their life or freedom was threatened in the sense of Article I, enter or are present in their territory without authorization, provided they present themselves without delay to the authorities and show good cause for their illegal entry or presence.

2. The Contracting States shall not apply to the movements of such refugees restrictions other than those which are necessary and such restrictions shall only be applied until their status in the country is regularized or they obtain admission into another country. The Contracting States shall allow such refugees a reasonable period and all the necessary facilities to obtain admission into another country.

ARTICLE 32
EXPULSION

1. The Contracting States shall not expel a refugee lawfully in their territory save on grounds of national security or public order.

2. The expulsion of such a refugee shall be only in pursuance of a decision reached in accordance with due process of law. Except where compelling reasons of national security otherwise require, the refugee shall be allowed to submit evidence to clear himself, and to appeal to and be represented for the purpose before competent authority or a person or persons specially designated by the competent authority.

3. The Contracting States shall allow such a refugee a reasonable period within which to seek legal admission into another country. The Contracting States reserve the right to apply during that period such internal measures as they may deem necessary.

ARTICLE 33
PROHIBITION OF EXPULSION OR RETURN ("REFOULEMENT")

1. No Contracting State shall expel or return ("refouler") a refugee in any manner whatsoever to the frontiers of territories where his life or freedom would be threatened on account of his race, religion, nationality, membership of a particular social group or political opinion.

2. The benefit of the present provision may not, however, be claimed by a refugee whom there are reasonable grounds for regarding as a danger to the security of the country in which he is, or who, having been convicted by a final judgment of a particularly serious crime, constitutes a danger to the community of that country.

ARTICLE 34
NATURALIZATION

The Contracting States shall as far as possible facilitate the assimilation and naturalization of refugees. They shall in particular make every effort to expedite naturalization proceedings and to reduce as far as possible the charges and costs of such proceedings.

CHAPTER VI
EXECUTORY AND TRANSITORY PROVISIONS

ARTICLE 35
CO-OPERATION OF THE NATIONAL AUTHORITIES WITH THE UNITED NATIONS

1. The Contracting States undertake to co-operate with the Office of the United Nations High Commissioner for Refugees, or any other agency of the United Nations which may succeed it, in the exercise of its functions, and shall in particular facilitate its duty of supervising the application of the provisions of this Convention.

2. In order to enable the Office of the High Commissioner or any other agency of the United Nations which may succeed it, to make reports to the Competent organs of the United Nations, the

Contracting States undertake to provide them in the appropriate form with information and statistical data requested concerning:

(a) the condition of refugees,
(b) the implementation of this Convention, and
(c) laws, regulations and decrees which are, or may hereafter be, in force relating to refugees.

ARTICLE 36
INFORMATION ON NATIONAL LEGISLATION

The Contracting States shall communicate to the Secretary-General of the United Nations the laws and regulations which they may adopt to ensure the application of this Convention.

ARTICLE 37
RELATION TO PREVIOUS CONVENTIONS

Without prejudice to Article 28, paragraph 2, of this Convention, this Convention replaces, as between parties to it, the Arrangements of 5 July 1922, 31 May 1924, 12 May 1926, 30 June 1928 and 30 July 1935, the Conventions of 28 October 1933 and 10 February 1938, the Protocol of 14 September 1939 and the Agreement of 15 October 1946.

CHAPTER VII
FINAL CLAUSES

ARTICLE 38
SETTLEMENT OF DISPUTES

Any dispute between parties to this Convention relating to its interpretation or application, which cannot be settled by other means, shall be referred to the International Court of Justice at the request of any one of the parties to the dispute.

ARTICLE 39
SIGNATURE, RATIFICATION AND ACCESSION

1. This Convention shall be opened for signature at Geneva on 28 July 1951 and shall thereafter be deposited with the Secretary-General of the United Nations. It shall be open for signature at the European Office of the United Nations from 28 July to 31 August 1951 and shall be re-opened for signature at the Headquarters of the United Nations from 17 September 1951 to 31 December 1952.

2. This Convention shall be open for signature on behalf of all States Members of the United Nations, and also on behalf of any other

State invited to attend the Conference of Plenipotentiaries on the Status of Refugees and Stateless Persons or to which an invitation to sign will have been addressed by the General Assembly. It shall be ratified and the instruments of ratification shall be deposited with the Secretary-General of the United Nations.

3. This Convention shall be open from 28 July 1951 for accession by the States referred to in paragraph 2 of this Article. Accession shall be effected by the deposit of an instrument of accession with the Secretary-General of the United Nations.

ARTICLE 40
TERRITORIAL APPLICATION CLAUSE

1. Any State may, at the time of signature, ratification or accession, declare that this Convention shall extend to all or any of the territories for the international relations of which it is responsible. Such a declaration shall take effect when the Convention enters into force for the State concerned.

2. At any time thereafter any such extension shall be made by notification addressed to the Secretary-General of the United Nations and shall take effect as from the ninetieth day after the day of receipt by the Secretary-General of the United Nations of this notification, or as from the date of entry into force of the Convention for the State concerned, whichever is the later.

3. With respect to those territories to which this Convention is not extended at the time of signature, ratification or accession, each State concerned shall consider the possibility of taking the necessary steps in order to extend the application of this Convention to such territories, subject, where necessary for constitutional reasons, to the consent of the governments of such territories.

ARTICLE 41
FEDERAL CLAUSE

In the case of a Federal or non-unitary State, the following provisions shall apply:

(a) With respect to those Articles of this Convention that come within the legislative jurisdiction of the federal legislative authority, the obligations of the Federal Government shall to this extent be the same as those of Parties which are not Federal States,

(b) With respect to those Articles of this Convention that come within the legislative jurisdiction of constituent States, provinces or cantons which are not, under the constitutional system of the federation, bound to take legislative action, the

Federal Government shall bring such Articles with a favourable recommendation to the notice of the appropriate authorities of States, provinces or cantons at the earliest possible moment.

(c) A Federal State Party to this Convention shall, at the request of any other Contracting State transmitted through the Secretary-General of the United Nations, supply a statement of the law and practice of the Federation and its constituent units in regard to any particular provision of the Convention showing the extent to which effect has been given to that provision by legislative or other action.

Article 42
Reservations

1. At the time of signature, ratification or accession, any State may make reservations to articles of the Convention other than to Articles 1, 3, 4, 16 (1), 33, 36-46 inclusive.

2. Any State making a reservation in accordance with paragraph 1 of this article may at any time withdraw the reservation by a communication to that effect addressed to the Secretary-General of the United Nations.

Article 43
Entry into force

1. This Convention shall come into force on the ninetieth day following the day of deposit of the sixth instrument of ratification or accession.

2. For each State ratifying or acceding to the Convention after the deposit of the sixth instrument of ratification or accession, the Convention shall enter into force on the ninetieth day following the date of deposit by such State of its instrument of ratification or accession.

Article 44
Denunciation

1. Any Contracting State may denounce this Convention at any time by a notification addressed to the Secretary-General of the United Nations.

2. Such denunciation shall take effect for the Contracting State concerned one year from the date upon which it is received by the Secretary-General of the United Nations.

3. Any State which has made a declaration or notification under Article 40 may, at any time thereafter, by a notification to the Secretary-General of the United Nations, declare that the Convention

shall cease to extend to such territory one year after the date of receipt of the notification by the Secretary-General.

ARTICLE 45
REVISION

1. Any Contracting State may request revision of this Convention at any time by a notification addressed to the Secretary-General of the United Nations.

2. The General Assembly of the United Nations shall recommend the steps, if any, to be taken in respect of such request.

ARTICLE 46
NOTIFICATIONS BY THE SECRETARY-GENERAL OF THE UNITED NATIONS

The Secretary-General of the United Nations shall inform all Members of the United Nations and non-member States referred to in Article 39:

(a) of declarations and notifications in accordance with Section B of Article 1;
(b) of signatures, ratifications and accessions in accordance with Article 39;
(c) of declarations and notifications in accordance with Article 40;
(d) of reservations and withdrawals in accordance with Article 42;
(e) of the date on which this Convention will come into force in accordance with Article 43;
(f) of denunciations and notifications in accordance with Article 44;
(g) of requests for revision in accordance with Article 45.

IN FAITH WHEREOF the undersigned, duly authorized, have signed this Convention on behalf of their respective Governments,

DONE at Geneva, this twenty-eighth day of July, one thousand nine hundred and fifty-one, in a single copy, of which the English and French texts are equally authentic and which shall remain deposited in the archives of the United Nations, and certified true copies of which shall be delivered to all Members of the United Nations and to the non-member States referred to in Article 39.

SCHEDULE

PARAGRAPH 1

1. The travel document referred to in Article 28 of this Convention shall be similar to the specimen annexed hereto.

2. The document shall be made out in at least two languages, one of which shall be English or French.

Paragraph 2

Subject to the regulations obtaining in the country of issue, children may be included in the travel document of a parent or, in exceptional circumstances, of another adult refugee.

Paragraph 3

The fees charged for issue of the document shall not exceed the lowest scale of charges for national passports.

Paragraph 4

Save in special or exceptional cases, the document shall be made valid for the largest possible number of countries.

Paragraph 5

The document shall have a validity of either one or two years, at the discretion of the issuing authority.

Paragraph 6

1. The renewal or extension of the validity of the document is a matter for the authority which issued it, so long as the holder has not established lawful residence in another territory and resides lawfully in the territory of the said authority. The issue of a new document is, under the same conditions, a matter for the authority which issued the former document.

2. Diplomatic or consular authorities, specially authorized for the purpose, shall be empowered to extend, for a period not exceeding six months, the validity of travel documents issued by their Governments.

3. The Contracting States shall give sympathetic consideration to renewing or extending the validity of travel documents or issuing new documents to refugees no longer lawfully resident in their territory who are unable to obtain a travel document from the country of their lawful residence.

Paragraph 7

The Contracting States shall recognize the validity of the documents issued in accordance with the provisions of Article 28 of this Convention.

Paragraph 8

The competent authorities of the country to which the refugee desires to proceed shall, if they are prepared to admit him and if a visa is required, affix a visa on the document of which he is the holder.

Paragraph 9

1. The Contracting States undertake to issue transit visas to refugees who have obtained visas for a territory of final destination.

2. The issue of such visas may be refused on grounds which would justify refusal of a visa to any alien.

Paragraph 10

The fees for the issue of exit, entry or transit visas shall not exceed the lowest scale of charges for visas on foreign passports.

Paragraph 11

When a refugee has lawfully taken up residence in the territory of another Contracting State, the responsibility for the issue of a new document, under the terms and conditions of Article 28, shall be that of the competent authority of that territory, to which the refugee shall be entitled to apply.

Paragraph 12

The authority issuing a new document shall withdraw the old document and shall return it to the country of issue, if it is stated in the document that it should be so returned; otherwise it shall withdraw and cancel the document.

Paragraph 13

1. Each Contracting State undertakes that the holder of a travel document issued by it in accordance with Article 28 of this Convention shall be re-admitted to its territory at any time during the period of its validity.

2. Subject to the provisions of the preceding sub-paragraph, a Contracting State may require the holder of the document to comply with such formalities as may be prescribed in regard to exit from or return to its territory.

3. The Contracting States reserve the right, in exceptional cases, or in cases where the refugee's stay is authorized for a specific period, when issuing the document, to limit the period during which the refugee may return to a period of not less than three months.

Paragraph 14

Subject only to the terms of paragraph 13, the provisions of this Schedule in no way affect the laws and regulations governing the conditions of admission to, transit through, residence and establishment in, and departure from, the territories of the Contracting States.

Paragraph 15

Neither the issue of the document nor the entries made thereon determine or affect the status of the holder, particularly as regards nationality.

Paragraph 16

The issue of the document does not in any way entitle the holder to the protection of the diplomatic or consular authorities of the country of issue, and does not confer on these authorities a right of protection.

ANNEX
SPECIMEN TRAVEL DOCUMENT

The document will be in booklet form (approximately 15 x 10 centimetres).

It is recommended that it be so printed that any erasure or alteration by chemical or other means can be readily detected, and that the words "Convention of 28 July 1951" be printed in continuous repetition on each page, in the language of the issuing country.

APPENDIX
FINAL ACT OF THE 1951 UNITED NATIONS CONFERENCE OF PLENIPOTENTIARIES ON THE STATUS OF REFUGEES AND STATELESS PERSONS

I

The General Assembly of the United Nations, by Resolution 429 (V) of 14 December 1950, decided to convene in Geneva a Conference of Plenipotentiaries to complete the drafting of, and to sign, a Convention relating to the Status of Refugees and a Protocol relating to the Status of Stateless Persons.

The Conference met at the European Office of the United Nations in Geneva from 2 to 25 July 1951.

The Governments of the following twenty-six States were represented by delegates who all submitted satisfactory credentials or other communications of appointment authorizing them to participate in the Conference:

Australia
Austria
Belgium
Brazil
Canada
Colombia
Denmark
Egypt
France
Germany, Federal Republic of
Greece
Holy See
Iraq
Israel
Italy
Luxembourg
Monaco
Netherlands
Norway
Sweden
Switzerland (the Swiss delegation also represented Liechtenstein)
Turkey
United Kingdom of Great Britain and Northern Ireland
United States of America
Venezuela
Yugoslavia

The Governments of the following two States were represented by observers

Cuba
Iran

Pursuant to the request of the General Assembly, the United Nations High Commissioner for Refugees participated, without the right to vote, in the deliberations of the Conference.

The International Labour Organisation and the International Refugee Organization were represented at the Conference without the right to vote.

The Conference invited a representative of the Council of Europe to be represented at the Conference without the right to vote.

Representatives of the following Non-Governmental Organizations in consultative relationship with the Economic and Social Council were also present as observers:

CATEGORY A

International Confederation of Free Trade Unions
International Federation of Christian Trade Unions
Inter-Parliamentary Union

CATEGORY B

Agudas Israel World Organization
Caritas Internationalis
Catholic International Union for Social Service
Commission of the Churches on International Affairs
Consultative Council of Jewish Organizations

Co-ordinating Board of Jewish Organizations
Friends' World Committee for Consultation
International Association of Penal Law
International Bureau for the Unification of Penal Law
International Committee of the Red Cross
International Council of Women
International Federation of Friends of Young Women
International League for the Rights of Man
International Social Service
International Union for Child Welfare
International Union of Catholic Women's Leagues
Pax Romana
Women's International League for Peace and Freedom
World Jewish Congress
World Union for Progressive Judaism
World Young Women's Christian Association

Register

International Relief Committee for Intellectual Workers
League of Red Cross Societies
Standing Conference of Voluntary Agencies
World Association of Girl Guides and Girl Scouts
World University Service

Representatives of Non-Governmental Organizations which have been granted consultative status by the Economic and Social Council as well as those entered by the Secretary-General on the Register referred to in Resolution 288 B (X) of the Economic and Social Council, paragraph 17, had under the rules of procedure adopted by the Conference the right to submit written or oral statements to the Conference.

The Conference elected Mr. Knud Larsen, of Denmark, as President, and Mr. A. Herment, of Belgium, and Mr. Talat Miras, of Turkey, as Vice-Presidents.

At its second meeting, the Conference, acting on a proposal of the representative of Egypt, unanimously decided to address an invitation to the Holy See to designate a plenipotentiary representative to participate in its work. A representative of the Holy See took his place at the Conference on 10 July 1951.

The Conference adopted as its agenda the Provisional Agenda drawn up by the Secretary-General (A/CONF.2/2/Rev.l). It also adopted the Provisional Rules of Procedure drawn up by the Secretary-General, with the addition of a provision which authorized a representative of the Council of Europe to be present at the Conference without the right to vote and to submit proposals (A/CONF.2/3/Rev.l).

In accordance with the Rules of Procedure of the Conference, the President and Vice-Presidents examined the credentials of representatives and on 17 July 1951 reported to the Conference the results of such examination, the Conference adopting the report.

The Conference used as the basis of its discussions the draft Convention relating to the Status of Refugees and the draft Protocol relating to the Status of Stateless Persons prepared by the ad hoc Committee on Refugees and Stateless Persons at its second session held in Geneva from 14 to 25 August 1950, with the exception of the preamble and Article 1 (Definition of the term "refugee") of the draft Convention. The text of the preamble before the Conference was that which was adopted by the Economic and Social Council on 11 August 1950 in Resolution 319 B 11 (Xl). The text of Article 1 before the Conference was that recommended by the General Assembly on 14 December 1950 and contained in the Annex to Resolution 429 (V). The latter was a modification of the text as it had been adopted by the Economic and Social Council in Resolution 319 B 11 (Xl).

The Conference adopted the Convention relating to the Status of Refugees in two readings. Prior to its second reading it established a Style Committee composed of the President and the representatives of Belgium, France, Israel, Italy, the United Kingdom of Great Britain and Northern Ireland and the United States of America, together with the High Commissioner for Refugees, which elected as its Chairman Mr. G. Warren, of the United States of America. The Style Committee re-drafted the text which had been adopted by the Conference on first reading, particularly from the point of view of language and of concordance between the English and French texts.

The Convention was adopted on 25 July by 24 votes to none with no abstentions and opened for signature at the European Office of the United Nations from 28 July to 31 August 1951. It will be re-opened for signature at the permanent headquarters of the United Nations in New York from 17 September 1951 to 31 December 1952. The English and French texts of the Convention, which are equally authentic, are appended to this Final Act.

II

The Conference decided, by 17 votes to 3 with 3 abstentions, that the titles of the chapters and of the articles of the Convention are included for practical purposes and do not constitute an element of interpretation.

III

With respect to the draft Protocol relating to the Status of Stateless Persons, the Conference adopted the following resolution:

The Conference,

Having considered the draft Protocol relating to the Status of Stateless Persons,

Considering that the subject still requires more detailed study,

Decides not to take a decision on the subject at the present Conference and refers the draft Protocol back to the appropriate organs of the United Nations for further study.

IV

The Conference adopted unanimously the following recommendations:

A. [Facilitation of refugee travels]

The Conference,

Considering that the issue and recognition of travel documents is necessary to facilitate the movement of refugees, and in particular their resettlement,

Urges Governments which are parties to the Inter-Governmental Agreement on Refugee Travel Documents signed in London on 15 October 1946, or which recognize travel documents issued in accordance with the Agreement, to continue to issue or to recognize such travel documents, and to extend the issue of such documents to refugees as defined in Article 1 of the Convention relating to the Status of Refugees or to recognize the travel documents so issued to such persons, until they shall have undertaken obligations under Article 28 of the said Convention.

B. [Principle of unity of the family]

The Conference,

Considering that the unity of the family, the natural and fundamental group unit of society, is an essential right of the refugee, and that such unity is constantly threatened, and

Noting with satisfaction that, according to the official commentary of the *ad hoc* Committee on Statelessness and Related Problems (E/1618, p. 40) the rights granted to a refugee are extended to members of his family,

Recommends Governments to take the necessary measures for the protection of the refugee's family, especially with a view to:

(1) Ensuring that the unity of the refugee's family is maintained particularly in cases where the head of the family has fulfilled the necessary conditions for admission to a particular country,

(2) The protection of refugees who are minors, in particular unaccompanied children and girls, with special reference to guardianship and adoption.

C. [Welfare services]

The Conference,

Considering that, in the moral, legal and material spheres, refugees need the help of suitable welfare services, especially that of appropriate non-governmental organizations,

Recommends Governments and inter-governmental bodies to facilitate, encourage and sustain the efforts of properly qualified organizations.

D. [International co-operation in the field of asylum and resettlement]

The Conference,

Considering that many persons still leave their country of origin for reasons of persecution and are entitled to special protection on account of their position,

Recommends that Governments continue to receive refugees in their territories and that they act in concert in a true spirit of international co-operation in order that these refugees may find asylum and the possibility of resettlement.

E. [Extension of treatment provided by the Convention]

The Conference,

Expresses the hope that the Convention relating to the Status of Refugees will have value as an example exceeding its contractual scope and that all nations will be guided by it in granting so far as possible to persons in their territory as refugees and who would not be covered by the terms of the Convention, the treatment for which it provides.

IN WITNESS WHEREOF the President, Vice-Presidents and the Executive Secretary of the Conference have signed this Final Act.

DONE at Geneva this twenty-eighth day of July one thousand nine hundred and fifty-one in a single copy in the English and French languages, each text being equally authentic. Translations of this Final Act into Chinese, Russian and Spanish will be prepared by the Secretary-General of the United Nations, who will, on request, send copies thereof to each of the Governments invited to attend the Conference.

The President of the Conference: Knud Larsen
The Vice-Presidents of the Conference: A. Herment Talat Miras
The Executive Secretary of the Conference: John P. Humphrey

The 1967 Protocol Relating to the Status of Refugees

The 1967 Protocol Relating to the Status of Refugees removed both the dateline and the geographical limitations of the 1951 UN convention, giving the convention a truly universal character. It had become apparent the movement of refugees was not a phenomenon confined to World War II and its aftermath. New refugee groups emerged, particularly in Africa, throughout the late 1950s and 1960s. It therefore became necessary to make the 1951 UN convention applicable in all such refugee situations.

The 1967 protocol is an independent instrument to which states may accede without becoming parties to the convention. States that accede to the protocol undertake to apply the provisions of the convention to refugees who meet the convention definition, but without the 1951 dateline. If a state accedes to the protocol alone, there is no possibility of introducing a geographical limitation.

When acceding to the convention and/or protocol, states may make reservations to articles they feel unable to apply. There are, however, certain articles to which no reservations are permitted, and acceding states must therefore accept. They are as follows:

Article 1, refugee definition

Article 3, nondiscrimination as to race, religion, or country of origin

Article 4, freedom to practice religion

Article 16 (1), free access to courts

Article 33, nonrefoulement

In recent years, the number of accessions to the convention and protocol has grown to over 120. Nevertheless, many major asylum states, including governments in Asia and the Middle East, have not yet signed the major refugee instruments. One of UNHCR's major and ongoing protection tasks is to encourage states to accede to international instruments for the protection of refugees, as well as to supervise their application.

Entry into force: 4 October 1967, in accordance with Article VIII

Text: United Nations Treaty Series No. 8791, Vol. 606, p. 267

The States Parties to the present Protocol,

Considering that the Convention relating to the Status of Refugees done at Geneva on 28 July 1951 (hereinafter referred to as the Convention) covers only those persons who have become refugees as a result of events occurring before 1 January 1951,

Considering that new refugee situations have arisen since the Convention was adopted and that the refugees concerned may therefore not fall within the scope of the Convention,

Considering that it is desirable that equal status should be enjoyed by all refugees covered by the definition in the Convention irrespective of the dateline 1 January 1951,

Have agreed as follows:

ARTICLE I
GENERAL PROVISION

1. The States Parties to the present Protocol undertake to apply Articles 2 to 34 inclusive of the Convention to refugees as hereinafter defined.

2. For the purpose of the present Protocol, the term "refugee" shall, except as regards the application of paragraph 3 of this Article, mean any person within the definition of Article 1 of the Convention as if the words "As a result of events occurring before 1 January 1951 and . . ." and the words ". . . as a result of such events", in Article 1 A (2) were omitted.

3. The present Protocol shall be applied by the States Parties hereto without any geographic limitation, save that existing declarations made by States already Parties to the Convention in accordance with Article 1 B (1) *(a)* of the Convention, shall, unless extended under Article 1 B (2) thereof, apply also under the present Protocol.

ARTICLE II
CO-OPERATION OF THE NATIONAL AUTHORITIES WITH THE UNITED NATIONS

1. The States Parties to the present Protocol undertake to co-operate with the Office of the United Nations High Commissioner for Refugees, or any other agency of the United Nations which may succeed it, in the exercise of its functions, and shall in particular facilitate its duty of supervising the application of the provisions of the present Protocol.

2. In order to enable the Office of the High Commissioner, or any other agency of the United Nations which may succeed it, to make reports to the competent organs of the United Nations, the States Parties to the present Protocol undertake to provide them with the information and statistical data requested, in the appropriate form, concerning:

(a) The condition of refugees;
(b) The implementation of the present Protocol;
(c) Laws, regulations and decrees which are, or may hereafter be, in force relating to refugees.

Article III
Information on national legislation

The States Parties to the present Protocol shall communicate to the Secretary-General of the United Nations the laws and regulations which they may adopt to ensure the application of the present Protocol.

Article IV
Settlement of disputes

Any dispute between States Parties to the present Protocol which relates to its interpretation or application and which cannot be settled by other means shall be referred to the International Court of Justice at the request of any one of the parties to the dispute.

Article V
Accession

The present Protocol shall be open for accession on behalf of all States Parties to the Convention and of any other State Member of the United Nations or member of any of the specialized agencies or to which an invitation to accede may have been addressed by the General Assembly of the United Nations. Accession shall be effected by the deposit of an instrument of accession with the Secretary-General of the United Nations.

Article VI
Federal clause

In the case of a Federal or non-unitary State, the following provisions shall apply:

(a) With respect to those articles of the Convention to be applied in accordance with Article I, paragraph 1, of the present Protocol that come within the legislative jurisdiction of the federal legislative authority, the obligations of the Federal Government shall to this extent be the same as those of States Parties which are not Federal States;
(b) With respect to those articles of the Convention to be applied in accordance with Article I, paragraph 1, of the present Protocol that come within the legislative jurisdiction of

constituent States, provinces or cantons which are not, under the constitutional system of the federation, bound to take legislative action, the Federal Government shall bring such articles with a favourable recommendation to the notice of the appropriate authorities of States, provinces or cantons at the earliest possible moment;

(c) A Federal State Party to the present Protocol shall, at the request of any other State Party hereto transmitted through the Secretary-General of the United Nations, supply a statement of the law and practice of the Federation and its constituent units in regard to any particular provision of the Convention to be applied in accordance with Article I, paragraph 1, of the present Protocol, showing the extent to which effect has been given to that provision by legislative or other action.

ARTICLE VII
RESERVATIONS AND DECLARATIONS

1. At the time of accession, any State may make reservations in respect of Article IV of the present Protocol and in respect of the application in accordance with Article I of the present Protocol of any provisions of the Convention other than those contained in Articles 1, 3, 4, 16 (1) and 33 thereof, provided that in the case of a State Party to the Convention reservations made under this Article shall not extend to refugees in respect of whom the Convention applies.

2. Reservations made by States Parties to the Convention in accordance with Article 42 thereof shall, unless withdrawn, be applicable in relation to their obligations under the present Protocol.

3. Any State making a reservation in accordance with paragraph 1 of this Article may at any time withdraw such reservation by a communication to that effect addressed to the Secretary-General of the United Nations.

4. Declarations made under Article 40, paragraphs 1 and 2, of the Convention by a State Party thereto which accedes to the present Protocol shall be deemed to apply in respect of the present Protocol, unless upon accession a notification to the contrary is addressed by the State Party concerned to the Secretary-General of the United Nations. The provisions of Article 40, paragraphs 2 and 3, and of Article 44, paragraph 3, of the Convention shall be deemed to apply *mutatis mutandis* to the present Protocol.

ARTICLE VIII
ENTRY INTO FORCE

1. The present Protocol shall come into force on the day of deposit of the sixth instrument of accession.

2. For each State acceding to the Protocol after the deposit of the sixth instrument of accession, the Protocol shall come into force on the date of deposit by such State of its instrument of accession.

ARTICLE IX
DENUNCIATION

1. Any State Party hereto may denounce this Protocol at any time by a notification addressed to the Secretary-General of the United Nations.

2. Such denunciation shall take effect for the State Party concerned one year from the date on which it is received by the Secretary-General of the United Nations.

ARTICLE X
NOTIFICATIONS BY THE SECRETARY-GENERAL OF THE UNITED NATIONS

The Secretary-General of the United Nations shall inform the States referred to in Article V above of the date of entry into force, accessions, reservations and withdrawals of reservations to and denunciations of the present Protocol, and of declarations and notifications relating hereto.

ARTICLE XI
DEPOSIT IN THE ARCHIVES OF THE SECRETARIAT OF THE UNITED NATIONS

A copy of the present Protocol, of which the Chinese, English, French, Russian and Spanish texts are equally authentic, signed by the President of the General Assembly and by the Secretary-General of the United Nations, shall be deposited in the archives of the Secretariat of the United Nations. The Secretary-General will transmit certified copies thereof to all States Members of the United Nations and to the other States referred to in Article V above.

APPENDIX
GENERAL ASSEMBLY RESOLUTION 2198(XXI)
Protocol relating to the Status of Refugees

The General Assembly,

Considering that the Convention relating to the Status of Refugees, signed at Geneva on 28 July 1951, covers only those persons who have become refugees as a result of events occurring before 1 January 1951,

Considering that new refugee situations have arisen since the Convention was adopted and that the refugees concerned may therefore not fall within the scope of the Convention,

Considering that it is desirable that equal status should be enjoyed by all refugees covered by the definition in the Convention, irrespective of the date-line of 1 January 1951,

Taking note of the recommendation of the Executive Committee of the Programme of the United Nations High Commissioner for Refugees that the draft Protocol relating to the Status of Refugees should be submitted to the General Assembly after consideration by the Economic and Social Council, in order that the Secretary-General might be authorized to open the Protocol for accession by Governments within the shortest possible time,

Considering that the Economic and Social Council, in its resolution 1186 (XLI) of 18 November 1966, took note with approval of the draft Protocol contained in the addendum to the report of the United Nations High Commissioner for Refugees and concerning measures to extend the personal scope of the Convention and transmitted the addendum to the General Assembly,

1. *Takes note* of the Protocol relating to the Status of Refugees, the text of which is contained in the addendum to the report of the United Nations High Commissioner for Refugees;
2. *Requests* the Secretary-General to transmit the text of the Protocol to the States mentioned in article V thereof, with a view to enabling them to accede to the Protocol.

1495th plenary meeting,
16 December 1966.

The United Nations Declaration on Territorial Asylum (1967)

The United Nations Declaration on Territorial Asylum (1967) recalls Articles 13 and 14 of the Universal Declaration of Human Rights and states the principle of nonrefoulement in broad terms, including nonrejection at the frontier. It also recognizes that the granting of asylum by a state is a peaceful and humanitarian act that cannot be regarded as unfriendly by another state.

Adopted by the General Assembly of the United Nations on 14 December 1967 (resolution 2312 (XXII))

The General Assembly,

Recalling its resolutions 1839 (XVII) of 19 December 1962, 2100 (XX) of 20 December 1965 and 2203 (XXI) of 16 December 1966 concerning a declaration on the right of asylum,

Considering the work of codification to be undertaken by the International Law Commission in accordance with General Assembly resolution 1400 (XIV) of 21 November 1959,

Adopts the following Declaration:

DECLARATION ON TERRITORIAL ASYLUM

The General Assembly,

Noting that the purposes proclaimed in the Charter of the United Nations are to maintain international peace and security, to develop friendly relations among all nations and to achieve international co-operation in solving international problems of an economic, social, cultural or humanitarian character and in promoting and encouraging respect for human rights and for fundamental freedoms for all without distinction as to race, sex, language or religion,

Mindful of the Universal Declaration of Human Rights, which declares in article 14 that:

> "1. Everyone has the right to seek and to enjoy in other countries asylum from persecution.
> 2. This right may not be invoked in the case of prosecutions genuinely arising from non-political crimes or from acts contrary to the purposes and principles of the United Nations,"

Recalling also article 13, paragraph 2, of the Universal Declaration of Human Rights, which states:

"Everyone has the right to leave any country, including his own, and to return to his country,"

Recognizing that the grant of asylum by a State to persons entitled to invoke article 14 of the Universal Declaration of Human Rights is a peaceful and humanitarian act and that, as such, it cannot be regarded as unfriendly by any other State,

Recommends that, without prejudice to existing instruments dealing with asylum and the status of refugees and stateless persons, States should base themselves in their practices relating to territorial asylum on the following principles:

ARTICLE 1

1. Asylum granted by a State, in the exercise of its sovereignty, to persons entitled to invoke article 14 of the Universal Declaration of Human Rights, including persons struggling against colonialism, shall be respected by all other States.

2. The right to seek and to enjoy asylum may not be invoked by any person with respect to whom there are serious reasons for considering that he has committed a crime against peace, a war crime or a crime against humanity, as defined in the international instruments drawn up to make provision in respect of such crimes.

3. It shall rest with the State granting asylum to evaluate the grounds for the grant of asylum.

ARTICLE 2

1. The situation of persons referred to in article 1, paragraph 1, is, without prejudice to the sovereignty of States and the purposes and principles of the United Nations, of concern to the international community.

2. Where a State finds difficulty in granting or continuing to grant asylum, States individually or jointly or through the United Nations shall consider, in a spirit of international solidarity, appropriate measures to lighten the burden on that State.

ARTICLE 3

1. No person referred to in article 1, paragraph 1, shall be subjected to measures such as rejection at the frontier or, if he has already entered the territory in which he seeks asylum, expulsion or compulsory return to any State where he may be subjected to persecution.

2. Exception may be made to the foregoing principle only for overriding reasons of national security or in order to safeguard the population, as in the case of a mass influx of persons.

3. Should a State decide in any case that exception to the principle stated in paragraph 1 of this article would be justified, it shall consider the possibility of granting to the person concerned, under such conditions as it may deem appropriate, an opportunity, whether by way of provisional asylum or otherwise, of going to another State.

ARTICLE 4

States granting asylum shall not permit persons who have received asylum to engage in activities contrary to the purposes and principles of the United Nations.

The Organization of African Unity Convention Governing the Specific Aspects of Refugee Problems in Africa

The Organization of African Unity (OAU) Convention Governing the Specific Aspects of Refugee Problems in Africa, adopted in 1969, is the most important of several regional refugee instruments. It contains a broader refugee definition than the internationally accepted definition found in the 1951 UN convention and the 1967 UN protocol. It does not include any temporal or geographical limitations or any reference to earlier categories of refugees. The OAU convention also regulates the question of asylum (Article II) and prohibits subversive activities by refugees

(Article III). In addition, it stipulates that repatriation must be a voluntary act (Article V).

Adopted by the Assembly of Heads of State and Government at its Sixth Ordinary Session (Addis Ababa, 10 September 1969)

Entry into Force: 20 June 1974, in accordance with Article XI

Text: United Nations Treaty Series No. 14 691

PREAMBLE

We, the Heads of State and Government assembled in the city of Addis Ababa, from 6-10 September 1969,

1. *Noting with concern* the constantly increasing numbers of refugees in Africa and desirous of finding ways and means of alleviating their misery and suffering as well as providing them with a better life and future,
2. *Recognizing* the need for and essentially humanitarian approach towards solving the problems of refugees,
3. *Aware,* however, that refugee problems are a source of friction among many Member States, and desirous of eliminating the source of such discord,
4. *Anxious* to make a distinction between a refugee who seeks a peaceful and normal life and a person fleeing his country for the sole purpose of fomenting subversion from outside,
5. *Determined* that the activities of such subversive elements should be discouraged in accordance with the Declaration on the Problem of Subversion and Resolution on the Problem of Refugees adopted at Accra in 1965,
6. *Bearing* in mind that the Charter of the United Nations and the Universal Declaration of Human Rights have affirmed the principle that human beings shall enjoy fundamental rights and freedoms without discrimination,
7. *Recalling* Resolution 2312 (XXII) of 14 December 1967 of the United Nations General Assembly, relating to the Declaration on Territorial Asylum,
8. *Convinced* that all the problems of our continent must be solved in the Spirit of the Charter of the Organization of African Unity and in the African context,
9. *Recognizing* that the United Nations Convention of 28 July 1951, as modified by the Protocol of 31 January 1967, constitutes the basic and universal instrument relating to the status of refugees and reflects the deep concern of States for refugees and their desire to establish common standards for their treatment,

10. *Recalling* Resolutions 26 and 104 of the OAU Assemblies of Heads of State and Government, calling upon Member States of the Organization who had not already done so to accede to the United Nations Convention of 1951 and to the Protocol of 1967 relating to the Status of Refugees, and meanwhile to apply their provisions to refugees in Africa,
11. *Convinced* that the efficiency of the measures recommended by the present Convention to solve the problem of refugees in Africa necessitates close and continuous collaboration between the Organization of African Unity and the Office of the United Nations High Commissioner for Refugees,

Have agreed as follows:

ARTICLE I
DEFINITION OF THE TERM "REFUGEE"

1. For the purposes of this Convention, the term "refugee" shall mean every person who, owing to well-founded fear of being persecuted for reasons of race, religion, nationality, membership of a particular social group or political opinion, is outside the country of his nationality and is unable or, owing to such fear, is unwilling to avail himself of the protection of that country, or who, not having a nationality and being outside the country of his former habitual residence as a result of such events is unable or, owing to such fear, is unwilling to return to it.

2. The term "refugee" shall also apply to every person who, owing to external aggression, occupation, foreign domination or events seriously disturbing public order in either part or the whole of his country of origin or nationality, is compelled to leave his place of habitual residence in order to seek refuge in another place outside his country of origin or nationality.

3. In the case of a person who has several nationalities, the term "a country of which he is a national" shall mean each of the countries of which he is a national, and a person shall not be deemed to be lacking the protection of the country of which he is a national if, without any valid reason based on well-founded fear, he has not availed himself of the protection of one of the countries of which he is a national.

4. This Convention shall cease to apply to any refugee if:

(a) he has voluntarily re-availed himself of the protection of the country of his nationality, or,
(b) having lost his nationality, he has voluntarily reacquired it, or,
(c) he has acquired a new nationality, and enjoys the protection of the country of his new nationality, or,

(d) he has voluntarily re-established himself in the country which he left or outside which he remained owing to fear of persecution, or,

(e) he can no longer, because the circumstances in connection with which he was recognized as a refugee have ceased to exist, continue to refuse to avail himself of the protection of the country of his nationality, or,

(f) he has committed a serious non-political crime outside his country of refuge after his admission to that country as a refuge, or,

(g) he has seriously infringed the purposes and objectives of this Convention.

5. The provisions of this Convention shall not apply to any person with respect to whom the country of asylum has serious reasons for considering that:

(a) he has committed a crime against peace, a war crime, or a crime against humanity, as defined in the international instruments drawn up to make provision in respect of such crimes;

(b) he committed a serious non-political crime outside the country of refuge prior to his admission to that country as a refugee;

(c) he has been guilty of acts contrary to the purposes and principles of the Organization of African Unity;

(d) he has been guilty of acts contrary to the purposes and principles of the United Nations.

6. For the purposes of this Convention, the Contracting State of Asylum shall determine whether an applicant is a refugee.

ARTICLE II
ASYLUM

1. Member States of the OAU shall use their best endeavours consistent with their respective legislations to receive refugees and to secure the settlement of those refugees who, for well-founded reasons, are unable or unwilling to return to their country of origin or nationality.

2. The grant of asylum to refugees is a peaceful and humanitarian act and shall not be regarded as an unfriendly act by any Member State.

3. No person shall be subjected by a Member State to measures such as rejection at the frontier, return or expulsion, which would compel him to return to or remain in a territory where his life, physical integrity or liberty would be threatened for the reasons set out in Article I, paragraphs 1 and 2.

4. Where a Member State finds difficulty in continuing to grant asylum to refugees, such Member State may appeal directly to other Member States and through the OAU, and such other Member States shall in the spirit of African solidarity and international co-operation take appropriate measures to lighten the burden of the Member State granting asylum.

5. Where a refugee has not received the right to reside in any country of asylum, he may be granted temporary residence in any country of asylum in which he first presented himself as a refugee pending arrangement for his resettlement in accordance with the preceding paragraph.

6. For reasons of security, countries of asylum shall, as far as possible settle refugees at a reasonable distance from the frontier of their country of origin.

ARTICLE III
PROHIBITION OF SUBVERSIVE ACTIVITIES

1. Every refugee has duties to the country in which he finds himself which require in particular that he conforms with its laws and regulations as well as with measures taken for the maintenance of public order. He shall also abstain from any subversive activities against any Member State of the OAU.

2. Signatory States undertake to prohibit refugees residing in their respective territories from attacking any State Member of the OAU, by any activity likely to cause tension between Member States, and in particular by use of arms, through the press, or by radio.

ARTICLE IV
NON-DISCRIMINATION

Member States undertake to apply the provisions of this Convention to all refugees without discrimination as to race, religion, nationality, membership of a particular social group or political opinions.

ARTICLE V
VOLUNTARY REPATRIATION

1. The essentially voluntary character of repatriation shall be respected in all cases and no refugee shall be repatriated against his will.

2. The country of asylum, in collaboration with the country of origin, shall make adequate arrangements for the safe return of refugees who request repatriation.

3. The country of origin, on receiving back refugees, shall facilitate their resettlement and grant them the full rights and privileges of nationals of the country, and subject them to the same obligations.

4. Refugees who voluntarily return to their country shall in no way be penalized for having left it for any of the reasons giving rise to refugee situations. Whenever necessary, an appeal shall be made through national information media and through the Administrative Secretary-General of the OAU, inviting refugees to return home and giving assurance that the new circumstances prevailing in their country of origin will enable them to return without risk and to take up a normal and peaceful life without fear of being disturbed or punished, and that the text of such appeal should be given to refugees and clearly explained to them by their country of asylum.

5. Refugees who freely decide to return to their homeland, as a result of such assurances or on their own initiative, shall be given every possible assistance by the country of asylum, the country of origin, voluntary agencies and international and intergovernmental organizations, to facilitate their return.

Article VI
Travel Documents

1. Subject to Article III, Member States shall issue to refugees lawfully staying in their territories travel documents in accordance with the United Nations Convention relating to the Status of Refugees and the Schedule and Annex thereto, for the purpose of travel outside their territory, unless compelling reasons of national security or public order otherwise require. Member States may issue such a travel document to any other refugee in their territory.

2. Where an African country of second asylum accepts a refugee from a country of first asylum, the country of first asylum may be dispensed from issuing a document with a return clause.

3. Travel documents issued to refugees under previous international agreements by States Parties thereto shall be recognized and treated by Member States in the same way as if they had been issued to refugees pursuant to this Article.

Article VII
Co-operation of the National Authorities with the Organization of African Unity

In order to enable the Administrative Secretary-General of the Organization of African Unity to make reports to the competent organs of the Organization of African Unity, Member States undertake to provide the Secretariat in the appropriate form with information and statistical data requested concerning:

(a) the condition of refugees;
(b) the implementation of this Convention, and

(c) laws, regulations and decrees which are, or may hereafter be, in force relating to refugees.

ARTICLE VIII
CO-OPERATION WITH THE OFFICE OF THE UNITED NATIONS HIGH COMMISSIONER FOR REFUGES

1. Member States shall co-operate with the Office of the United Nations High Commissioner for Refugees.

2. The present Convention shall be the effective regional complement in Africa of the 1951 United Nations Convention on the Status of Refugees.

ARTICLE IX
SETTLEMENT OF DISPUTES

Any dispute between States signatories to this Convention relating to its interpretation or application, which cannot be settled by other means, shall be referred to the Commission for Mediation, Conciliation and Arbitration of the Organization of African Unity, at the request of any one of the Parties to the dispute.

ARTICLE X
SIGNATURE AND RATIFICATION

1. This Convention is open for signature and accession by all Member States of the Organization of African Unity and shall be ratified by signatory States in accordance with their respective constitutional processes. The instruments of ratification shall be deposited with the Administrative Secretary-General of the Organization of African Unity.

2. The original instrument, done if possible in African languages, and in English and French, all texts being equally authentic, shall be deposited with the Administrative Secretary-General of the Organization of African Unity.

3. Any independent African State, Member of the Organization of African Unity, may at any time notify the Administrative Secretary-General of the Organization of African Unity of its accession to this Convention.

ARTICLE XI
ENTRY INTO FORCE

This Convention shall come into force upon deposit of instruments of ratification by one-third of the Member States of the Organization of African Unity.

Article XII
Amendment

This Convention may be amended or revised if any member State makes a written request to the Administrative Secretary-General to that effect, provided however that the proposed amendment shall not be submitted to the Assembly of Heads of State and Government for consideration until all Member States have been duly notified of it and a period of one year has elapsed. Such an amendment shall not be effective unless approved by at least two-thirds of the Member States Parties to the present Convention.

Article XIII
Denunciation

1. Any Member State Party to this Convention may denounce its provisions by a written notification to the Administrative Secretary-General.

2. At the end of one year from the date of such notification, if not withdrawn, the Convention shall cease to apply with respect to the denouncing State.

Article XIV

Upon entry into force of this Convention, the Administrative Secretary-General of the OAU shall register it with the Secretary-General of the United Nations, in accordance with Article 102 of the Charter of the United Nations.

Article XV
Notifications by the Administrative Secretary-General of the Organization of African Unity

The Administrative Secretary-General of the Organization of African Unity shall inform all Members of the Organization:

(a) of signatures, ratifications and accessions in accordance with Article X;
(b) of entry into force, in accordance with Article XI;
(c) of requests for amendments submitted under the terms of Article XII;
(d) of denunciations, in accordance with Article XIII.

IN WITNESS WHEREOF we, the Heads of African State and Government, have signed this Convention.

1. Algeria
2. Botswana
3. Burundi
4. Cameroon
5. Central African Republic
6. Chad
7. Congo (Brazaville)
8. Congo (Kinshasa)
9. Dahomey
10. Equatorial Guinea
11. Ethiopia
12. Gabon
13. Gambia
14. Ghana
15. Guinea
16. Ivory Coast
17. Kenya
18. Lesotho
19. Liberia
20. Libya
21. Madagascar
22. Malawi
23. Mali
24. Mauritania
25. Mauritius
26. Morocco
27. Niger
28. Nigeria
29. Rwanda
30. Senegal
31. Sierra Leone
32. Somalia
33. Sudan
34. Swaziland
35. Togo
36. Tunisia
37. Uganda
38. United Arab Republic
39. United Republic of Tanzania
40. Upper Volta
41. Zambia

DONE in the City of Addis Ababa this 10th day of September 1969.

The Convention on Territorial Asylum of 1954

The Convention on Territorial Asylum of 1954 is one of a series of instruments on territorial and diplomatic asylum in Latin America. It reaffirms the territorial state's sovereign right to grant asylum, the duty of other states to respect such asylum, and the state's exemption from any obligation to surrender or expel persons "sought for political offenses" or "persecuted for political reasons or offenses."

Signed in Caracas on March 28, 1954
at the Tenth Inter-American Conference

Entry into force: 29 December 1954, in accordance with Article 14

Text: OAS Official Records, OEA/Ser.X/I. Treaty Series 34

The Governments of the Member States of the Organization of American States, desirous of concluding a Convention regarding Territorial Asylum, have agreed to the following articles:

ARTICLE 1

Every State has the right, in the exercise of its sovereignty, to admit into its territory such persons as it deems advisable, without, through the exercise of this right, giving rise to complaint by any other State.

ARTICLE 2

The respect which, according to international law, is due to the jurisdictional right of each State over the inhabitants in its territory, is equally due, without any restriction whatsoever, to that which it has over persons who enter it proceeding from a State in which they are persecuted for their beliefs, opinions, or political affiliations, or for acts which may be considered as political offenses.

Any violation of sovereignty that consists of acts committed by a government or its agents in another State against the life or security of an individual, carried out on the territory of another State, may not be considered attenuated because the persecution began outside its boundaries or is due to political considerations or reasons of state.

ARTICLE 3

No state is under the obligation to surrender to another State, or to expel from its own territory, persons persecuted for political reasons or offenses.

ARTICLE 4

The right of extradition is not applicable in connection with persons who, in accordance with the qualifications of the solicited State, are sought for political offenses, or for common offenses committed for political ends, or when extradition is solicited for predominantly political motives.

ARTICLE 5

The fact that a person has entered into the territorial jurisdiction of a State surreptitiously or irregularly does not affect the provisions of this Convention.

ARTICLE 6

Without prejudice to the provisions of the following articles, no State is under the obligation to establish any distinction in its legislation, or in its regulations or administrative acts applicable to aliens, solely because of the fact that they are political asylees or refugees.

ARTICLE 7

Freedom of expression of thought, recognized by domestic law for all inhabitants of a State, may not be ground of complaint by a third State on the basis of opinions expressed publicly against it or its government by asylees or refugees, except when these concepts constitute systematic propaganda through which they incite to the use of force or violence against the government of the complaining State.

ARTICLE 8

No State has the right to request that another State restrict for the political asylees or refugees the freedom of assembly or association which the latter States's internal legislation grants to all aliens within its territory, unless such assembly or association has as its purpose fomenting the use of force or violence against the government of the soliciting State.

ARTICLE 9

At the request of the interested State, the State that has granted refuge or asylum shall take steps to keep watch over, or to intern at a reasonable distance from its border, those political refugees or asylees who are notorious leaders of a subversive movement, as well as those against whom there is evidence that they are disposed to join it.

Determination of the reasonable distance from the border, for the purpose of internment, shall depend upon the judgment of the authorities of the State of refuge.

All expenses incurred as a result of the internment of political asylees and refugees shall be chargeable to the State that makes the request.

ARTICLE 10

The political internees referred to in the preceding article shall advise the government of the host State whenever they wish to leave its territory. Departure therefrom will be granted, under the condition that they are not to go to the country from which they came and the interested government is to be notified.

ARTICLE 11

In all cases in which a complaint or request is permissible in accordance with this Convention, the admissibility of evidence presented by the demanding State shall depend on the judgment of the solicited State.

ARTICLE 12

This Convention remains open to the signature of the Member States of the Organization of American States, and shall be ratified by the signatory States in accordance with their respective constitutional procedures.

ARTICLE 13

The original instrument, whose texts in the English, French, Portuguese, and Spanish languages are equally authentic, shall be deposited in the Pan American Union, which shall send certified copies to the governments for the purpose of ratification. The instruments of ratification shall be deposited in the Pan American Union; this organization shall notify the signatory governments of said deposit.

Article 14

This Convention shall take effect among the States that ratify it in the order in which their respective ratifications are deposited.

Article 15

This Convention shall remain effective indefinitely, but may be denounced by any of the signatory States by giving advance notice of one year, at the end of which period it shall cease to have effect for the denouncing State, remaining, however, in force among the remaining signatory States. The denunciation shall be forwarded to the Pan American Union which shall notify the other signatory States thereof.

IN WITNESS WHEREOF, the undersigned Plenipotentiaries, having presented their plenary powers which have been found in good and satisfactory form, sign this Convention, in the name of their respective Governments, in the city of Caracas, this twenty-eighth day of March, one thousand nine hundred and fifty-four.

Here follow the signatures of the Plenipotentiaries.

RESERVATIONS

Guatemala

We make express reservation to Article 3 (three) wherein it refers to the surrender of persons persecuted for political reasons or offenses; because according to the provisions of our Political Constitution, we maintain that such surrender of persons persecuted for political reasons may never be carried out.

We affirm, likewise, that the term "internment" in Article 9 means merely location at a distance from the border.

Dominican Republic

The delegation of the Dominican Republic subscribes to the Convention on Territorial Asylum, with the following reservations:

> Article 1. The Dominican Republic accepts the general principle embodied in that article in the sense that "Every State has the right to admit into its territory such persons as it deems

advisable", but it does not renounce the right to make diplomatic representation to any other State, if for considerations of national security it deems this advisable.

Article 2. It accepts the second paragraph of this article with the understanding that the latter does not affect the regulations of the frontier police.

Article 10. The Dominican Republic does not renounce the right to resort to the procedures for pacific settlement of international disputes that may arise from the exercise of territorial asylum.

MEXICO

The delegation of Mexico makes express reservation to Articles 9 and 10 of the Convention regarding territorial asylum because they are contrary to the individual guarantees enjoyed by all the inhabitants of the Republic in accordance with the Political Constitution of Mexico.

PERU

The delegation of Peru makes reservation to the text of Article 7 of the Convention regarding Territorial Asylum, insofar as it differs from Article 6 of the draft proposal of the Inter-American Council of Jurists, with which the delegation concurs.

HONDURAS

The delegation of Honduras gives its approval to the Convention regarding Territorial Asylum with reservations with respect to those articles opposed to the Constitution and to the laws in force in the Republic of Honduras.

ARGENTINA

The delegation of Argentina has voted in favor of the Convention regarding Territorial Asylum, but makes express reservations in regard to Article 7, as it believes that the latter does not duly consider nor satisfactorily resolve the problem arising from the exercise, on the part of political asylees, of the right of freedom of expression of thought.

The Convention on Diplomatic Asylum Signed in Caracas, March 28, 1954 at the Tenth Inter-American Conference

The Convention on Diplomatic Asylum, signed in 1954, is another of several major refugee instruments in Latin America, a continent with a long history of political asylum. While acknowledging that "every state has a right to grant asylum," the Convention on Diplomatic Asylum stresses that an asylum country "is not obligated to do so or state its reasons for refusing [asylum]" and that it remains with "the state granting asylum to determine the nature of the offense or the motives for the persecution."

Entry into force: 29 December 1954, in accordance with Article 23

Text: OAS Official Records, OEA/Ser.X/I. Treaty Series 34

The Governments of the Member States of the Organization of American States, desirous of concluding a Convention on Diplomatic Asylum, have agreed to the following articles:

Article 1

Asylum granted in legations, war vessels, and military camps or aircraft, to persons being sought for political reasons or for political offenses shall be respected by the territorial State in accordance with the provisions of this Convention.

For the purposes of this Convention, a legation is any seat of a regular diplomatic mission, the residence of chiefs of mission, and the premises provided by them for the dwelling places of asylees when the number of the latter exceeds the normal capacity of the buildings.

War vessels or military aircraft that may be temporarily in shipyards, arsenals, or shops for repair may not constitute a place of asylum.

Article 2

Every State has the right to grant asylum; but it is not obligated to do so or to state its reasons for refusing it.

Article 3

It is not lawful to grant asylum to persons who, at the time of requesting it, are under indictment or on trial for common offenses or have been convicted by competent regular courts and have not served the respective sentence, nor to deserters from land, sea, and air forces, save when the acts giving rise to the request for asylum, whatever the case may be, are clearly of a political nature.

Persons included in the foregoing paragraph who de facto enter a place that is suitable as an asylum shall be invited to leave or, as the case may be, shall be surrendered to the local authorities, who may not try them for political offenses committed prior to the time of the surrender.

ARTICLE 4

It shall rest with the State granting asylum to determine the nature of the offense or the motives for the persecution.

ARTICLE 5

Asylum may not be granted except in urgent cases and for the period of time strictly necessary for the asylee to depart from the country with the guarantees granted by the Government of the territorial State, to the end that his life, liberty, or personal integrity may not be endangered, or that the asylee's safety is ensured in some other way.

ARTICLE 6

Urgent cases are understood to be those, among others, in which the individual is being sought by persons or mobs over whom the authorities have lost control, or by the authorities themselves, and is in danger of being deprived of his life or liberty because of political persecution and cannot, without risk, ensure his safety in any other way.

ARTICLE 7

If a case of urgency is involved, it shall rest with the State granting asylum to determine the degree of urgency of the case.

ARTICLE 8

The diplomatic representative, commander of a warship, military camp, or military airship, shall, as soon as possible after asylum has been granted, report the fact to the Minister of Foreign Affairs of the territorial State, or to the local administrative authority if the case arose outside the Capital.

ARTICLE 9

The official furnishing asylum shall take into account the information furnished to him by the territorial government in forming his judgment as to the nature of the offense or the existence of related common crimes; but this decision to continue the asylum or to demand a safe-conduct for the asylee shall be respected.

ARTICLE 10

The fact that the Government of the territorial State is not recognized by the State granting asylum shall not prejudice the application of the present Convention, and no act carried out by virtue of this Convention shall imply recognition.

ARTICLE 11

The Government of the territorial State, may, at any time, demand that the asylee be withdrawn from the country, for which purpose the said State shall grant a safe-conduct and the guarantees stipulated in Article 5.

ARTICLE 12

Once asylum has been granted, the State granting asylum may request that the asylee be allowed to depart for foreign territory, and the territorial State is under obligation to grant immediately, except in case of force majeure, the necessary guarantees, referred to in Article 5, as well as the corresponding safe-conduct.

ARTICLE 13

In the cases referred to in the preceding articles the State granting asylum may require that the guarantees be given in writing, and may take into account, in determining the rapidity of the journey, the actual conditions of danger involved in the departure of the asylee.

The State granting asylum has the right to transfer the asylee out of the country. The territorial State may point out the preferable route for the departure of the asylee, but this does not imply determining the country of destination.

If the asylum is granted on board a warship or military airship, departure may be made therein, but complying with the previous requisite of obtaining the appropriate safe-conduct.

ARTICLE 14

The State granting asylum cannot be held responsible for the prolongation of asylum caused by the need for obtaining the information required to determine whether or not the said asylum is proper, or whether there are circumstances that might endanger the safety of the asylee during the journey to a foreign country.

ARTICLE 15

When, in order to transfer an asylee to another country it may be necessary to traverse the territory of a State that is a party to this Convention, transit shall be authorized by the latter, the only requisite being the presentation, through diplomatic channels, of a safe-conduct, duly countersigned and bearing a notation of his status as asylee by the diplomatic mission that granted asylum.

En route, the asylee shall be considered under the protection of the State granting asylum.

ARTICLE 16

Asylees may not be landed at any point in the territorial State or at any place near thereto, except for exigencies of transportation.

ARTICLE 17

Once the departure of the asylee has been carried out, the State granting asylum is not bound to settle him in its territory; but it may not return him to his country of origin, unless this is the express wish of the asylee.

If the territorial State informs the official granting asylum of its intention to request the subsequent extradition of the asylee, this shall not prejudice the application of any provision of the present Convention. In that event, the asylee shall remain in the territory of the State granting asylum until such time as the formal request for extradition is received, in accordance with the juridical principles governing that institution in the State granting asylum. Preventive surveillance over the asylee may not exceed thirty days.

Payment of the expenses incurred by such transfer and of preventive control shall devolve upon the requesting State.

ARTICLE 18

The official furnishing asylum may not allow the asylee to perform acts contrary to the public peace or to interfere in the internal politics of the territorial State.

ARTICLE 19

If as a consequence of a rupture of diplomatic relations the diplomatic representative who granted asylum must leave the territorial State, he shall abandon it with the asylees. If this is not possible for reasons independent of the wish of the asylee or the diplomatic representative, he must surrender them to the diplomatic mission of a third State, which is a party to this Convention, under the guarantees established in the Convention. If this is also not possible, he shall surrender them to a State that is not a party to this Convention and that agrees to maintain the asylum. The territorial State is to respect the said asylum.

ARTICLE 20

Diplomatic asylum shall not be subject to reciprocity. Every person is under its protection, whatever his nationality.

ARTICLE 21

The present Convention shall be open for signature by the Member States of the Organization of American States and shall be ratified by the signatory States in accordance with their respective constitutional procedures.

ARTICLE 22

The original instrument, whose texts in the English, French, Spanish, and Portuguese languages are equally authentic, shall be deposited in the Pan American Union, which shall send certified copies to the governments for the purpose of ratification. The instruments of ratification shall be deposited in the Pan American Union, and the said organization shall notify the signatory governments of the said deposit.

ARTICLE 23

The present Convention shall enter into force among the States that ratify it in the order in which their respective ratifications are deposited.

ARTICLE 24

The present Convention shall remain in force indefinitely, but may be denounced by any of the signatory States by giving advance notice of one year, at the end of which period it shall cease to have effect for the denouncing State, remaining in force, however, among the remaining signatory States. The denunciation shall be transmitted to the Pan American Union, which shall inform the other signatory States thereof.

IN WITNESS WHEREOF, the undersigned Plenipotentiaries, having presented their plenary powers, which have been found in good and due form, sign this Convention, in the name of their respective Governments, in the city of Caracas, this twenty-eighth day of March, one thousand nine hundred and fifty-four.

Here follow the signatures of the Plenipotentiaries.

RESERVATIONS

GUATEMALA

We make an express reservation to Article 2 wherein it declares that the States are not obligated to grant asylum; because we uphold a broad, firm concept of the right to asylum.

Likewise, we make an express reservation to the final paragraph of Article 20 (Twenty), because we maintain that any person, without any discrimination whatsoever, has the right to the protection of asylum.

Uruguay

The government of Uruguay makes a reservation to Article 2, in the part that stipulates that the authority granting asylum, is, in no case, obligated to grant asylum nor to state its reasons for refusing it. It likewise makes a reservation to that part of Article 15 that stipulates: ". . . the only requisite being the presentation, through diplomatic channels, of a safe-conduct, duly countersigned and bearing a notation of his status as asylee by the diplomatic mission that granted asylum. En route, the asylee shall be considered under the protection of the State granting asylum." Finally, it makes a reservation to the second paragraph of Article 20, since the government of Uruguay understands that all persons have the right to asylum, whatever their sex, nationality, belief, or religion.

Dominican Republic

The Dominican Republic subscribes to the above Convention with the following reservations:

First: The Dominican Republic does not agree to the provisions contained in Article 7 and those following with respect to the unilateral determination of the urgency by the State granting asylum; and

Second: The provisions of this Convention shall not be applicable, consequently, insofar as the Dominican Republic is concerned, to any controversies that may arise between the territorial State and the State granting asylum, that refer specifically to the absence of a serious situation or the non-existence of a true act of persecution against the asylee by the local authorities.

Honduras

The delegation of Honduras subscribes to the Convention on Diplomatic Asylum with reservations with respect to those articles that are in violation of the Constitution and laws in force in the Republic of Honduras.

Other Significant Universal Refugee Instruments

In addition to the key legal refugee instruments listed above, there have been a number of other significant refugee instruments at both the universal and regional levels. Because of the limited space available, these texts are not reproduced here. The full documents can be found in UNHCR, *Collection of International Instruments concerning Refugees* (1979); Guy Goodwin-Gill, *The Refugee in Intenational Law* (1983); and UN Center for Human Rights, *Human Rights Bibliography: United Nations Documents and*

Publications, 1980–1990) (1993). Many of the most important ones are summarized below.

Convention Relating to the Status of Stateless Persons (1954)

This convention defines the standards of treatment to be accorded to stateless persons, which are, broadly speaking, the same as those for refugees.

Convention on the Reduction of Statelessness (1961)

This document seeks mainly to avoid statelessness at birth by granting the nationality of the acceding state to persons born in their territory who would otherwise be stateless. It also provides, subject to certain exceptions, that a person should not be deprived of his or her nationality if this would result in making them stateless, and specifies that a person shall not be deprived of his or her nationality on racial, religious, or political grounds.

Fourth Geneva Convention Relative to the Protection of Civilian Persons in Time of War (1949)

The Fourth Geneva Convention contains an article dealing with refugees and displaced persons. This Protocol Additional (1977) provides specifically (Article 73) that refugees and stateless persons shall be protected persons under the meaning of Parts I and III of the Fourth Geneva Convention. These legal instruments, the so-called laws of warfare, have become increasingly important with the mounting number of internal conflicts in recent years.

Other Significant Regional Refugee Instruments

Cartagena Declaration on Refugees of 1984

This declaration, like the 1969 OAU convention (see Text 5 above), broadens the definition of the term *refugee* found in the 1951 UN convention to include those persons who have fled their country because their lives, safety, or freedom have been threatened by generalized violence, foreign aggression, internal conflicts, massive violation of human rights, or other circumstances that have seriously disturbed public order (Conclusion 3). Although a nonbinding instrument, the Cartagena Declaration has been accepted and is being applied by Latin American states to the degree that it has entered the domain of international law.

Dublin Convention

The Convention Determining the State Responsible for Examining Applications for Asylum Lodged in One of the Member States of the European Community was signed by the member states of the European Community at Dublin on 15 June 1990 in what is known as the Dublin Convention. It is one of the collective measures taken by member states towards the realization of a single market and the elimination of controls at internal European Union borders.

In the preamble, the signatories to the Dublin Convention express their determination to guarantee adequate protection to refugees in keeping with their common humanitarian tradition. The Dublin Convention also contains an expression of the signatories' awareness of the need to take measures to avoid leaving applicants for asylum in doubt for too long as regards the likely outcome of their applications. The signatories also state their concern to provide all asylum applicants with a guarantee that their applications will be examined by one of the member states and to ensure that applicants are not referred successively from one member state to another.

In accordance with these objectives, the Dublin Convention sets rules for determining the state responsible for examining applications for asylum. It also elaborates on the circumstances and the conditions that govern the transfer or readmission of applicants between member states. It provides, moreover, for the mutual exchange between member states of general information as well as information on individual cases. A number of safeguards are included concerning the protection of personal data.

In Article 2 of the Dublin Convention, member states of the European Union reaffirm their obligations under the 1951 UN convention and the 1967 UN Protocol Relating to the Status of Refugees, with no geographic restriction of the scope of these instruments, and restate their commitment to cooperate with the United Nations High Commissioner for Refugees in applying them.

Schengen Agreement (1990)

Signed by the Benelux countries (Germany, France, Italy, Spain, and Portugal) but not ratified as of 1994, this agreement contains criteria similar to the Dublin Convention, within the context of the progressive abolition of frontier controls between countries of the European Union.

The Schengen Agreement contains provisions establishing uniform principles for controlling member states' common borders and for harmonizing conditions of entry and visa requirements. In an effort to prevent unsuccessful applicants from lodging successive asylum claims in the same or other countries, the Schengen Agreement also includes a formula for determining which country is responsible for receiving an asylum request. Finally, the agreement specifies that a permanent information system, known as the Schengen Information System, is to be set up and computerized.

International Human Rights Instruments and Their Significance

There is a close link between the protection of refugees and the broader context of human rights. The link is confirmed, moreover, in the preamble to the 1951 UN Convention Relating to the Status of Refugees, which makes reference to the principle that all human beings shall enjoy fundamental rights and freedoms without discrimination. The preamble also recalls that the United Nations has, on various occasions, manifested its profound concern for refugees and endeavored to assure refugees the widest possible exercise of these fundamental rights and freedoms. Therefore, a number of key human rights instruments must be added to the various legal texts of direct or indirect relevance to the protection of refugees. The major ones are as follows:

The Universal Declaration of Human Rights

Adopted and proclaimed by United Nations General Assembly Resolution 217 A(III) of 10 December 1948, this document stipulates:

1. No one shall be subjected to arbitrary arrest, detention or exile. (Article 9)
2. Everyone has the right to freedom of movement and residence within the borders of each state; and every one has the right to leave any country, including his own, and to return to his country. (Article 13)
3. Everyone has the right to seek and enjoy in other countries asylum from persecution. (Article 14)
4. Everyone has the right to a nationality; and no one shall be arbitrarily deprived of his nationality or denied the right to change his nationality. (Article 15)

The United Nations has set international human rights standards in about 70 covenants, conventions, and treaties. The International Covenant on Economic, Social and Cultural Rights and the International Covenant on Civil and Political Rights are among the UN treaties that impose legally binding obligations on states concerning the rights of people under their jurisdiction. These two covenants were adopted by the UN General Assembly and opened for signature in December 1966. Both were entered into force in early 1976.

International Covenant on Civil and Political Rights

The International Covenant on Civil and Political Rights states that:

1. Each State Party to the present Covenant undertakes to respect and to ensure to all individuals within its territory and subject to its jurisdiction the rights recognized in the present Covenant, without distinction of any kind, such as race, color, sex, language, religion, political or other opinion, national or social origin, property, birth or other status. (Article 2)
2. Everyone lawfully within the territory of a State shall, within that territory, have the right to liberty of movement and freedom to choose his residence; Everyone shall be free to leave any country, including his own; The above-mentioned rights shall not be subject to any restrictions except those which are provided by law, are necessary to protect national security, public order (order public) public health or morals or the rights and freedoms of others, and are consistent with the other rights recognized in the present Covenant; No one shall be arbitrarily deprived of the right to enter his own country. (Article 12)
3. An alien lawfully in the territory of a State Party to the present Covenant may be expelled therefrom only in pursuance of a decision reached in accordance with law and shall, except where compelling reasons of national security otherwise require, be allowed to submit the reasons against his expulsion and to have his case reviewed by, and be represented for the purpose before, the competent authority or a person or persons especially designated by the competent authority. (Article 13)

The Covenant against Torture and Other Cruel, Inhuman or Degrading Treatment or Punishment

This document, approved by consensus by the UN General Assembly on 10 December 1984 as Annex to UN General Assembly Resolution 39/46, states:

> No State Party shall expel, return ("refouler") or extradite a person to another State where there are substantial grounds for believing that he would be in danger of being subjected to torture. For the purpose of determining whether there are such grounds, the competent authorities shall take into account all relevant considerations including, where applicable, the existence in the State concerned of a consistent pattern of gross, flagrant or mass violations of human rights. (Article 3)

The United Nations Convention on the Elimination of All Forms of Discrimination against Women

Signed in 1979, this document contains a series of provisions for the benefit of women. It is considered to be a cornerstone for the protection of refugee women.

The United Nations Convention on the Rights of the Child

This document, approved in 1989, makes special provision for refugee children. It stipulates:

> States Parties shall take appropriate measures to ensure that a child who is seeking refugee status or who is considered a refugee . . . shall . . . receive appropriate protection and humanitarian assistance . . . " (Article 22)

The African Charter on Human and People's Rights

Adopted by the 18th Assembly of the Heads of State and Government of the Organization of African Unity (OAU) on 27 June 1981 at Nairobi, this charter states:

> Every individual shall have the right, when persecuted, to seek and obtain asylum in other countries in accordance with the law of those countries and international conventions. (Article 12)

The American Convention on Human Rights

Signed on 22 November 1969 at the Inter-American Specialized Conference on Human Rights, held at San Jose, Costa Rica, this document states:

> Every person has the right to leave any country freely, including his own; No one can be expelled from the territory of the state of which

> he is a national or be deprived of the right to enter it; Every person has the right to seek and granted asylum in a foreign territory, in accordance with the legislation of the state and international conventions, in the event he is being pursued for political offenses or related common crimes; In no case may an alien be deported or returned to a country, regardless of whether or not it is his country of origin, if in that country his right to life or personal freedom is in danger of being violated because of his race, nationality, religion, social status or political opinion. (Article 22)

The European Convention for Protection of Human Rights and Fundamental Freedoms

This document, signed in Rome in 1950 and enhanced by several additional protocols, details certain rights that bear on refugees:

> Liberty of movement and freedom to choose one's residence (Fourth Protocol, Article 2);
>
> Freedom from exile and the right to enter the country of which one is a national (Fourth Protocol, Article 3);
>
> Prohibition of the collective expulsion of aliens (Fourth Protocol, Article 4);
>
> The right of an alien not to be expelled from a state without due process of law (Seventh Protocol, Article 1).

Recent Significant Developments

In recent years there have been several new developments in the international protection and assistance offered refugees and displaced persons. In particular, the international community has established two new mechanisms of relevance to refugees worldwide: (1) the creation within the United Nations of an emergency coordinator for humanitarian assistance and an under secretary-general for humanitarian assistance within the newly established Department of Humanitarian Affairs and (2) the appointment of a special representative of the UN secretary-general for internally displaced persons.

The office of emergency coordinator was created in December 1991 in order to strengthen and expedite international action in humanitarian emergencies, especially in cases where governments refuse to cooperate. The new office fills an important gap by integrating the activities of the wide array of UN agencies and imposing a structural approach that will include long-term strategies to refugee problems where only short-term ad hoc humanitarian efforts now exist. The coordinator will facilitate the relief work of the different UN agencies, make contact with outside organizations, and negotiate access for such agencies in an emergency situation without waiting for a formal government request. UN General Assembly Resolution (46/182), which established the new mechanism, allows humanitarian aid to be provided with "the consent of the affected country" rather than at its request, as was the case in the past.

The emergency relief coordinator reports directly to the UN secretary-general and is mandated to coordinate all relief measures within the UN system and among other organizations. To support the coordinator, a central funding mechanism has been established at a cost of $50 million. The coordinator is also responsible for coordinating appeals for financial assistance for emergencies from donor governments. Finally, an Interagency Standing Committee coordinates the relief activities of all UN agencies (including UNHCR) and the International Committee of the Red Cross, the Federation of Red Cross and Red Crescent Societies, and the Inter-Governmental Committee for Migration.

The special representative of the UN secretary-general for internally displaced persons has helped put the issue of protection and assistance to internally displaced persons on the international agenda. The position was created when the UN Human Rights Commission passed a resolution (1992/73) at its 48th session (5 March 1992) calling on the UN secretary-general to "designate a representative to seek to gain views and information from all governments on the human rights issues related to internally displaced persons, including an examination of existing international human rights, humanitarian and refugee law and standards and their applicability to protection of and relief assistance to internally displaced persons. . . ."

The UN secretary-general subsequently appointed Francis Deng, a former Sudanese ambassador, as his special representative for the internally displaced. Ambassador Deng presented a comprehensive study of internally displaced persons to the 49th session of the UN Human Rights Commission in 1993. At this session, the UN Human Rights Commission passed a further resolution (1993/105) requesting "the Secretary-General to mandate his Representative for a period of two years to continue his work aimed at a better understanding of the general problems faced by internally displaced persons and their possible long-term solutions, with a view to identify, where required, ways and means for improved protection for and assistance to internally displaced persons."

Future Directions

Despite the impressive array of legal instruments and institutions directed to the protection and assistance of refugees and other forcibly displaced persons, increasing numbers of commentators and advocates view the international treaty regime that protects refugees as inadequate to ensure respect for the basic human rights of those forced to migrate. The need to strengthen refugee protection at the international level is pressing, particularly to address issues such as guaranteeing initial asylum to those in flight from persecution and violence, respecting the human rights of asylum-seekers, including the right to be free from arbitrary detention, and extending of refugee rights to those displaced within countries as a result of persecution and violence. Governments, acting through the United Nations and regional intergovernmental organizations, must not only expand the coverage of international law but also improve its enforcement. Until governments establish comprehensive international standards and meaningful mechanisms, many refugees and asylum-seekers will simply remain insecure and subject to human rights violations.

5

Organizations and Government Agencies

THE FOLLOWING ARE SELECTED international, governmental, and private organizations providing information about or assistance and protection for refugees. It should be noted that most countries and states and even some larger cities have an agency, department, or commission concerned with refugees.

International Organizations

Centre for Documentation on Refugees (CDR)
case postale 2500
CH-1211 Geneva 2 Dépôt
Switzerland
(41-22) 739-8111
Fax: (41-22) 739-8682
E-mail: UNHCR.CDR@OLN.COMLINK.APC.ORG

A computer-based documentation center, CDR gathers, stores, and disseminates information on all aspects of refugee protection, reception, resettlement, and integration. It is part of UNHCR, but it also serves outside users. CDR also houses the coordinating unit of the International Refugee Documentation Network (IRDN) and maintains the International Refugee Electronic Network (IRENE) bulletin boards.

PUBLICATIONS: *Refugee Abstracts* (quarterly) and ad hoc bibliographies.

European Council on Refugees and Exiles (ECRE)
Bondway House, 3–9 Bondway
London SW8
England
(44-71) 582-9928
General Secretary: Philip Rudge

ECRE is an international forum for 60 West European nongovernmental organizations that either assist refugees or are concerned with refugee and asylum policy. It monitors national and international developments, promotes legal and information networks, and advocates progressive standards for treatment of refugees and asylum-seekers. The European Legal Network on Asylum (ELENA), a forum for legal counselors, is a project of ECRE.

International Committee of the Red Cross (ICRC)
19 Avenue de la Paix
CH-1202 Geneva
Switzerland
(41-22) 734-6001
Fax: (41-22) 733-2057
Telex: 414-226
President: Cornelio Sommaruga

In the United States:
780 Third Avenue, 28th Floor
New York, NY 10017
(212) 371-0770
Fax: (212) 838-5397

Founder of the Red Cross and Red Crescent Movement, ICRC promotes international humanitarian law and has delegations in 47 countries. ICRC is an independent and neutral organization with an internationally recognized role of acting as a humanitarian intermediary between belligerents during armed conflicts. ICRC protects and assists victims of civil and international wars and victims of internal disturbances and tensions by providing medical aid and relief supplies; serves as a tracing and information agency for prisoners of war and missing persons; provides a service for transmitting family messages; and visits civilian internees, prisoners of war, and political detainees. The ICRC maintains observer status to the UN General Assembly.

International Council of Voluntary Agencies (ICVA)
case postale 216
CH-1211 Geneva 21
Switzerland
(41-22) 732-6600
Fax: (41-22) 738-9904

Cable: VOLAG (Geneva)
Telex: 412-586 ICVA-CH
Executive Director: Delmar Blasco

Founded in 1962 to provide a forum for voluntary agencies active in the fields of humanitarian assistance and development cooperation, the ICVA currently has 87 members comprising international, national, and regional voluntary agencies.

International Federation of Red Cross and Red Crescent Societies
17 Chemin des Crets
case postale 372
CH-1211 Geneva 19
Switzerland
(41-22) 734-5580
Fax: (41-22) 733-0395
Telex: 22555 LRCS-CH
Secretary-General: Par Stenback

This is the international federation of 149 National Red Cross and Red Crescent Societies. It contributes to the humanitarian activities of its member societies, coordinates relief operations for natural disaster victims, cares for refugees outside areas of conflict, and aims to promote peace in the world. In refugee situations, the secretariat mobilizes the federation's own financial and in-kind contributions, as well as its health and managerial staff, to supplement resources of the UNHCR and national Red Cross and Red Crescent Societies.

International Organization for Migration (IOM, formerly ICM)
17 route des Morillons
case postale 71
CH-1211 Geneva 19
Switzerland
(41-22) 717-9111
Fax: (41-22) 798-6150
Director General: James N. Purcell, Jr.

Representatives:
New York—Richard Scott
1123 Broadway, Room 717
New York, NY 10010
(212) 463-8422

California—James Gildea
The Adam Grant Building, Suite 1225
114 Sansome Street
San Francisco, CA 94104
(415) 391-9796

Washington—Hans Petter Boe
1750 K Street, NW, Suite 1110
Washington, DC 20006
(202) 862-1826

Chicago—Pannee Peiffer
O'Hare Corporate Tower 1, Suite 329
10400 West Higging Road
Rosemont, IL 60018
(708) 296-3583

Miami—Ada Peralte
4471 N.W. 36th Street, Suite 236
Miami Springs, FL 33166
(305) 885-5426

IOM was established in 1951 to arrange resettlement processing and transportation for refugees and migrants. The organization conducts related programs for medical screenings, language training, and cultural orientation. IOM also plans and implements programs for the transfer of specialized human resources through migration to developing countries. Represented in 55 countries worldwide, IOM undertakes research projects and organizes biennial international seminars on major migration themes.

Office of the United Nations High Commissioner for Refugees (UNHCR)
case postale 2500
CH-1200 Geneva 2 Dépôt
Switzerland
(41-22) 739-8111
High Commissioner: Sadako Ogata

UNHCR Liaison Office to the United Nations Headquarters
UN Plaza
New York, NY 10017
(212) 963-6200

UNHCR Branch Office for the United States
1718 Connecticut Avenue, NW
Washington, DC 20009
(202) 387-8546
Representative: Rene van Rooyen

The UNHCR was established in 1951 to provide international protection to refugees who fall within the scope of its statute and to seek durable solutions for the problems of refugees. It also coordinates assistance programs for displaced persons in accordance with various subsequent General Assembly resolutions. It has representation in over 100 countries.

United Nations Children's Fund (UNICEF)
3 UN Plaza
New York, NY 10017
(212) 326-7000
Fax: (212) 888-7465
Executive Director: James Grant

Since 1946, UNICEF has cooperated with developing countries in providing child assistance programs involving nutrition, primary health care, water and sanitation, and education. It provides emergency humanitarian assistance to victims of natural and man-made disasters.

United Nations Department of Humanitarian Affairs (DHA)
Palais des Nations
CH-1211 Geneva 10
Switzerland
(41-22) 917-2142
Fax: (41-22) 917-0023
Telex: 4142DHA

UN Headquarters
UN Plaza
New York, NY 10017
(212) 963-1392
Fax: (212) 963-9489 or (212) 963-1312

Created in 1992, this UN department is the center for facilitating action on emergencies by coordinating UN action, fielding assessment missions, issuing appeals for the funding of humanitarian relief programs, publishing situation reports, and monitoring the status of donor contributions. It administers the Central Emergency Revolving Fund, which is used to facilitate rapid humanitarian action in emergency situations. It incorporates the previous office of the UN Disaster Relief Coordinator and the secretariat of the International Decade for Natural Disaster Reduction.

United Nations Relief and Works Agency for Palestine Refugees in the Near East (UNRWA)
Vienna International Centre
P.O. Box 700, A-1400
Vienna, Austria
(43-1) 21131, Ext. 4530
Commissioner-General: Ilter Turkmen

New York Liaison Office:
UN Building, Room DC2-0550
New York, NY 10017
(212) 963-2255
Director: William Lee

Since 1950, UNRWA has provided assistance to registered Palestinian refugees, now numbering more than 2 million, in Lebanon, Jordan, Syria, and the occupied territories of the West Bank and Gaza Strip. It offers basic health and relief services to eligible refugees, education to children, and vocational and teacher training. It also provides emergency relief services to Palestinian refugees displaced by war and violence, as it has been doing continuously since 1975 in Lebanon. UNRWA has provided additional emergency aid to refugees in the West Bank and Gaza Strip, where the Palestinian uprising broke out in December 1987.

World Council of Churches, Refugee and Migration Service
case postale 2100
CH-1211 Geneva 2
Switzerland
(41-22) 791-6111
Fax: (41-22) 791-0361
Telex: 415 730 OIK CH
Coordinator: Melaku Kifle

This organization works with local churches in about 70 countries in support of their refugee service, including both emergency and long-term assistance. Also, in cooperation with local churches, it advocates on behalf of refugees, provides resettlement services, provides public information and training, and facilitates meetings between churches on refugee issues.

World Food Program (WFP)
Via Cristoforo Colombo 426
00145 Rome, Italy
(39-6) 522-821
Fax: (39-6) 512-3700
Telex: (39-6) 626675 WFP1
Executive Director: Catherine Bertini

Liaison Office at United Nations Headquarters
(212) 963-8364
Fax: (212) 963-8019

The food aid arm of the United Nations system, with offices in 80 developing countries, WFP provides both long-term development assistance and emergency aid. A major share of the program's resources is channeled to protracted and emergency feeding operations for refugees and displaced persons, done in close cooperation with the United Nations High Commissioner for Refugees. WFP coordinates food aid deliveries and assists bilateral donors with procurement and transport of food, and it helps developing countries with logistics problems in food emergency situations.

U.S. Government Organizations

Department of Health and Human Services, Centers for Disease Control and Prevention (CDC)
1600 Clifton Road, NE
Atlanta, GA 30333
(404) 639-2101
Fax: (404) 639-0277
Associate Director for International Health: Joe H. Davis, M.D.

CDC provides technical assistance in refugee health to U.S. government agencies, multilateral organizations, nongovernmental organizations, and other agencies involved in refugee care. This technical assistance includes rapid needs assessment in health and nutrition, epidemiologic evaluation, disease outbreak investigation and control, and the establishment of disease surveillance systems in refugee populations. CDC also conducts training in refugee health.

Department of Health and Human Services, Office of Refugee Resettlement (ORR)
Administration for Children and Families
370 L'Enfant Promenade SW, 6th Floor
Washington, DC 20447
(202) 401-9246
Director: Lavinia Limon

The ORR assists refugees in achieving economic self-sufficiency following their arrival in the United States. Assistance is primarily provided through state-administered resettlement programs. The office reimburses states for some costs incurred in providing cash and medical assistance to newly arrived refugees in need. It also provides social service grants to states primarily for making English language and employment training services available to refugees.

Department of Justice, Immigration and Naturalization Service (INS)
425 I Street, NW
Washington, DC 20536
(202) 514-2000
Commissioner: Doris Meissner

The INS administers immigration and naturalization laws relating to the admission, exclusion, deportation, and naturalization of aliens, including refugees and asylees.

Department of State, Bureau for Refugee Programs (BRP)
2201 C Street, NW, Room 5824
Washington, DC 20520
(202) 647-5822
Director: Phyllis Oakley

The BRP formulates, implements, and directs U.S. refugee and migration policies and programs. The basic mission comprises international refugee protection and assistance as well as management of the U.S. admissions program.

House Judiciary Committee
2138 Rayburn House Office Building
Washington, DC 20515
(202) 225-3951
Chairman: Jack Brooks

Subcommittee on International Law, Immigration, and Refugees
Chairman: Romano L. Mazzoli

The House Judiciary Committee studies and makes recommendations on immigration and naturalization, citizenship, admission of refugees, treaties and international agreements, and other appropriate matters.

Senate Judiciary Committee
224 Dirksen Senate Office Building
Washington, DC 20510
(202) 224-5225
Chairman: Joseph Biden

Subcommittee on Immigration and Refugee Policy
518 Dirksen Senate Office Building
Washington, DC 20510
(202) 224-7878
Chairman: Edward M. Kennedy

The Senate Judiciary Committee studies and makes recommendations on the problems of refugees and has jurisdiction over immigration and naturalization legislation.

U.S. Resettlement Agencies

The following are selected, private, voluntary agencies in the United States that participate in programs to resettle refugees.

American Council for Nationalities Service (ACNS)
95 Madison Avenue
New York, NY 10016
(212) 532-5858
Executive Director: Roger Winter

ACNS is a nonsectarian organization with a 74-year history of service to refugees, immigrants, and others in migration. Forty community-based affiliates located throughout the United States provide refugee resettlement, immigration counseling, and other supportive services meant to ease the burden of transition for both newcomers and the communities receiving them. Agencies provide asylum representation and advocate on behalf of the rights of immigrants and refugees. International Social Service/American Branch, providing intercountry casework services to families and children around the world, is an ACNS program. The U.S. Committee for Refugees is the public information arm of ACNS.

Church World Service/Immigration and Refugee Program
475 Riverside Drive
New York, NY 10115
(212) 870-3300
Fax: (212) 870-2132
Director: Dr. Elizabeth G. Ferris

A part of the National Council of Churches, the Church World Service, through its Immigration and Refugee Program, provides refugee resettlement and first asylum services in the United States and responds to human need around the world. It works with ecumenical agencies worldwide, including the World Council of Churches.

Episcopal Migration Ministries
815 Second Avenue
New York, NY 10017
(212) 922-5198
Senior Program Executive Director: Diane Porter

Formerly the Presiding Bishop's Fund for World Relief/Refugee Migration Affairs, the Episcopal Migration Ministries is the official channel through which the Episcopal Church responds to relief and development needs of refugees, migrants, displaced persons, and asylum-seekers globally. It resettles refugees and assists immigrants and asylum-seekers in the United States through 98 Episcopal dioceses. It assists refugees worldwide in concert with the Anglican Communion and partner agencies, in cooperation with the Presiding Bishop's Fund for World Relief. It also advocates for legislation to respond to the protection and resettlement needs of refugees and displaced persons.

Hebrew Immigrant Aid Society, Inc. (HIAS)
333 Seventh Avenue
New York, NY 10001-5004
(212) 674-6800
Executive Vice President: Martin A. Wenick

HIAS is the refugee and migration agency of the organized American Jewish community. It assists Jewish refugees and migrants from Eastern Europe, the Middle East, North Africa, and elsewhere. HIAS also assists Indochinese, Ethiopian, Afghan, and other non-Jewish refugees through programs in cooperation with the U.S. government. It has a global network of offices and affiliated organizations in 45 countries on six continents.

International Rescue Committee (IRC)
122 East 42nd Street, 12th Floor
New York, NY 10168-1289
(212) 551-3000
President: Robert P. DeVecchi

The IRC, a nonsectarian voluntary agency, was founded in 1933. It provides resettlement services to refugees from Indochina, the former Soviet Union, Eastern Europe, Cuba, Central America, Afghanistan, Iran, Ethiopia, and other countries. It maintains a domestic resettlement network of 16 offices as well as 5 European offices. Overseas, it provides emergency relief and assistance to refugees and internally displaced victims of civil strife and conflict. Its services include medical aid, public health, education, and other related forms of assistance. International Rescue Committee programs are presently operating in Thailand, Pakistan, Jordan, Sudan, Malawi, Costa Rica, and El Salvador.

Lutheran Immigration and Refugee Service (LIRS)
390 Park Avenue South
New York, NY 10016-8803
(212) 532-6350
Executive Director: Ralston Deffenbaugh, Jr.

The LIRS is the national agency of Lutheran churches in the United States for ministry with refugees, asylum-seekers, undocumented persons, and immigrants. Founded in 1939 to resettle World War II refugees, it now serves in advocacy for protection and humane treatment for uprooted people worldwide as well as in immigration services and resettlement. It works through 26 regional affiliate social service agency offices that support the direct assistance of church and community volunteers. It has 19 partner agencies to help unaccompanied minor children, is involved in more than 40 ecumenical community-based projects to help asylum-seekers, and provides immigration training to assist service providers.

Tolstoy Foundation, Inc.
200 Park Avenue South, Suite 1612
New York, NY 10003
(212) 677-7770
Executive Director: Alexis Troubetzkoy

The Tolstoy Foundation was originally founded in 1939 to assist Russian refugees, but its scope has broadened to provide services to refugees from Eastern Europe, the Near East, Southeast Asia, and Africa. Oppressed minorities such as Tibetans, Circassians, and Armenians have also received assistance from the Tolstoy Foundation. European headquarters in Munich and South American headquarters in Buenos Aires oversee offices in these regions. Six regional offices in the United States provide resettlement services.

United States Catholic Conference Migration and Refugee Services (USCC/MRS)
3211 Fourth Street, NE
Washington, DC 20017-1194
(202) 541-3315
Fax: (202) 541-3245
Executive Director: Rev. Richard Ryscavage, S. J.

One of the public policy and social action agencies of the United States Catholic Conference, MRS carries out church policy on migration, refugee, and immigration issues. It provides program support and regional coordination for a network of more than 140 diocesan refugee resettlement offices. The network was able to resettle over 27,000 refugees of all faiths in 1992 alone. Within MRS, the Office for the Pastoral Care of Migrants and Refugees provides the pastoral foundation for all of MRS's programs and assists bishops in encouraging the integration of immigrants, migrants, and refugees into the life and mission of the local church. MRS also advocates generous immigration, asylum, refugee admission, and assistance policies. The Catholic Legal Immigration Network, Inc. (CLINIC) was established in 1988 to ensure that all newcomers have access to affordable immigration related services. CLINIC supports the diocesan network with technical assistance, consultation services, and a national immigration support network.

World Relief of the National Association of Evangelicals
201 Route 9W North
Congers, NY 10920
(914) 268-4135
Director of United States Ministries: Donald N. Hammond

World Relief of the National Association of Evangelicals has programs both overseas and in the United States. Overseas, it provides relief and development assistance in countries of first asylum. Domestically, it provides resettlement services to refugees, aiding more than 10,000 individuals in 1992 alone. It also provides orientation and training to sponsoring churches, community groups, families, and individuals to assist the evangelical community to meet the needs of refugees. World Relief has a network of 29 offices throughout the United States.

Aid and Information Organizations

The following are selected U.S. and international voluntary agencies and human rights and educational organizations that provide assistance to or information about refugees.

Africare, Inc.
440 R Street, NW
Washington, DC 20001
(202) 462-3614
Executive Director: C. Payne Lucas

Africare is dedicated to improving the quality of life in rural Africa through the development of water resources, increased food production, health services, and refugee assistance. It currently operates more than 220 programs in Eastern, Southern, and Francophone Africa, along with many development education programs in the United States.

Alien Rights Law Project (ARLP)
Washington Lawyers' Committee for Civil Rights under Law
1400 I Street, NW, Suite 450
Washington, DC 20005
(202) 682-5900
Acting Director: Deborah Sanders

Started in 1978 by the Washington Lawyers' Committee for Civil Rights under Law, the ARLP provides legal assistance to aliens. Its focus is on asylum and refugee issues, as well as those cases where aliens suffer employment or housing discrimination due to their immigration status.

American Friends Service Committee (AFSC)
1501 Cherry Street
Philadelphia, PA 19102
(215) 241-7000
Fax: (215) 241-7026
Executive Director: Kara Newell

A Quaker organization founded in 1917, AFSC supports reconciliation and development worldwide, especially in situations of conflict. It provides relief and rehabilitation assistance to refugees in the context of community development and advocates for resolution of conflicts and refugee rights in the United States.

American Jewish Joint Distribution Committee, Inc. (JDC)
711 Third Avenue
New York, NY 10017
(212) 687-6200
Executive Vice President: Michael Schneider

Established in 1914 and funded predominantly by the campaigns of the United Jewish Appeal (UJA), the JDC serves as the overseas arm of the organized American Jewish community, providing for rescue, relief, and rehabilitation of Jewish communities around the world. Its current programs, operating in 35 countries, deal with Soviet Jewish émigrés, Israel's social needs, glasnost-facilitated expansions in Eastern Europe and the former USSR, and nonsectarian development and disaster relief worldwide.

American Jewish Philanthropic Fund
c/o Tanenbaum
27 East 61st Street
New York, NY 10021
(212) 755-5640
President: Charles J. Tanenbaum

The American Jewish Philanthropic Fund provides relief, resettlement, and retraining services to Jewish refugees in Europe and the United States through programs administered by the International Rescue Committee.

American Red Cross
17th & D Streets, NW
Washington, DC 20006
(202) 639-3306
Chairman: George F. Moody

International Social Services Division
Director: Mary-Lou McCutcheon
(202) 639-3308

American Red Cross works in cooperation with the 149 Red Cross/Red Crescent societies, the International Committee of the Red Cross, and the Federation of Red Cross and Red Crescent Societies. It assists refugees in locating missing family members through its Tracing Services. Other Red Cross programs include disaster preparedness and relief and the strengthening of programs of other national Red Cross/Red Crescent societies.

American Refugee Committee (ARC)
Headquarters:
2344 Nicollet Avenue, Room 350
Minneapolis, MN 55404
(612) 872-7060

Chicago Office:
317 Howard Street
Evanston, IL 60202
President and CEO: Anthony J. Kozlowski

Internationally, ARC provides medical volunteers for refugee camps in Thailand and in Malawi (Africa), where it provides direct care, medical training, and child survival programs for Indochinese and Mozambican refugees. In 1991, it initiated program activities in Cambodia. The Illinois program focuses on public/mental health training and English language/ citizenship training. The Minnesota program uses volunteer American mentors with traditional education experiences to move refugee youth, women, and elders toward self-reliance.

Amnesty International (AI)
International Secretariat
1 Easton Street
London WCIX 8DJ
England
Secretary General: Pierre Sané

U.S. Section:
322 Eighth Avenue
New York, NY 10001
Executive Director: William F. Schulz

Address requests for assistance to:
National Refugee Office
500 Sansome Street, Suite 615
San Francisco, CA 94111
(415) 291-0601
Fax: (415) 291-8722

Amnesty International is a human rights organization working for the release of prisoners of conscience, for fair and prompt trials for all political prisoners, and to abolish torture and executions worldwide. It provides information for political asylum applications and opposes refoulement of persons who might reasonably be expected to be tortured, killed, or incarcerated as prisoners of conscience.

PUBLICATIONS: Amnesty International publishes an annual report, newsletter, and country and special reports on worldwide human rights conditions.

Armenian Assembly of America
122 C Street, NW, Suite 350
Washington, DC 20001
(202) 393-3434
Fax: (202) 638-4904
Executive Director: Ross Vartian

Through the Armenian Refugee Coordinating Committee (ARCC), the Armenian Assembly of America advocates a humane and appropriate response to the plight of Armenian refugees, provides direct assistance, and serves as a resource for the public and private sectors and media for information about Armenian refugees and émigrés. In 1988, the Armenian Assembly of America operated direct assistance programs in Belgium, Greece, and Pakistan.

Boat People S.O.S., Inc.
P.O. Box 2652
Merrifield, VA 22116
(703) 204-2662
Fax: (703) 204-2662
Executive Director: Dr. Thang Dinh Nguyen
Chairperson: Mr. Nguyen Ngoc Bich

The mission of the Boat People S.O.S. is to help Vietnamese refugees in refugee camps or on the open sea. It has offices throughout the United States and branches in Canada, Australia, Japan, and Europe.

CARE
151 Ellis Street, NE
Atlanta, GA 30303
(404) 681-2552
President: Dr. Philip Johnston

CARE, an international aid and self-help development organization, responds to the needs of refugees and displaced persons in emergency situations through effective delivery systems facilitating food distribution and other aid. It also implements long-term development programs in health and nutrition education and natural resource management to improve living conditions and to facilitate self-sufficiency among refugees, displaced persons, and repatriates. It has refugee programs in Sierra Leone, Somalia, Sudan, and Thailand, and programs for the displaced in Chad, Mali, Niger, Sudan, Ethiopia, and Mozambique.

Catholic Relief Services (CRS)
209 West Fayette Street
Baltimore, MD 21201-3443
(410) 625-2220
Fax: (410) 685-1635
Executive Director: Kenneth E. Hackett

CRS is the overseas relief and development agency of the U.S. Catholic community. Active in over 70 countries with nutrition programs, water and agricultural projects, small enterprise development and community promotion, its major refugee foci are Africa and Central America. Its refugee and resettlement assistance in 1989 was valued at $15 million—6 percent of the CRS program expenditure.

Center for Applied Linguistics
1118 22nd Street, NW
Washington, DC 20037
(202) 429-9292
President: G. Richard Tucker

The Center for Applied Linguistics operates the Refugee Service Center in Washington, D.C., under a cooperative agreement with the U.S. Department of State. It acts as a liaison between the State Department–funded Overseas Refugee Training Program sites in Southeast Asia and educators, social service providers, and others assisting refugees in the United States. It produces resettlement guides for newly arrived refugees; conducts surveys to gather information on refugees' resettlement experiences; gives presentations and workshops in the United States, at resettlement sites and professional conferences; and publishes information for staff in the Overseas Refugee Training Program.

Center for Migration Studies (CMS)
209 Flagg Place
Staten Island, NY 10304-1199
(718) 351-8800
Fax: (718) 667-4598
Executive Director: Lydio F. Tomasi

Founded in 1964, CMS encourages the interdisciplinary study of human migration and refugee movements everywhere through scientific research projects. It operates a specialized library and archives on migration and refugees. The CMS Annual National Legal Conference on Immigration and Refugee Policy is held in Washington, D.C.

PUBLICATIONS: CMS publishes the quarterly *International Migration Review* and the bimonthly *Migration World Magazine,* as well as books, papers, and a newsletter.

Cultural Survival, Inc.
215 First Street
Cambridge, MA 02142
(617) 621-3818
Fax: (617) 621-3814
Executive Director: Alexander H. See

Cultural Survival provides research and analysis concerning the survival of indigenous peoples and ethnic groups. It examines ethnic persecution as a cause of refugee flows and is involved in maintaining the land and the health care necessary for the survival of threatened groups.

Direct Relief International
27 La Patera Lane
P.O. Box 30820
Santa Barbara, CA 93130
(805) 964-4767
President: Ann W. Carlos

Direct Relief International receives and donates contributions of pharmaceuticals, medical supplies, and equipment to assist needy health facilities in medically less-developed areas of the world, and it also assists refugees and other victims of natural disaster and civil strife.

Documentation Exchange, Refugee Legal Support Service (RLSS)
Box 2327
Austin, Texas 78768
(512) 476-9841
Director: Jill McRae

Established in 1983, RLSS provides political asylum documentation for refugees from all Central American countries. Information is obtained from an extensive human rights database of computer-indexed U.S., Central American, and international human rights reports, news clipping services, and church and government reports. Referrals are made to direct service organizations and to attorneys with comparable cases.

Eritrean Relief Committee, Inc.
1325 15th Street, NW, Suite 112
Washington, DC 20005
(202) 387-5001
Fax: (202) 387-5006
Executive Director: Dr. Amdetsion Kidane

Founded in 1976, the Eritrean Relief Committee aids Eritreans affected by war, drought, and famine, including people displaced internally and refugees in the Sudan. The Eritrean Relief Committee is a U.S. partner agency of the indigenous Eritrean Relief and Rehabilitation Association (ERRA), which focuses on self-help and grassroots initiatives. Emergency assistance includes food, medicine, shelter, and pest control. Development support includes an agricultural rehabilitation program, rural healthcare facilities, and vocational and academic education projects.

Ethiopian Community Development Council, Inc.
1038 South Highland Street
Arlington, VA 22204
(703) 685-0510
Fax: (703) 685-0529
Director: Tsehaye Teferra

A private, nonprofit organization established in 1983, the Ethiopian Community Development Council administers a refugee resettlement program and engages in programs that promote the economic, educational, and social development of the Ethiopian community in the United States. It provides Ethiopians and other refugees with the means to gain the knowledge and skills necessary to become self-sufficient, and it disseminates information concerning Ethiopia and the Ethiopian community in the United States.

Exodus World Service
P.O. Box 620
Itasca, IL 60143-0620
(708) 775-1500 or (312) REFUGEE
Fax: (708) 775-1505
Executive Director: Heidi Moll Schoedel

Exodus World Service is an international humanitarian agency that provides educational services to individuals and churches to heighten their knowledge and awareness of refugees. It also works through media and volunteer networks to gain material and service assistance from the private sector for refugee families resettling in the United States.

Georgetown University Center for Immigration Policy and Refugee Assistance (CIPRA)
P.O. Box 2298
Georgetown University
Washington, DC 20057
(202) 298-0200
Director: Fr. Julio Giulietti, S.J.

CIPRA provides research, training, and consultation to contribute to the development of humane, reasonable, and enforceable immigration and refugee policies. It sponsors lectures, seminars, and public meetings on refugee policy and administers educational programs offering internships in refugee assistance. Its tutorial programs offer community service to refugees, immigrants, and at-risk youth. CIPRA also conducts research on migration in the Americas and on U.S. immigration legislation and its effects.

Grassroots International
P.O. Box 312
Cambridge, MA 02139
(617) 497-9180

Grassroots International provides humanitarian assistance to Third World peoples and social movements as a basis for building awareness and activism among North Americans in support of equity, justice, and peace. It sends funds and material aid to local partner organizations linked to broad-based movements for change in crisis areas—currently South Africa, the Philippines, the Horn of Africa, and the Middle East. All projects supported by Grassroots International are community-based, with emphasis on community organizing and empowerment.

Holt International Children's Services, Inc.
1195 City View, Box 2880
Eugene, OR 97402
(503) 687-2202
Executive Director: David H. Kim

An international child-caring agency serving children in Korea, the Philippines, Thailand, India, and Latin America, Holt International Children's Services works with affiliate agencies in providing a wide range of services to homeless children.

Human Rights Internet
c/o Human Rights Centre
University of Ottawa
57 Louis Pasteur
Ottawa, Ontario K1N 6N5
Canada
(613) 564-3492
Fax: (613) 564-4054
Executive Director: Laurie S. Wiseberg

Human Rights Internet is an international communications network and clearinghouse that serves the information needs of the human rights community: scholars, activists, and policymakers concerned with the promotion and protection of internationally recognized human rights.

PUBLICATIONS: Human Rights Internet publishes *Human Rights Internet Reporter,* a comprehensive reference work on humanitarian activity worldwide. It also publishes directories describing the work of worldwide human rights organizations.

Human Rights Watch
485 Fifth Avenue
New York, NY 10017
(212) 972-8400
Fax: (212) 972-0905
Executive Director: Kenneth Roth

Washington Office:
1522 K Street, NW
(202) 371-6592
Washington, DC 20005
Director: Holly Burkhalter

Human Rights Watch is a U.S. human rights organization that monitors the human rights practices of governments. It is composed of five regional divisions—Africa Watch, America Watch, Asia Watch, Helsinki Watch, and Middle East Watch—plus the Fund for Free Expression.

Institute for Education and Advocacy
1403 Harmon Place
Minneapolis, MN 55403
(612) 341-8082

St. Paul Office:
1550 Summit Avenue
St. Paul, MN 55105
(612) 698-8509

The Institute for Education and Advocacy builds the capacity of refugees and immigrants to participate actively in the social, economic, and political life of Minnesota. It operates a network of education and self-reliance programs under the auspices of the Episcopal Diocese of Minnesota.

InterAction (American Council for Voluntary International Action)
1717 Massachusetts Avenue, NW, 8th Floor
Washington, DC 20036
(202) 667-8227
President and CEO: Julia Taft
Program Officer, Refugee Affairs: Timothy M. McCully

InterAction is a broadly based membership association of 120 U.S. private and voluntary organizations working in international development; humanitarian and emergency relief; refugee relief, assistance, and resettlement; public policy and federal relations; and development education. Member agencies participate in any or all of six working committees: Development Assistance, Migration and Refugee Affairs, Disaster Response and Resources, Public Policy, Development Education, and Private Funding.

International Alert
1 Glyn Street
London SE11 5HT
England
(44-71) 793-8383
Secretary-General: Kumar Rupesinghe

International Alert is an independent, international, nongovernmental organization established in 1985 by Martin Ennals. Its objectives are: to help bring peace in internal conflicts; to seek and to propose constitutional provisions that protect and respect ethnic, religious, linguistic, and other minorities; to promote the human rights and development of groups and individuals within national borders and internationally; to alert opinion to danger areas of actual and potential conflict, mass killings, and genocide; and to provide opportunities for dialogue and discussion with a view to ending ethnic conflicts.

PUBLICATIONS: International Alert puts out a publication entitled *Update*.

International Catholic Migration Commission (ICMC)
37–39 rue de Vermont
case postale 96
CH-1211 Geneva 20 CIC
Switzerland
(41-22) 733-4150
Secretary General: Dr. Andre Van Chau
President: Mr. Michael Whiteley

U.S. Address:
1319 F Street, NW, Suite 820
Washington, DC 20004

ICMC links Catholic assistance agencies in both first-asylum and refugee resettlement countries, providing logistical and sometimes financial support for their emigration processing activities. Since 1951, it has administered a series of travel loan funds for refugees and migrants. It acts as Joint Voluntary Agency Representative in six countries and administers the U.S. component of the Orderly Departure Program. ICMC also promotes local settlement activities through project assistance and training of refugee officers.

International Social Service
American Branch:
95 Madison Avenue
New York, NY 10016
(212) 532-5858
Executive Director: Wells C. Klein
Director: Marie Mercer

Established in 1924, International Social Service is a liaison between social agencies in the United States and agencies abroad. It is designed to resolve, on a case-by-case basis, problems that derive from international migration and the separation of families by national boundaries. Its special emphasis is on services and protection for children in migration, intercountry adoption planning, and family reunification, including refugee families. The General Secretariat of International Social Service is based in Geneva. Since 1983, it has been affiliated with the American Council for Nationalities Service.

Jesuit Refugee Service (JRS)
1424 16th Street, NW, Suite 300
Washington, DC 20036
(202) 462-5200
Director: Rev. Robert W. McChesney, S.J.

Founded in 1981 under the auspices of the Society of Jesus, JRS is the central coordinating office in the United States for the International Jesuit Refugee Service, which operates programs for refugees and internally displaced persons in over 25 countries in Asia, Africa, Central and North America, Europe, and Australia. Its major program foci include pastoral care, legal assistance, research, health, education, and human rights protection.

Lawyers Committee for Human Rights (LCHR)
330 Seventh Avenue, 10th Floor
New York, NY 10001
(212) 629-6170
Executive Director: Michael Posner
Director, Asylum Representation Program: Stephanie Marks

Washington Office:
100 Maryland Avenue, Room 502
Washington, DC 20002
(202) 547-5692
Staff Attorney: Elisa Massimino

The Lawyers Committee for Human Rights is a public interest law center in the fields of international human rights and refugee law. It monitors human rights in countries around the world, including those receiving U.S. foreign aid. It works to ensure that persons seeking refuge in the United States receive the protections they are guaranteed under the U.S. Constitution and international law. Legal representation is provided by volunteer attorneys for individual asylum applicants who cannot afford counsel.

Lutheran World Relief
390 Park Avenue South
New York, NY 10016
(212) 532-6350
Executive Director: Katherine F. Wolford

Lutheran World Relief serves as the overseas development and relief agency to assist with long-term and emergency help for people around the world, especially in Asia, Africa, and Latin America. Refugee assistance is often channelled through programs of the Lutheran World Federation.

Mennonite Central Committee
21 South 12th Street
Akron, PA 17501
(717) 859-1151

Canada Office:
134 Plaza Drive
Winnipeg, Manitoba R3T 5K9
Canada
(204) 261-6381
Executive Secretary: John A. Lapp

The Mennonite Central Committee is a cooperative relief and service agency for Mennonites and Brethren in Christ in North America. It provides material aid and development assistance to refugees from man-made and natural disasters. Its current work includes assistance to refugees in the Horn of Africa, Central America, Southeast Asia, and the Middle East.

Minnesota Advocates for Human Rights
200 Second Avenue South
Suite 1050
Minneapolis, Minnesota 55401
Director: Barbara Frey

Formerly known as the Minnesota Lawyers International Human Rights Committee, this organization undertakes studies and advocacy on international human rights and refugee issues.

PUBLICATION: Minnesota Advocates for Human Rights publishes *Human Rights Observer.*

Minority Rights Group
379 Brixton Road
London SW9 7DE
England
(44-71) 978-9498
Fax: (44-71) 738-6265

An independent, international human rights information and education body, Minority Rights Group provides written material on the subject and carries out advocacy on minority rights at the United Nations and other international fora. It has sister groups outside the United Kingdom.

PUBLICATIONS: Minority Rights Group publishes reports on minority groups worldwide and thematic reports on issues concerning minorities and human rights.

National Coalition for Haitian Refugees (NCHR)
16 East 42nd Street, 3rd Floor
New York, NY 10017
(212) 867-0020
Fax: (212) 867-1668
Executive Director: Mr. Jocelyn McCalla

Established in 1982, the NCHR is an alliance of nearly 40 prominent U.S. civil rights, labor, human rights, religious, and immigrants' rights organizations. NCHR acts in accord with both U.S. and international law to uphold the rights of refugees fleeing repression in Haiti and traveling to the United States. It advocates for Haitian refugees by facilitating cooperation among various agencies providing humanitarian service, and also by promoting democratic institution-building in Haiti.

National Immigration Refugee, and Citizenship Forum
220 I Street, NE, Suite 220
Washington, DC 20002
(202) 544-0004
Director: Frank Sharry

A national, nonprofit, educational organization with a broad multi-institutional and multiethnic membership, the National Immigration, Refugee, and Citizenship Forum was formed to establish positive working relationships among the diverse communities represented by its membership and to promote the pro-immigrant, pro-refugee philosophy embodied in its statement of principles.

Operation USA
8320 Melrose Avenue, #200
Los Angeles, CA 90069
(213) 658-8876
Fax: (213) 653-7846
Telex: 295252 OPCAUR
President: Richard Walden

Operation USA is a nonprofit organization founded in 1979. Its objectives are to collect and transport high-priority emergency relief supplies to areas of need. It has been active in Somalia, Ethiopia, Sudan, Tibet, Cambodia, Malaysia, Thailand, Vietnam, the Philippines, Honduras, Guatemala, Nicaragua, El Salvador, Ecuador, Mexico, Lebanon, Poland, and the United States.

Oxfam America
26 West Street
Boston, MA 02111-1206
(617) 482-1211
Executive Director: Dr. John Hammock

Oxfam America is a nonprofit, international agency that funds self-help development and disaster relief projects in poor countries in Africa, Asia, Latin America, and the Caribbean. Founded in 1970, Oxfam America is one of seven autonomous Oxfam organizations worldwide.

PUBLICATIONS: Oxfam America publishes and distributes educational materials on issues of hunger and development.

Rav Tov, Inc.
International Jewish Rescue Organization
500 Bedford Avenue
Brooklyn, NY 11211
(718) 963-1991
Executive Director: David Niederman

Through its network of overseas offices, Rav Tov provides care and maintenance, medical assistance, visa documentation, and premigration planning to refugees while in transit. In countries of resettlement, it provides a full range of services, including reception, housing, medical care, language training, education, employment counseling, and maintenance assistance.

Refugee Policy Group (RPG)
1424 16th Street, NW, Suite 401
Washington, DC 20036
(202) 387-3015
Executive Director: Dennis Gallagher

RPG serves as an independent center of policy analysis and research on domestic and international refugee issues. It houses a refugee resource library and contributes to policy analysis, research, and program development in the refugee field.

Refugee Studies Programme (RSP)
Oxford University
Queen Elizabeth House
21 St. Giles
Oxford OX1 3LA
(44-865) 270-722
Fax: (44-865) 270-721
E-mail: RSP@VAX.OXFORD.AC.UK
Director: Dr. Barbara Harrell-Bond

The RSP is a center for multidisciplinary research, teaching, and training of practitioners in the field of involuntary migration. In addition to disseminating public information, RSP conducts weekly seminars and annual international symposia to provide a forum for dialogue between academics, refugees, host government officials, and agency workers.

PUBLICATIONS: RSP's publications include *Directory of Current Research on Refugee and Other Forced Migrants,* the *Journal of Refugee Studies, Refugee Participation Network,* and *Displaced People and Refugees: A Resource Guide.*

Refugee Voices, Inc.
3041 4th Street, NE
Washington, DC 20017-1102
(202) 832-0020 or (800) 688-REFUGEE
Fax: (202) 832-5616
Director: Frank Moan, S.J.

Refugee Voices is a public education organization that, through various media, works to inform Americans of the plight of refugees in the United States and those in camps worldwide.

Refugee Women in Development (RefWID)
810 First Street, NE, Suite 300
Washington, DC 20002
(202) 289-1104
Fax: (202) 887-0812
Executive Director: Sima Wali

RefWID is the only national organization established to address the needs and concerns of Third World refugee women who have settled in the United States. Its priorities include conducting training on the protection needs of refugee women, particularly in regard to domestic violence; developing practical program models for leadership development and coalition building; and carrying out education and advocacy with refugee and mainstream organizations, policymakers, and the general public.

Refugees International
21 Dupont Circle, NW
Washington, DC 20036
(202) 828-0110
Executive Director: Lionel Rosenblatt

Refugees International monitors refugee situations worldwide to ensure that refugees' basic needs for protection and care are met. It provides information to both policymakers and the public, advocates fair refugee policy at home and abroad, and organizes letter-writing campaigns.

PUBLICATION: Refugees International publishes a newsletter.

Relief and Development Institute
1 Ferdinand Place
London NWI 8EE
England
(44-71) 485-0944
Fax: (44-71) 284-0244
Director: Edward Clay

Relief and Development Institute researches all aspects of disaster relief and management, including refugee communities. It hosts workshops and briefing and training courses for field staff, and it also acts as an information center.

PUBLICATIONS: Relief and Development Institute publishes *Disasters*, a quarterly journal.

The Salvation Army World Service Office (SAWSO)
615 Slaters Lane, 3rd Floor
Alexandria, VA 22313
(703) 684-5528
Executive Director: Dean B. Seiler

As a development arm of the Salvation Army, SAWSO provides technical and financial assistance in support of self-help, relief, and training programs. Assistance, including aid to disaster victims, refugees, and displaced persons, is available to the 93 countries and territories in which the Salvation Army operates.

Save the Children Federation, Inc.
54 Wilton Road
Westport, CT 06880
(203) 221-4000
President: Charles F. MacCormack

Founded in 1932, Save the Children Federation serves children through community development in 43 countries, including the United States. In its refugee programs, it provides humanitarian assistance with an emphasis on making refugees self-sufficient and providing a base on which long-term development can take place. Agriculture, nutrition, health care, sanitation, education, and small-scale enterprise are program components in Somalia, Zimbabwe, Sudan, and Pakistan. Training in literacy, language, cultural orientation, employment skills, and secondary and primary education are program components in Thailand and Indonesia.

Southeast Asia Resource Action Center (SEARAC)
1628 16th Street, NW, 3rd Floor
Washington, DC 20009
(202) 667-4690
Executive Director: Le Xuan Khoa

SEARAC assists Southeast Asians in the United States in making the transition from refugee status to productive Asian Americans. Its major activities include public education and advocacy, leadership and citizenship development, capacity-building for Indochinese self-help organizations, and economic development.

United States Committee for Refugees (USCR)
1717 Massachusetts Avenue, NW, Suite 701
Washington, DC 20036
(202) 347-3507
Fax: (202) 347-3418
Director: Roger Winter

The U.S. Committee for Refugees is the public information and advocacy program of the American Council for Nationalities Service. It issues publications and provides information about refugees worldwide, and it participates actively as a refugee advocate in the development of U.S. policy with respect to refugees in the United States and abroad. It also supports specialized UN agencies working to ensure refugee protection and assistance.

PUBLICATIONS: USCR publishes *World Refugee Survey* and *Refugee Reports,* a monthly news service on refugee issues.

United States Committee for UNICEF
333 East 38th Street
New York, NY 10016
(212) 686-5522
Executive Vice President: Tsugiko Y. Scullion

Established in 1947, the U.S. Committee for UNICEF is the oldest and largest of 32 national UNICEF committees. It informs Americans about UNICEF's efforts to meet the needs of the developing world's children and their mothers in the areas of nutrition, primary health care, clean water and sanitation, education, social services, and emergency relief and rehabilitation. It also raises funds for UNICEF through greeting card sales, contributions, and special events.

Women's Commission for Refugee Women and Children
c/o International Rescue Committee
122 East 42nd Street, 12th Floor
New York, NY 10168-1289
(212) 551-3000
Director: Mary Diaz

Founded in 1989 under the auspices of the International Rescue Committee, the mission of the Women's Commission for Refugee Women and Children is to speak on behalf of the millions of women and children worldwide who have been forced to flee from their homes because of war, civil strife, famine, or persecution. It dispatches fact-finding delegations of distinguished women to refugee areas all over the world and testifies before Congress. It also presents its findings to the U.S. State Department, UN officials, and other governments.

World Concern International
P.O. Box 33000
19303 Fremont Avenue North
Seattle, WA 98133
(206) 546-7201
Executive Director: Fred Gregory

World Concern International provides emergency relief, but focuses primarily on long-term development to refugee and nonrefugee populations in Asia, Africa, and the Americas. Indigenous agencies supply most of the aid through technical assistance, grants, and commodities.

World Learning, Inc.
Southeast Asia Programs
Box 676
Brattleboro, VT 05302
(802) 258-3124
Vice President: Claude Del Pepin

In a consortium with Save the Children and World Education, World Learning offers English as a Second Language (ESL), cultural work orientation, and other programs to Indochinese living in Phanat Nikhom, Thailand. It provides education, literacy, and limited ESL to Indochinese refugees and asylum-seekers in Galang, Indonesia; administers repatriation programs in Laos; and offers job development and reintegration employment skills training projects in Vietnam. In addition, World Learning assists Afghan refugees in Pakistan to generate income and obtain education.

World Vision, Inc.
919 West Huntington Drive
Monrovia, CA 91016
(818) 305-7836
President: Dr. Robert A. Seiple
Director, Refugee Programs: Rev. "Duke" Duc X. Nguyen

World Vision was established in 1950 and is an international Christian child relief agency and a development agency. Today it supports over 6,000 projects in 94 countries. U.S. programs work with children who are at risk, the urban poor, and Asian Americans. The organization benefits nearly 17 million people through child sponsorship, primary health care, agricultural development, and community leadership projects.

6

Selected Print Resources

THERE ARE THOUSANDS OF PUBLICATIONS on refugees, and the number is rapidly expanding. In this chapter we offer a brief annotated bibliography of the leading journals, major references, books, and reports in the field so readers can quickly identify the sources most important and useful to them.

Principal Journals

There are many periodicals that carry material related to refugees, a highly interdisciplinary topic. Several academic journals in the following list, however, are specifically dedicated to refugees and offer essential research and reference sources.

AWR Bulletin
Association for the Study of the World Refugee Problem
Wilhelm Braumüller
Universitäts-Verlagsbuchhandlung
A-1092 Vienna
Servite-casse 5
Austria

This quarterly publication is devoted to the study of refugee problems. It includes articles, speeches, book reviews, legislative materials, and other writings of concern to refugees.

Human Rights Internet Reporter
Human Rights Internet
University of Ottawa
57 Louis Pasteur
Ottawa
Canada K1N 6N5

This publication is a comprehensive reference work on humanitarian activity worldwide.

Human Rights Quarterly
The Johns Hopkins University Press
701 West 40th Street, Suite 275
Baltimore, Maryland 21211-2190

This quarterly journal specializes in human rights, including refugee issues.

Immigrants and Minorities
Frank Cass, Gainsborough House
11 Gainsborough Road
London E11 1RS
England

Immigrants and Minorities is a British quarterly that focuses on immigrant minorities in Western societies.

International Migration
International Organization for Migration
P.O. Box 71
CH-1211 Geneva 19
Switzerland

This intergovernmental quarterly includes documents, conference reports, and articles.

International Migration Review
Center for Migration Studies
209 Flagg Place
Staten Island, NY 10034

The leading quarterly journal in the field of migration, *International Migration Review* contains current research articles, book reviews, documents, and bibliographies.

International Review of the Red Cross
International Committee of the Red Cross
17 avenue de la paix
CH-1211 Geneva
Switzerland

This journal, published six times a year, contains articles on international humanitarian law.

Journal of International Refugee Law
Oxford University Press
Walton Street
Oxford OX2 6DP
England

This quarterly journal publishes articles about refugee law and policy. It also includes legislation, documentation, and abstracts of recent publications in the field.

Journal of Refugee Studies
Refugee Studies Programme
Oxford University Press
Walton Street
Oxford OX2 6DP
England

The quarterly *Journal of Refugee Studies* covers all aspects of refugee issues from a multidisciplinary perspective.

Migration
Berlin Institute for Social Research
Postfach 1125
1000 Berlin 30
Germany

Migration is a European journal of international migration and ethnic relations.

Migration World
Center for Migration Studies
209 Flagg Place
Staten Island, NY 10304

This journal publishes articles and information about migration and refugee problems worldwide. It is written in a readable and accessible way and is a good source of information for school and college reports.

Monday
Church World Service
455 Riverside Drive
New York, NY 10115

A weekly newsletter, *Monday* discusses refugee and immigration issues of both national and international significance.

Netherlands Quarterly of Human Rights
Kluwer Publishers
675 Massachusetts Avenue
Cambridge, MA 02139

This quarterly journal covers refugees and other human rights issues and problems.

Refuge
Centre for Refugee Studies
York University
322 York Lanes
North York, Ontario
Canada M3J 1P3

This publication discusses Canadian refugee policy and reviews recent developments in refugee problems around the world.

Refugee Participation Network
Refugee Studies Programme
Queen Elizabeth House
21 St. Giles
Oxford OX1 3LA
England

Refugee Participation Network disseminates research findings and provides a forum for debate among the personnel of humanitarian agencies and refugees themselves.

Refugee Reports
U.S. Committee for Refugees
1717 Massachusetts Avenue, NW, Suite 701
Washington, DC 20036

Refugee Reports is an essential monthly source of information and documentation about refugees and legislation and programs affecting them. A special year-end statistical issue is published every December.

Revue Européene des migrations internationales
University of Poitiers
Poitiers 86022
France

Issues of this biannual publication, published by the university's geography department, focus on subjects such as Antilleans in Europe and immigration in the Americas.

World Disasters Report
International Federation of Red Cross and Red Crescent Societies
17 Chenin des Crets
case postale 372
CH-1211 Geneva 19
Switzerland

This report is the only annual report focusing on disasters—from earthquakes to epidemics and conflict to economic crises—and on the millions of people affected by them.

World Refugee Survey
U.S. Committee for Refugees
1717 Massachusetts Avenue, NW, Suite 701
Washington, DC 20036

World Refugee Survey is an indispensable annual survey that identifies and reviews refugee problems in the world and provides authoritative statistics.

Important Document Sources

INS Reporter
Immigration and Naturalization Service
U.S. Department of Justice
425 I Street, NW
Washington, DC 20536

This quarterly publication provides a brief survey of recent developments in U.S. immigration law.

Refugee Survey Quarterly
Center for Documentation on Refugees
United Nations High Commissioner for Refugees (UNHCR)
case postale 2500
1211-Geneva 2 Dépôt
Switzerland

This quarterly lists the abstracts of many of the publications about refugees. In addition, it contains a selection of country reports and a section on refugee- or human rights–related legal documentation.

Refugee Report
Bureau for Refugee Programs
Department of State
Room 5824
2201 C Street, NW
Washington, DC 20520

This is the official annual report to Congress concerning the world refugee situation.

SOPEMI: Continuous Reporting on Migration
Organization for Economic Cooperation and Development
2 rue André-Pascal
75775 Paris Cedex 16
France

This annual publication has articles and important statistical information on migration flows into the industrialized states of the world.

Sri Lanka Monitor
The Refugee Council
3–9 Bondway
London SW8
England

Sri Lanka Monitor contains information about Tamil refugees and developments in Sri Lanka affecting refugee flows.

The State of World Population
UN Population Fund
United Nations
UN Plaza
New York, NY 10017

This annual publication discusses world population growth and related problems, and it contains useful statistics. UN Population Fund also publishes: *World Population Trends, Reports, World Foreign-Born Populations,* and *World Migration Studies.*

Reference Works

This section provides a select listing of key reference resources that are useful in the study of refugees. Although some of the titles may not deal specifically with refugees, they are included here because they have sections on refugees or are valuable introductions to refugee-related issues.

Aitchison, Jean. **International Thesaurus of Refugee Terminology.** Dordrecht, Netherlands: Martinus Nijhoff, 1989. 476p. ISBN 0-7923-0504-3.

This thesaurus covers a wide range of subjects central to or impinging on the field of refugees. It is intended for use by organizations that are active in documentation work concerning refugees.

American Immigrant Lawyers Association. **The Law of Asylum: A Manual for Practitioners and Adjudicators.** Washington, DC: American Immigrant Lawyers Association, 1989. 81p.

An indispensable resource for lawyers involved in asylum work, this resource analyzes and explains the legal basis for asylum, the withholding of deportation and application processes, cessation of asylum status, the rights of applicants, and the handling of persecution claims.

Berlin Institute for Comparative Social Research. **German Literature on Flight and Asylum.** Berlin: Edition Parabolis, 1992. 312p.

This publication lists the German language literature on assimilation problems of German refugees and expellees, asylum legislation, and the integration of migrants in Germany.

———. **Refugees in Africa.** Berlin: Edition Parabolis, 1993. 140p.

This bibliography includes the major works on refugee movements in Africa.

———. **Refugees in Asia and Australia/Oceania.** Berlin: Edition Parabolis, 1992. 144p.

This is a listing of 1,283 titles covering refugee movements in Asia and Australasia since the end of World War II.

———. **Refugees in Latin America and the Caribbean.** Berlin: Edition Parabolis, 1993. 140p.

This is a bibliography of the research on refugees in Latin America and the Caribbean.

———. **Refugees in Northern America.** Berlin: Edition Parabolis, 1993. 300p.

This listing of books, articles, research reports, dissertations, and reports of aid agencies on refugee issues covers all of North America.

———. **Refugees in Western Europe.** Berlin: Edition Parabolis, 1992. 176p.

Refugees in Western Europe lists the literature on the refugee and asylum issue in Western Europe, excluding Germany. It includes studies on refugee movements, immigration and asylum policy, the social situation of refugees, and their integration and legal status.

Boyer, Laura M. **The Older Generation of Southeast Asian Refugees, An Annotated Bibliography.** Minneapolis, MN: Southeast Asian Refugee Studies Project, Center for Urban and Regional Affairs, University of Minnesota, 1991. 61p.

This is an annotated listing of sources on older Southeast Asian refugees.

Center for Human Rights, United Nations. **Human Rights Bibliography: United Nations Documents and Publications, 1980–1990.** New York: United Nations, 1993. 5 volumes. ISBN 92-1-100377-6.

This bibliography presents all UN instruments, documents, and publications on human rights.

Center for the Study of Human Rights, Columbia University, New York. **Human Rights: A Topical Bibliography.** Boulder, CO: Westview Press, 1983. 297p. ISBN 0-86531-571-X.

A bibliography consisting of scholarly books and articles on human rights, *Human Rights* draws primarily from the disciplines of law, the social sciences, and philosophy. It includes a list of the agencies that provide documentary resource materials on a continuing basis.

Central America Refugee Policy Research Project. **Sourcebook on Central American Refugee Policy: A Bibliography.** Austin, TX: Lyndon B. Johnson School of Public Affairs, University of Texas, 1985. 68p.

This bibliography contains almost 800 items, including books, articles, newsletters, and other reports and resources on Central American refugees.

Davies, Julian, and Refugee Studies Programme, University of Oxford. **Displaced Peoples and Refugee Studies, A Resource Guide.** London: Hans Zell Publishers, 1990. 219p. ISBN 0-905450-76-0.

This resource guide includes a comprehensive and well-annotated list of manuals, reference works, periodicals, dissertations, and books. There are also useful directories of libraries, documentation centers, research and teaching centers, and organizations concerned with all aspects of the refugee issue, arranged alphabetically by country of location.

Enrostat. **Asylum Seekers and Refugees: A Statistical Report.** Luxembourg: Office for Official Publications of the European Communities, 1994. 157p. ISBN 92-826-7623-4.

This publication is an important resource of statistics providing up-to-date figures on asylum-seekers and refugees for the European Union and European Free Trade Association countries.

Fenton, Thomas, and Mary Heffron, eds. **Third World Resource Directory.** Maryknoll, New York: Orbis Books, 1984. 283p. ISBN 0-88344-509-3.

This comprehensive resource guide is divided into geographical areas and themes. It covers resources, organizations, and printed and audio-visual materials.

Hammond, Ruth E., and Glenn L. Hendricks, eds. **Southeast Asian Refugee Youth: An Annotated Bibliography.** Minneapolis, MN: Southeast Asian Refugee Studies Project, Center for Urban and Regional Affairs, University of Minnesota, 1988. 143p. Publication No. CURA 88-2.

This annotated bibliography lists 372 works about Southeast Asian young people who are refugees in the United States.

Human Rights Internet. **Africa: Human Rights Directory and Bibliography.** Ottawa: Human Rights Internet, University of Ottawa, 1989. 304p. ISBN 0-939338-04-1.

This directory of human rights organizations in Africa is concerned with human rights and social justice.

———. **Human Rights Directory: Eastern Europe.** Ottawa: Human Rights Internet, University of Ottawa, 1987. 210p. ISBN 0-939338-03-3.

This resource lists organizations in Eastern Europe that are working on human rights and social justice.

———. **Human Rights Directory: Latin America and the Caribbean.** Ottawa: Human Rights Internet, University of Ottawa, 1990. 526p. ISBN 0-939338-05-X.

This directory describes nearly 800 organizations concerned with human rights and humanitarian issues in Latin America and the Caribbean. Available in English and Spanish, it is an excellent source for networking, research, and policymaking.

———. **Human Rights Directory: North America.** Ottawa: Human Rights Internet, University of Ottawa, 1984. 300p. ISBN 0-939338-02-5.

This directory lists organizations in North America concerned with human rights and social justice.

———. **Human Rights Directory: Western Europe.** Ottawa: Human Rights Internet, University of Ottawa, 1982. 335p. ISBN 0-939338-01-7.

This directory focuses on organizations in Western Europe that deal with human rights and social justice issues.

International Committee of the Red Cross (ICRC). **Bibliography of International Humanitarian Law Applicable in Armed Conflicts.** Geneva: ICRC and Henry Dunant Institute, 1987. 605p. ISBN 2-88044-017-3.

An indispensable bibliography, this book covers international humanitarian law, international armed conficts, noninternational armed conflicts, and protection of noncombatants in warfare.

International Refugee Integration Resource Centre (IRIRC). **International Bibliography of Refugee Literature.** Geneva: IRIRC, 1985. 152p.

This bibliography includes 850 titles covering refugee situations according to the following categories: international organizations, exodus, asylum, resettlement, and integration.

Newman, Frank, and David Weissbrodt, eds. **Selected International Human Rights Instruments.** Cincinnati: Anderson Publishing Co., 1990. 812p. ISBN 0-87084-368-0.

This handbook lists and describes the principal international human rights instruments.

Refugee Studies Programme, University of Oxford. **The Directory of Research on Refugees and Other Forced Migrants,** 3d ed. Oxford: Refugee Studies Programme, 1993. 184p. ISBN 0-9512260-0-2.

This directory contains information on the research and publications of about 400 scholars working in the refugee field. It gives the cultural origin, discipline, and research topic for each entry and provides telephone and fax numbers where applicable. Cross-referencing is facilitated by lists based on geographical area and discipline of each person listed.

Segal, Aaron. **An Atlas of International Migration.** London: Hans Zell, 1993. 233p. ISBN 1-873836-30-9.

This atlas details various kinds of migration patterns and their effects on sending and receiving countries. It contains much useful documentation.

Schorr, Alan. **Refugee and Immigrant Resource Directory, 1990–1991.** Juneau, AK: Denali Press, 1990. 349p. ISBN 0-938737-19-8.

This invaluable resource includes information on 958 local, regional, and national organizations, research centers, academic programs, foundations, museums, government agencies, and other groups in the United States that offer services or provide information about refugees and immigrants.

United Nations High Commissioner for Refugees (UNHCR). **Collection of International Instruments concerning Refugees.** Geneva: UNHCR, 1979. 335p.

This is a collection of the international legal instruments (concerning refugees, stateless persons, and human rights), regional legal instruments (for Africa, Europe, and the Americas), and other instruments.

———. **Conclusions on the International Protection of Refugees Adopted by the Executive Committee on International Protection of Refugees of the UNHCR Program.** Geneva: UNHCR, 1980. 91p.

This compendium comprises the conclusions on the international protection of refugees as adopted by UNHCR's Executive Committee up to 1980.

UNHCR Centre for Documentation on Refugees and Refugee Policy Group. **Bibliography on Refugee Children.** Geneva: UNHCR, 1987. 138p.

This is an annotated bibliography on refugee children categorized under protection and assistance; national policies; refugee camps; placement and fostering; integration; education; health; and psychological problems.

———. **Bibliography on Refugee Women.** Geneva: UNHCR, 1989. 122p.

This annotated bibliography focuses on current research on refugee women and is arranged geographically.

———. **Bibliography Prepared for the Excom Working Group on Solutions and Protection.** Geneva: UNHCR, 1990. 85p.

This is an annotated bibliography of literature on refugees divided into four sections: (1) refugee and related migratory movements; (2) solutions; (3) early warning and prevention; and (4) refugee law and policies.

UNHCR Liaison Section with Non-Governmental Organizations. **Directory of Non-Governmental Organizations.** Geneva: UNHCR, 1992. 240p.

This directory contains the names and addresses of over 500 institutions working with refugees and asylum-seekers.

Williams, Carolyn. **An Annotated Bibliography on Refugee Mental Health.** Washington, DC: Department of Health and Human Services, 1987. 335p. DHHS Publication No. (ADM) 87-1517.

This bibliography of 666 items is organized under four main headings: (1) understanding refugees in context; (2) specific mental health issues and refugees; (3) concerns of selected subgroups of refugees; and (4) other bibliographies on refugees or related topics.

Books

Adelman, Howard, ed. **Refugee Policy: Canada and the United States.** Toronto: York Lanes Press, 1991. 455p. ISBN 0-9343733-64-3.

This book, a collection of papers presented at a conference at York University in 1990, compares the refugee policies of Canada and the United States. It includes contributions by many of the leading North American researchers in refugee studies and has chapters on the normative and political aspects of refugee policy, root causes, refugee relief and development assistance, refugee law and practice, and resettlement policies.

Baker, Ron, ed. **The Psychological Problems of Refugees.** London: The British Refugee Council, 1983. 250p. ISBN 0-946787-00-X.

This book provides data on the mental health problems experienced by many refugees.

Basoglu, Metin. **Torture and Its Consequences.** Cambridge: Cambridge University Press, 1992. 355p. ISBN 0521-39299-3.

Basoglu gives an account of victims of torture, many of whom are refugees, and the challenges of providing treatment for these individuals.

Bramwell, Anna, ed. **Refugees in the Age of Total War: Twentieth Century Case-Studies of Refugees in Europe and the Middle East.** London: Unwin Hyman, 1987. 359p. ISBN 004-445194-6.

These 20 chapters analyze refugee movements in Europe and the Middle East generated by the two world wars and their aftermaths. They also examine the responses of international organizations and governments to the movements.

Bread for the World Institute on Hunger and Development. **Hunger 1993: Uprooted People.** Washington, DC: Bread for the World Institute on Hunger and Development, 1992. 204p. ISBN 1-9628058-6-6.

This book focuses on the special circumstances of refugees and displaced people and the problems of hunger and malnutrition. It is a useful overview of the issues and contains many helpful tables and graphs, as well as a bibliography.

Cahill, Kevin, ed. **A Framework for Survival: Health, Human Rights, and Humanitarian Assistance in Conflicts and Disasters.** New York: Basic Books and the Council on Foreign Relations, 1993. 340p. ISBN 0-465-02513-7.

This book, with 20 chapters by practitioners, focuses on legal and economic issues, health issues, and the responses of private voluntary agencies and the United Nations to humanitarian crises. It illustrates the interdependence of conflict, famine, health care, and refugee crises and underscores the importance of a comprehensive approach to these problems.

Collinson, Sarah. **Beyond Borders: West European Migration Policy towards the 21st Century.** London: Royal Institute of International Affairs and Wyndham Place Trust, 1993. 116p. ISBN 0-905031.

This book focuses on some of the major policy challenges confronting European governments: immigrant integration, immigration controls, proposals to alleviate the root causes of migration, and refugee and asylum policies.

———. **Europe and International Migration.** London: Pinter Publishers, 1993. 189p. ISBN 1-85567-049-6.

This book highlights elements of continuity and change in European states' involvement in migration policies. It places the problem of migration within an international, historical process and focuses on the integration of immigrant and ethnic minorities. Finally, it discusses Europe's efforts to harmonize their asylum and migration policies.

Crew, Linda. **Children of the River.** New York: Dell Publishing, 1991. 213p. ISBN 0-440-21022-4.

Children of the River is a novel for young adults about Sundra, a teenage Cambodian refugee, who is torn between her loyalty to her family and cultural traditions and her love for an American boy.

Damrosch, Lori. **Enforcing Restraint: Collective Intervention in Internal Conflicts.** New York: Council on Foreign Relations Press, 1993. 403p. ISBN 0-87609-155-9.

This is a collection of case studies—from the former Yugoslavia, Somalia, Haiti, Liberia, and Cambodia—that examines the efforts by the international community to intervene to end political conflict and provide humanitarian relief in the post–Cold War era.

Deng, Francis. **Protecting the Dispossessed: A Challenge for the International Community.** Washington, DC: The Brookings Institution, 1993. 175p. ISBN 0-8157-1825-X.

This book details the difficulties the international community confronts trying to protect the approximately 25 million internally displaced people in the world today. It includes case studies from the former Yugoslavia, Russia, Somalia, Sudan, El Salvador, and Cambodia.

Dowty, Alan. **Closed Borders: The Contemporary Assault on Freedom of Movement.** New Haven: Yale University Press, 1987. 270p. ISBN 0-300-03824-0.

Dowty traces how different governments throughout history have dealt with populations both entering and exiting their countries and explores the reasons for past and present government policies designed to restrict entry. He also analyzes the political and economic consequences of such policies and argues for a policy of open borders that would allow individuals to emigrate or immigrate at will.

Druke, Louise. **Preventive Action for Refugee-Producing Situations.** Frankfurt: Peter Lang, 1990. 271p. ISBN 3-631-42243-1.

Preventive Action for Refugee-Producing Situations examines situations where refugees are exploited as a weapon for political purposes and suggests ways to prevent situations that lead to refugee flows.

Ferris, Elizabeth. **Beyond Borders: Refugees, Migrants and Human Rights in the Post–Cold War Era.** Geneva: World Council of Churches Publications, 1993. 310p. ISBN 2-8254-1095-0.

This book examines the international context within which forced migration occurs and discusses the role of international organizations, governments, and nongovernmental organizations in assisting and protecting refugees.

Forbes Martin, Susan. **Refugee Women.** London: Zed Books, 1992. 195p. ISBN 1-85649-001-7.

This book focuses on the particular circumstances of refugee women and shows how they have to cope with additional traumas, such as rape.

Frank, Anne. **The Diary of a Young Girl.** New York: Random House, 1990. 285p. ISBN 1-55736-098-7.

This is the remarkable story of a young Jewish girl and two families who hid from the Nazis in a house in Amsterdam from 1942 to 1944. It is a poignant account of the thoughts and expressions of a young teenager living under extraordinarily difficult conditions.

Gallagher, Dennis, ed. **Refugees: Issues and Directions.** *International Migration Review.* Volume 20. New York: Center for Migration Studies, 1986. 541p. ISSN 0197-9183.

This is a special edition of the *International Migration Review* dealing with refugees. Eighteen essays by refugee specialists analyze the causes and characteristics of refugee movements worldwide, asylum and protection issues, refugee issues in developing countries, and adjustment and resettlement matters.

Gibney, Mark ed. **Open Borders? Closed Societies? The Ethical and Political Questions.** Westport, CT: Greenwood Press, 1988. 199p. ISBN 0-313-25578-4.

This collection of essays addresses many of the legal and ethical questions regarding policy on immigration and refugee admissions. Although these issues are of concern to most states, the focus of the authors in this volume is American policy.

Goodwin-Gill, Guy. **The Refugee in International Law.** Oxford: Clarendon Press, 1983. 317p. ISBN 0-19-825518-7.

This is a classic sourcebook for international refugee law. It describes the framework of refugee law and covers the definitions of terms such as *refugee, refoulement, refugee asylum,* and *refugee protection.* The author examines the evolution and effectiveness of treaties and organizations, state policies, and responsibilities, and he includes an appendix of key texts.

Gordenker, Leon. **Refugees in International Politics.** New York: Columbia University Press, 1987. 227p. ISBN 0-7099-3848-9.

This study explores the nature of forced migration and sets forth a framework that examines the causes of refugee movements. The author also covers the responses of states and international organizations to refugee flows and examines the traditional solutions—repatriation, local resettlement, and third-country resettlement—to refugee incidents. The study concludes with recommendations regarding early warning and a preventive framework for dealing with future refugee flows.

Gorman, R. F. **Coping with Africa's Refugee Burden: A Time for Solutions.** Dordrecht, Netherlands: Martinus Nijhoff, 1987. 206p. ISBN 90-247-3457-6.

This book focuses on the recommendations of the Second International Conference on Assistance to Refugees in Africa (ICARA II). The author analyzes the policies, organizational constraints, and roles of international agencies, governments, and nongovernmental organizations in responding to the refugee crisis, as well as the related development needs of host countries.

Grahl-Madsen, Atle. **The Status of Refugees in International Law.** Leyden, Netherlands: A. W. Sijthoff, 1966. 2 vols. 499p. ISBN 0-3192070-60.

This two-volume work investigates the international framework of refugee law. It examines refugee status determination, refugee definitions, refugee rights and obligations, and international and national law.

Hakovirta, H. **Third World Conflicts and Refugeeism: Dimensions, Dynamics and Trends of the World Refugee Problem.** Helsinki: Finnish Society of Science and Letters, 1986. 160p. ISBN 95-165-3140-7.

This study attempts to develop a social science model for analyzing the causes, dimensions, trends, and consequences of contemporary refugee movements.

Hannum, H. **The Right To Leave and Return in International Law and Practice.** Leyden, Netherlands: Martinus Nijhoff, 1987. 189p. ISBN 90-247-3445-2.

This study examines the international formulation, historical evolution, and jurisprudence of the right to leave and return. The author also analyzes state practice toward the right to movement in various countries throughout the world.

Hansen, Art, and A. Oliver-Smith, eds. **Involuntary Migration and Resettlement: The Problems and Responses of Dislocated People.** Boulder, CO: Westview Press, 1982. 333p. ISBN 0-8915-89767.

This volume examines a number of migration and resettlement schemes. The authors look at individual, group, and state reactions to the stresses of involuntary dislocation and resettlement and compare these to the stresses of voluntary migration.

Harrell-Bond, Barbara. **Imposing Aid: Emergency Assistance to Refugees.** Oxford: Oxford University Press, 1986. 440p. ISBN 0-19-261543-2.

This study appraises the assistance program mounted by international agencies in response to an emergency influx of Ugandan refugees into Sudan starting in early 1982. Using the findings of this case study, the author questions the effectiveness of current refugee assistance strategies. In particular, the book argues that relief workers easily become part of the problem they set out to solve and finds that in the search for solutions the needs and skills of refugees are often overlooked.

Hathaway, James. **The Law of Refugee Status.** Toronto: Butterworths, 1991. 252p. ISBN 0-409-91479-7.

This book explains the scope of the definition of the term *refugee* as embodied in the United Nations Convention Relating to the Status of Refugees (1951) and as it has evolved in practice. This is an excellent resource for international refugee law and is particularly useful to those concerned about the legal determination of refugee status.

Hitchcox, Linda. **Refugees.** New York: Franklin Watts, 1990. 32p. ISBN 0-531-17242-2.

One of the "Issues" series on current problems, this work is aimed at primary school children. It uses text, maps, and photographs to present the subject and includes a section on refugee children, a page of useful facts and statistics, and an index.

Holborn, Louise W. **The International Refugee Organization: A Specialized Agency of the United Nations, Its History and Work, 1946–1952.** Oxford: Oxford University Press, 1956. 819p.

This book details the history and activities of the United Nations' first refugee organization, the International Refugee Organization, between 1946 and 1952.

———. **Refugees: A Problem of Our Time: The Work of the United Nations High Commissioner for Refugees.** Metuchen, NJ: Scarecrow Press, 1975. 2 vols. 1,525p. ISBN 0-8108-0746-7.

These two volumes detail the history of the first 20 years of the Office of the United Nations High Commissioner for Refugees (UNHCR). Considered to be the official history of the early development of UNHCR, it contains extensive country-by-country case studies and provides useful historical documentation.

Holm, Anne. **North to Freedom.** San Diego, CA: Harcourt Brace Jovanovich, 1965. 239p. ISBN 0-15-257553-7.

This novel for young adults recounts the story of David, a 12-year-old boy, who escapes from a prison camp in Eastern Europe during the Cold War and makes his way on foot across Europe until he finds freedom.

Independent Commission on International Humanitarian Issues. **Refugees: Dynamics of Displacement.** London: Zed Books, 1986. 152p. ISBN 0-86232-697-4.

This is the official report on refugees from the Independent Commission on International Humanitarian Issues. The report focuses on mass expulsion, forcible relocation programs, and internally displaced people. It also highlights the increasingly restrictive policies of Western governments toward asylum-seekers, the responsibilities of governments worldwide in causing involuntary migration, and the inadequacy of international law in the prevention and resolution of problems of involuntary migration.

Joly, Daniele, Clive Nettleton, and H. Poulton. **Refugees: Asylum in Europe?** London: Minority Rights Publications, 1992. 180p. ISBN 1-873194-10-2.

This book examines the causes of refugee flight in both Western and Eastern Europe, the acceptance and settlement of refugees, international conventions and state legislation, and the racist backlash against refugees. It suggests how individuals, organizations, and governments can protect and assist refugees.

Kent, Randolph. **The Anatomy of Disaster Relief: The International Network in Action.** London: Pinter Publishers, 1987. 201p. ISBN 0-86187-294-0.

This study analyzes the causes and consequences of disasters, including man-made ones, and investigates the structure of the international disaster relief process. The author discusses specifically the role of international organizations and governments. He argues that some disaster relief aid is ineffective because many aid workers have skills unsuited to the disaster environment, pay little attention to the culture and traditions of aid recipients, and fail to learn from earlier mistakes.

Kibreab, Gaim. **African Refugees: Reflections on the African Refugee Problem.** Trenton, NJ: Red Sea Press, 1985. 132p. ISBN 0-86543-007-1.

This work critically examines assumptions about refugee rehabilitation in African host countries and suggests the adoption of measures to make refugees active and useful participants in the development process.

Kidd, Diana. **Onion Tears.** New York: Orchard Books, 1989. 62p. ISBN 0-531-08470-0.

This novel for young readers tells the story of Nam-Houng, a Vietnamese refugee, and the difficult adjustments she has to make integrating into her new homeland in the United States.

Koehn, Peter. **Refugees from Revolution: U.S. Policy and Third World Migration.** Boulder, CO: Westview Press, 1991. ISBN 0-8133-7719-6.

This study examines the causes of recent refugee migrations to the United States and the underlying connections between U.S. foreign and domestic policies regarding immigration, refugee resettlement, and human rights. The author focuses on Cuban, Indochinese, Ethiopian, Eritrean, and Iranian exile communities in the United States and examines their treatment under U.S. policy, their social and economic adaptation, and the factors that influence their decisions to return home.

Kritz, Mary, ed. **U.S. Immigration and Refugee Policy: Global and Domestic Issues.** Lexington, MA: D. C. Heath, 1983. 415p. ISBN 0-669-05543-3.

This book is an anthology of many theoretical and policy issues that confront scholars concerned with international migration. The editor stresses the importance of identifying the causes of population flows.

Kunz, Egon F. **Displaced Persons: Calwell's New Australians.** Sydney: Australian National University Press, 1988. 285p. ISBN 0-080-034406-2.

This history details Australia's immigration policy during and after World War II, when displaced Estonians, Latvians, Lithuanians, Poles, Ukranians, Russians, Czechs, Slovaks, Hungarians, Croats, Serbs, and Bulgarians were transported to Australia to increase its population and work force.

Lake, Anthony, et al., eds. **After the Wars: Reconstruction in Afghanistan, Indochina, Central America, Southern Africa and the Horn of Africa.** New Brunswick, NJ: Transaction Publishers, 1991. 197p. ISBN 0-887-738880-9.

Five policy analysts examine the political and economic costs of rebuilding the regions that experienced geopolitical rivalries and long-standing and destructive wars during the 1980s. Policy suggestions include creating an international fund to finance the reconstruction of war-torn areas of the Third World.

Larkin, Mary Ann, Frederick Cuny, and Barry Stein. **Repatriation under Conflict in Central America.** Washington, DC, and Dallas: Georgetown University and Intertecht, 1991. 231p. ISBN 0-924046-17-1.

This multiauthored volume examines the issue of repatriation in Central America. Experts examine the motivations of Salvadoran, Guatemalan, and Nicaraguan refugees from their initial flight through repatriation. Conditions in exile and at home, as well as assistance policies, are analyzed in light of their influence on the repatriation decision.

Lawless, Richard, and Laila Monahan, eds. **War and Refugees: The Western Sahara Conflict.** London: Pinter Publishers, 1987. 201p. ISBN 0-86187-900-7.

This is a study of the Western Sahara conflict and the long-standing refugee problem it created. The book analyzes the economic and political interests behind the war and the legal basis for occupation by Morocco, and it describes the life of a largely forgotten group of refugees.

Loescher, Gil. **Beyond Charity: International Cooperation and the Global Refugee Crisis.** New York: Oxford University Press, 1993. 260p. ISBN 0-19-508183-8.

This book is an extensive overview of the global refugee situation in the post–Cold War era. The author presents the contemporary crisis in a historical framework, examining both the rise of refugee problems in the last 70 years and the roles of international agencies, particularly the UNHCR, in responding to those problems. The book concludes with short- and long-term measures that might help address various aspects of the refugee problem.

———. **Refugee Movements and International Security.** Adelphi Paper 268. London: Brassey's for International Institute for Strategic Studies, 1992. 83p. ISBN 1-85-753-022-5.

This study examines the relationship between refugee movements and national and international security in the post–Cold War period. The author offers an overview of the contemporary refugee situation, outlines the political and strategic causes and consequences of refugee flows, and suggests a policy framework for dealing with the global refugee problem.

———, ed. **Refugees and the Asylum Dilemma in the West.** University Park, PA: Pennsylvania State University Press, 1992. 119p. ISBN 0-271-00856-3.

This book examines the historical background and contemporary significance of the asylum and refugee issue confronting Western governments and draws lessons for future policymaking. Seven experts look at asylum policy in the United States, Canada, and Western Europe and the development of an international response to the global refugee problem.

Loescher, Gil, and Ann Loescher. **The World's Refugees, A Test of Humanity.** San Diego, CA: Harcourt Brace Jovanovich, 1982. 145p. ISBN 0-15-299650-8.

Written for high school students and the uninitiated, this book provides an insightful introduction to the world refugee problem. It looks at what life is like for refugees in different regions of the world and at the international response to the problem. It also includes useful appendixes.

Loescher, Gil, and Laila Monahan, eds. **Refugees and International Relations.** Oxford: Oxford University Press, 1989. 430p. ISBN 0-19-827564-1.

This study contains 17 essays by experts in the field of refugee protection and assistance. It examines the international context and the political, legal, and economic dimensions of the global refugee problem, as well as the search for appropriate policy responses to this growing problem. Among the specific subjects addressed are military attacks on refugee camps, voluntary repatriation, restrictionism in Europe, women refugees, the role of the churches, the future of third-country settlement, and the problems of development and repatriation.

Loescher, Gil, and John Scanlan. **Calculated Kindness: Refugees and America's Half Open Door, 1945–Present.** New York: Free Press, 1986. 346p. ISBN 0-02-927340-4.

This study documents the political history of American refugee policy from 1945 until 1986. The authors focus on the factors that have influenced the refugee admissions policy of the United States: Cold War foreign policy that views refugees as symbols and instruments of anticommunism, restrictionist forces that contend that refugees are difficult to assimilate and that they take jobs away from Americans, religious and ethnic groups that lobby for displaced persons and coethnics abroad, and humanitarian interests that advocate admission for persecuted groups and individuals abroad.

———, eds. **The Global Refugee Problem: U.S. and World Response.** Special Issue of the Annals of American Academy of Political and Social Science 467. Beverly Hills, CA: Sage Publications, 1983. 256p. ISBN 0-8039-2015-6.

This collection of 13 essays by leading experts in the field addresses the causes and consequences of refugee movements in the United States and the world as they appeared in the early 1980s. Chapters focus on the scope of the problem, the international framework, the politics of refugee flows, and legal and resettlement issues.

Macalister-Smith, Peter. **International Humanitarian Assistance: Disaster Relief Action in International Law and Organisation.** Dordrecht, Netherlands: Martinus Nijhoff, 1985. 244p. ISBN 90-247-2993-9.

This book details the legal principles and instruments applied in historical and contemporary relief operations, with particular reference to the operations of the International Committee of the Red Cross, the Federation of Red Cross and Red Crescent Societies, and various agencies of the United Nations, including the UNHCR. It also offers suggestions about how to improve the implementation of international humanitarian norms.

Marrus, Michael R. **The Unwanted: European Refugees in the Twentieth Century.** Oxford: Oxford University Press, 1985. 415p. ISBN 0-19-503615-8.

This book tells the story of the refugee problem throughout the twentieth century, particularly during the Nazi era. It examines the impact of refugee movements on the conduct of international relations and diplomacy, outlines the growth of international agencies designed to help refugees, and assesses the work of those agencies.

Martin, David A., ed. **The New Asylum-Seekers: Refugee Law in the 1980s.** Dordrecht, Netherlands: Martinus Nijhoff, 1989. 217p. ISBN 90-247-3730-3.

This book addresses the legal and political issues raised by growing numbers of asylum-seekers and the increasingly restrictive measures introduced by Western governments during the 1980s.

Mason, Linda, and Roger Brown. **Rice, Rivalry and Politics.** South Bend, IN: University of Notre Dame Press, 1983. 218p. ISBN 02-680-1616-X.

The Khmer Rouge reign of terror and the subsequent invasion of Cambodia by Vietnam generated hundreds of thousands of refugees. This book tells the story of the international relief effort for these people, focusing in particular on the Thai-Cambodian border.

Minear, Larry. **Humanitarian Action in Times of War.** Boulder, CO: Lynne Rienner, 1993, 107p. ISBN 1-55587-437-1.

This is a handbook for practitioners providing humanitarian relief in armed conflict situations around the world.

Morgan, Scott, and Elizabeth Colson, eds. **People in Upheaval.** Staten Island, NJ: Center for Migration Studies, 1987. 241p. ISBN 0-934733-16-3.

This collection of 11 essays addresses the issue of displaced people. Key topics include the ambiguity between involuntary and voluntary migration, the interaction of refugees and host communities, the growth of national and international agencies, the support of kin and community, and the effects of resettlement.

Morris, Benny. **The Birth of the Palestinian Refugee Problem, 1947–1949.** Cambridge: Cambridge University Press, 1987. 380p. ISBN 0-521-33889-1.

Palestinian refugees constitute one of the oldest continuous refugee problems in the world. This book examines the roots of the Palestinian refugee problem by examining the exodus of 1947 to 1949 in the context of the first Arab-Israeli War. The author analyzes the reasons behind the Palestinian flight and uncovers some new views about it.

Muntarbhorn, Vitit. **The Status of Refugees in Asia.** Oxford: Oxford University Press, 1992. 210p. ISBN 0-19-825668-X.

This work is an analysis of the national laws and regulations concerning the admission and treatment of refugees and aliens in Asia. It provides useful documentation.

Nichols, Bruce. **The Uneasy Alliance: Religion, Refugee Work and U.S. Foreign Policy.** New York: Oxford University Press, 1988. 351p. ISBN 0-19-504274-3.

U.S. refugee policy has always relied on the successful cooperation of government and voluntary agencies, especially religious groups. This study traces the history of cooperation and conflict between government policy and religious agencies regarding refugee work. The author claims that the increasingly political and moral disagreement between the U.S. government and the religious community over refugee assistance during the latter part of the Cold War threatened the American tradition of humanitarian assistance and reflected the loss of consensus in American foreign policy.

Nichols, Bruce, and Gil Loescher, eds. **The Moral Nation: Humanitarianism and U.S. Foreign Policy Today.** South Bend, IN: University of Notre Dame Press, 1989. 321p. ISBN 0-268-01398-5.

This book critically examines the roles of U.S. government and private agencies in providing relief to human rights victims, refugees, and famine victims. Contributors examine the moral and political philosophy of humanitarianism and its relationship to the conduct of U.S. foreign policy, the political and legal factors involved in the formulation of humanitarian policy, and case studies involving asylum, sanctuary, and famine relief in Central America and the Horn of Africa.

Plender, Richard, ed. **Basic Documents on International Migration Law.** Dordrecht, Netherlands: Martinus Nijhoff, 1988. 424p. ISBN 90-247-3667-6.

This book lists the principal international conventions, declarations, and instruments governing the laws of international migration. It includes extracts from some of the instruments governing human rights and full texts of the principal treatises and declarations governing nationality, the protection of refugees, and migrant labor. There are also texts of the principal items of legislation of the European Communities and the instruments adopted by the Council of Europe, the Benelux Community, and the economic communities of West and Central Africa and the Caribbean.

———. **International Migration Law.** Dordrecht, Netherlands: Martinus Nijhoff, 1988. 339p. ISBN 90-286-01627.

This is a comprehensive review of the rights of aliens under international law. It not only includes chapters on the rights of aliens but also on the powers of states to restrict aliens. The book also includes a table of cases, statutes, and other internal instruments regarding migration.

Ressler, Everett Neil Boothby, and David Steinbeck. **Unaccompanied Children: Care and Placement in Wars, Natural Disasters and Refugee Movements.** Oxford: Oxford University Press, 1987. 421p. ISBN 0-19-504937-3.

This book provides a history of unaccompanied children and the assistance given them in the past. Based upon research conducted on the Thai-Cambodian border, the authors explain child development both within the family and community and outside these frameworks; the major legal issues involved concerning this group; and the roles of international and voluntary organizations.

Rogers, Rosemarie, and Emily Copeland. **Forced Migration: Policy Issues in the Post–Cold War World.** Medford, MA: The Fletcher School of Law and Diplomacy, Tufts University, 1993. 151p. ISBN 0-9636445-1-3.

This book is a good introduction to many of the policy issues involved in forced migration. It discusses the international political context of population movements and the limitations of traditional responses to refugee problems. It also proposes a more comprehensive approach to refugees for the future. The book has useful tables and references.

Rutter, Jill. **We Left Because We Had To: An Educational Book for 14–18 Year Olds.** London: Refugee Council, 1991. 148p. ISBN 0-946787-04-2.

This is an excellent educational resource for teachers offering lessons or courses on refugees. It discusses who refugees are, the causes of refugee movements, and the difficulties most refugees encounter as they resettle into new homelands.

Shawcross, William. **The Quality of Mercy: Cambodia, Holocaust and Modern Conscience.** New York: Simon & Schuster, 1984. 464p. ISBN 0-671-44022-5.

Written by a British journalist, this book examines the political disputes surrounding the worldwide relief effort aimed at Cambodia from the late 1970s to 1983. Shawcross tells the story of the workings of major relief agencies such as UNHCR and UNICEF and the political pressures exerted on them by the Thai, Vietnamese, and Western governments, as well as by the coalition government promoted by the various resistance groups within Cambodia.

Simpson, John Hope. **The Refugee Problem.** London: Oxford University Press, 1939. 637p.

This book is an account written in 1939 of the refugee problems in Europe during the preceding 20 years and of the international community's response to these problems.

Skran, Claudena. **Refugees in Inter-War Europe.** Oxford: Clarendon Press, 1994. 282p. ISBN 0-19-827392-4.

An analysis of the refugee problem in Europe from 1921 to 1939, this volume gives a particularly useful account of the growth and evolution of the international community's response to refugees during the interwar period.

Stoessinger, John. **The Refugee in the World Community.** Minneapolis, MN: University of Minnesota Press, 1956. 239p.

This book is a history of the International Refugee Organization, which resettled over 1 million displaced persons between 1947 and 1951, and the motivations of states in accepting large numbers of refugees as immigrants.

Strom, Margot Stern, and William Parsons. **Facing History and Ourselves: Holocaust and Human Behavior.** Watertown, MA: Intentional Educations, Inc., 1982. 400p.

This educational book, aimed at high school and older students, considers the holocaust of Armenians at the hands of the Ottoman Empire and of Jews at the hands of the Third Reich. An important feature of this book is the material on the social and political attitudes that lead to persecution of minorities and to political tyranny.

Sutter, Valerie. **The Indochinese Refugee Dilemma.** Baton Rouge: Louisiana State University Press, 1990. 256p. ISBN 0-8071-1556-8.

Between 1975 and 1990, well over 1.5 million refugees poured out of Indochina. This book offers a concise history of the complex national issues surrounding the Indochina refugee problem. It examines the domestic and foreign policy interests of the Indochinese states, Thailand and other Southeast Asian states, China, the United States, and the Soviet Union.

United Nations High Commissioner for Refugees (UNHCR). **The State of the World's Refugees: The Challenge of Protection.** New York: Penguin Books, 1993. 191p. ISBN 0-14-023487-X.

The first of UNHCR's biennal reports on the state of the world's refugees, this book focuses on the challenge of refugee protection. It has chapters on the meaning of protection, the causes of displacement, the crisis of asylum, the role of the media, and the particular problems of protection in armed conflict, refugee emergencies, and repatriation. The book also provides extensive documentation, statistics, charts, and maps.

Vernant, Jacques. **The Refugee in the Post-War World.** New Haven, CT: Yale University Press, 1953. 827p.

This is an account of the growth of refugee problems in the early post–World War II period, when large numbers of refugees fled communist regimes in Europe and the Soviet Union.

Weiner, Myron, ed. **International Migration and Security.** Boulder, CO: Westview Press, 1993. 333p. ISBN 0-8133-8774-4.

This collection of essays analyzes the security consequences of international population movements. There are individual chapters on Europe, the former Soviet Union, Asia, Africa, and Central America.

Williams, Carolyn, and Joseph Westermayer, eds. **Refugee Mental Health in Resettlement Countries.** Washington, DC: Hemisphere Publishing Corporation, 1986. 267p. ISBN 08-911-64456.

Refugees often suffer trauma and severe psychological problems as a result of being uprooted and displaced. This work summarizes research literature dealing with refugee health problems and explains the acculturation process, highlighting the behavioral and mental health problems of refugees. Case studies include Cambodians, the Falasha of Israel, Laotians, and Cubans. The book also offers suggestions for treatment and assessment.

Woodbridge, George. **The History of UNRRA.** New York: Columbia University Press, 1950. 3 vols. 1,639p.

This is a history of the United Nations Relief and Rehabilitation Administration (UNRRA), which provided relief assistance to war victims and displaced people in Europe from 1943 to 1947. The book also recounts the repatriation of East Europeans and Russians after the end of World War II.

Wyman, David. **The Abandonment of the Jews: America and the Holocaust, 1941–1945.** New York: Pantheon, 1985. 444p. ISBN 0-39442-913-7.

This is a critical analysis of the failure of the United States to rescue more Jews from certain death in the Holocaust from 1941 to 1945.

———. **Paper Walls: America and the Refugee Crisis, 1938–1941.** Amherst, MA: University of Massachusetts Press, 1968. 306p.

This is a moving and critical account of the ineffective and harsh U.S. policy toward Jews in Germany and the rest of Europe during the early years of World War II.

Zolberg, Aristide R., Astri Suhrke, and Sergio Aguayo. **Escape from Violence: Conflict and the Refugee Crises in the Developing World.** New York: Oxford University Press, 1989. 380p. ISBN 0-19-505592-6.

This book is one of the most systematic analyses of refugee movements in the Third World up to the late 1980s. The authors attempt a comprehensive, theoretically grounded, structural explanation for refugee movements and highlight the relationship between social conflict and refugee flows. All major regions of the world are covered, except the Middle East, Eastern Europe, and the former Soviet Union.

Zucker, Norman, and Naomi Zucker. **The Guarded Gate: The Reality of American Refugee Policy.** San Diego, CA: Harcourt Brace Jovanovich, 1987. 342p. ISBN 0-15-137575-5.

This book tells the story of U.S. refugee and asylum policy up to the mid-1980s. The authors trace the origins of U.S. refugee policy to immigration restrictionism in American history and offer constructive suggestions for reform in refugee and asylum policy.

Reports

Amnesty International. **Amnesty International Report 1994.** London: Amnesty International, 1994.

This annual report of worldwide human rights violations is produced by a prominent human rights monitoring organization.

Burr, Millard. **Sudan 1990–1992: Food Aid, Famine and Failure.** Washington, DC: U.S. Committee for Refugees, 1993.

About 5 million Sudanese have been internally displaced and more than half a million are refugees. This report provides a detailed historical review of Western food relief efforts and diplomatic maneuvering toward Sudan and looks at the Sudanese government policies that have persistently undermined relief efforts.

Chesnais, Jean-Claude. **Migration from Eastern to Western Europe, Past (1946–1989) and Future (1990–2000).** Strasbourg: Council of Europe, 1990.

This is an analysis of past and future trends of East-West flows. The main objective of this work is to reduce some of the uncertainty about the potential size of such movements in the future. It includes tables and documentation.

Childers, Erskine, and Brian Urquhart. **Strengthening International Response to Humanitarian Emergencies.** New York: Ford Foundation, 1991.

Two experienced former UN officials propose a comprehensive set of policy recommendations to expedite and make more effective the response of international organizations to humanitarian crises in the post–Cold War era.

Clark, Jeffrey. **Famine in Somalia and the International Response: Collective Failure.** Washington, DC: U.S. Committee for Refugees, 1992.

This paper reviews the history of missed opportunities and strategic and operational blunders in Somalia during 1990–1992.

Cohen, Roberta. **Human Rights Protection for Internally Displaced Persons.** Washington, DC: Refugee Policy Group, 1991.

This report analyzes the dimensions of the human rights problems confronting people displaced within their own countries and the lack of national and international protection for these people. It proposes a number of institutional and legal changes that would improve the protection of the internally displaced.

———. **United Nations Human Rights Bodies: An Agenda for Humanitarian Action.** Washington, DC: Refugee Policy Group, 1992.

This is an analysis of the ways in which United Nations human rights bodies can more effectively respond to the humanitarian problems of the post–Cold War period.

Forbes Martin, Susan. **Emigration, Immigration and Changing East-West Relations.** Washington, DC: Refugee Policy Group, 1989.

This report examines the massive flow of refugees from Eastern Europe toward the West in 1989, the policy responses to this situation by Western countries, the movement of refugees within Eastern Europe, and the institutional and policy structures available for dealing with refugee matters.

Frelick, Bill. **Croatia's Crucible: Providing Asylum for Refugees from Bosnia and Herzegovina.** Washington, DC: U.S. Committee for Refugees, 1992.

This report discusses the failures of the United Nations, the European Community, and the United States to respond to the humanitarian challenges in the former Yugoslavia.

Human Rights Watch. **Human Rights Watch Report 1994.** New York: Human Rights Watch, 1994.

This annual report by a prominent human rights organization documents human rights violations worldwide.

Jacobson, Jodi. **Environmental Refugees: A Yardstick of Habitability.** Washington, DC: World Watch Institute, 1988.

Throughout the world, vast areas are becoming unfit for human habitation. This report argues that the growing number of people fleeing from environmental degradation adds a new dimension to the global refugee problem.

Joly, Daniele, and Clive Nettleton. **Refugees in Europe.** London: Minority Rights Group, 1990.

This report offers a useful outline of some of the issues surrounding the current situation faced by refugees in Europe.

Keely, Charles. **Global Refugee Policy: The Case for a Development Oriented Strategy.** New York: Population Council, 1981.

This report was one of the first accounts that drew attention to the need to provide refugees with long-term development assistance rather than short-term relief assistance.

Kirk, Robin. **The Decade of Chaqwa: Peru's Internal Refugees.** Washington, DC: U.S. Committee for Refugees, 1991.

This report describes the causes of internal displacement in Peru and the plight of indigenous populations at the center of the fighting between the government and guerrillas.

———. **Feeding the Tiger: Colombia's Internally Displaced People.** Washington, DC: U.S. Committee for Refugees, 1993.

Kirk discusses the plight of internally displaced people in Colombia, the causes of their flight, and the inadequacies of the responses by Colombia and the international community.

Lawyers' Committee for International Human Rights. **The Implementation of the Refugee Act of 1980: A Decade of Experience.** New York: Lawyers' Committee for International Human Rights, 1990.

This is a critical review of the first ten years of U.S. asylum policy after the passage of the Refugee Act of 1980.

———. **Refugee Refoulement: The Forced Return of Haitians under the U.S. Haitian Interdiction Agreement.** New York: Lawyers' Committee for International Human Rights, 1990.

This report discusses the U.S. policy of interdicting Haitian boat people and returning them to Port-au-Prince.

———. **Uncertain Haven.** New York: Lawyers' Committee for International Human Rights, 1991.

A critical assessment of asylum and refugee policy in the 1980s in Asia, Africa, Latin America, Western Europe, and North America, this report also discusses the difficulties confronting the United Nations High Commissioner for Refugees (UNHCR) in providing protection.

———. **The UNHCR at 40: Refugee Protection at the Crossroads.** New York: Lawyers' Committee for International Human Rights, 1991.

This report examines the work of the Office of the United Nations High Commissioner for Refugees (UNHCR) at the time of its 40th anniversary. It focuses on the 1980s and discusses the institutional organization of the UNHCR, recent arrangements regarding its funding and oversight by governments, and efforts to work with nongovernmental organizations.

Loescher, Gil. **Forced Migration within and from the Former USSR: The Policy Challenges Ahead.** Santa Monica, CA: The Rand Corporation, 1993.

This report examines displacement within the former Soviet Union and the policy challenges it poses to the West. It sets out the range of policy responses that the international community should consider in the future.

Ruiz, Hiram. **Left Out in the Cold: The Perilous Homecoming of Afghan Refugees.** Washington, DC: U.S. Committee for Refugees, 1992.

This report analyzes the plight of Afghan refugees who have returned home following the withdrawal of Soviet forces from their country. It also documents the donor countries' poor financial support, which has left returnees, displaced people, and other war victims at risk in Afghanistan.

———. **Repatriation: Tackling Protection and Assistance Concerns.** Washington, DC: U.S. Committee for Refugees, 1993.

This report discusses many of the issues surrounding the return home of refugees, in particular the problems of assisting and protecting them.

———. ***El Retorno:* Guatemalans' Risky Repatriation Begins.** Washington, DC: U.S. Committee for Refugees, 1993.

This documents the problems and risks associated with the repatriation of Guatemalan refugees during a time of continued conflict and political uncertainty in Guatemala.

———. **Uprooted Liberians: Casualties of a Brutal War.** Washington, DC: U.S. Committee for Refugees, 1992.

This report reviews and analyzes the situation of Liberian refugees both inside their home country and in neighboring Sierra Leone, Guinea, and the Ivory Coast.

Women's Commission for Refugee Women and Children. **Balkan Trail of Tears Revisited: Living with the Nightmare.** New York: International Rescue Committee, 1992.

This report on former Yugoslavia focuses on the use of rape as a weapon of war and on the current needs of refugee and internally displaced women and children.

———. **Going Home: the Prospect of Repatriation for Refugee Women and Children.** New York: International Rescue Committee, 1992.

This report contains the proceedings of a conference held to investigate the problems that refugee women and children face when returning home after years, or sometimes decades, of war.

7

Selected Nonprint Resources

Electronic Databases

By far, the best electronic databases on refugees are held by the Center for Documentation for Refugees (CDR) at the office of the United Nations High Commissioner for Refugees (UNHCR) in Geneva, Switzerland. At present, access to these databases is provided to UNHCR branch offices, international organizations, nongovernmental organizations, and governments. In the United States and Canada, questions about access should be directed to the branch office of the UNHCR; the Research Information Center of the Immigration and Naturalization Service of the United States; or the Documentation, Information and Research Branch of the Immigration and Refugee Board of Canada.

Some of the principal electronic databases or infobases of CDR are listed below.

EXCOM Conclusions

This database includes all of the conclusions of the Executive Committee of the UNHCR from 1975 through 1992.

REFCAS: The International Case Law Infobase

This infobase collection includes all case abstracts of higher court decisions regarding refugee matters from Canada, Belgium, France, the Netherlands, the United Kingdom, and the United States.

REFINT: Information on Legal Issues

This infobase provides information such as whether or not a particular country is a signatory to any of the international treaties aimed at the protection of refugees and asylum-seekers, and it also includes a list of state ratifications with reservations or declarations.

REFLAP: Refugee Law and Policy

This infobase contains the full text of documents from the Division of Protection of the UNHCR and the United Nations including: (1) UNHCR Executive Committee conclusions from 1975 to 1991; (2) Internal Office Memoranda/Field Office Memoranda Protection directives from 1986 to 1992; (3) UN General Assembly resolutions; (4) UN Economic and Social Council resolutions since 1982 relating to UNHCR; (5) selected speeches of the high commissioner; and (6) internal Division of International Protection background papers on protection issues.

REFLEG: The Legislation Infobase

This infobase collection contains the full texts of national legislation worldwide on national procedures for the determination of refugee status; the acquisition and loss of citizenship; the entry, residence, and movement of aliens and displaced persons; and the fundamental rights and freedoms of citizens.

REFLIT: The Refugee Literature Infobase

This database contains abstracts of literature, papers, and other documents about refugees. Individual works can be searched by author, subject, or title.

THESAURUS: The Infobase on Refugee Terminology

This infobase contains standardized terminology or keywords on issues relating to refugees.

UNDOCS: United Nations Documents and Resolutions

This infobase contains all resolutions of the UN Security Council from January 1991 to the present; all General Assembly resolutions from the 45th session (1990–1991) to the present; and selected reports submitted to the UN Commission on Human Rights from its 1992 session to the present.

WRITENET: Country Reports and Chronologies

This infobase contains reports and summaries of current events concerning refugee developments worldwide.

Videotapes

VHS techonology has almost completely replaced all other forms of audiovisual materials. As a result, the following list is of VHS materials only.

This bibliography does not include costs of renting or purchasing the videos because prices change frequently. Please check with the sources for current prices. Generally, videos available from the United Nations High Commissioner for Refugees (UNHCR) and the United Nations Relief and Works Agency for Palestine Refugees in the Near East (UNRWA) can be rented free of charge.

Ambassador of Goodwill
Length: 14 min.
Date: 1991
Source: UNHCR
UN Plaza
New York, NY 10017
(212) 963-6200

This is a short film about the work of the UNHCR; it includes scenes from refugee camps around the world.

An American Tail
Length: 78 min.
Date: 1986
Source: Most video-renting establishments

This is a feature-length cartoon about mice who represent persecuted minorities in Russia escaping to New York. The film is about leaving home and adjusting to unfamiliar surroundings and culture, and it is best suited to children in the elementary grades.

Are You Listening/Indochina Refugees
Length: 60 min.
Date: 1982
Source: Martha Stuart Communications
P.O. Box 246
2 Anthony Street
Hillside, NY 12529

This film includes interviews with Southeast Asian refugees who are resettled in the United States. They talk about their experiences of flight, life in refugee camps, and problems of resettlement.

Are You Listening/Palestinians

Length: 28 min.
Date: 1983
Source: Martha Stuart Communications
P.O. Box 246
2 Anthony Street
Hillside, NY 12529

This video centers around the celebration of a marriage between Palestinian refugees in Paris. The marriage brings together family members from the United States, the Middle East, and Europe, and the film examines their loss of country and national identity.

Belize—Land of Refuge

Length: 20 min.
Date: 1988
Source: UNHCR
UN Plaza
New York, NY 10017
(212) 963-6200

This video looks at the program in Belize that encourages refugees from El Salvador to emigrate and become members of society, living and working with the people of Belize.

Blue Collar and Buddha

Length: 57 min.
Date: 1990
Source: Filmmakers Library, Inc.
124 East 40th Street, No. 901
New York, NY 10016
(212) 808-4980
Fax: (212) 808-4983

This video explores the problems facing Laotian refugees who have been resettled in Rockford, Illinois. They must try to strike a balance between preserving their own culture and adapting to their new environment. Their problems of readjustment have been complicated by the intolerance of their working-class neighbors.

Camino Triste: The Hard Journey of the Guatemalan Refugees

Length: 30 min.
Date: 1983
Source: Icarus Films
123 West 93rd Street, No. 5B
New York, NY 10025
(212) 674-3375

This documentary looks at the counterinsurgency campaign in Guatemala that caused over 100,000 Guatemalan Indians to flee to southern Mexico. It also considers the difficulties they have suffered as refugees in Mexican camps.

Central American Refugees: The Church Response

Length: 28 min.
Date: 1988
Source: Maryknoll World Video Library
P.O. Box 308
Maryknoll, NY 10545-0308
(800) 277-8523; (914) 945-0670

This video looks at the plight of Central American refugees who seek asylum in the United States, the help given them by churches, and the problems this causes with immigration authorities.

The Double Crossing: The Story of the *St. Louis*

Length: 29 min.
Date: 1992
Source: Ergo Media, Inc.
668 Front Street
P.O. Box 2037
Teaneck, NJ 07666
(201) 692-0404
Fax: (201) 692-0663

This video follows the fate of the *St. Louis,* a ship that left Nazi Germany with over 900 Jewish refugees on board. They were refused permission to land in Cuba and in the United States and were eventually returned to Europe, where they found refuge in a number of countries.

The Exiles

Length: 116 min.
Date: 1989
Source: Filmmakers Library Inc.
124 East 40th Street
New York, NY 10016
(212) 808-4980
Fax: (212) 808-4983

This video looks at the impact that intellectuals and artists who were refugees from Nazism have had on American culture. It traces their fates through interviews, reinactments, and historical film footage.

From Survival to Adaptation: The Adolescent Refugee Experience

Length: 22 min.

Date: 1988
Source: The International Counseling Center
3000 Connecticut Avenue
Washington, DC 20008

This video is not only useful as a training film but also for general audiences. It gives insight into the particular problems and hopes of adolescents who are also refugees. It includes interviews with young people in the United States who are refugees from Afghanistan, Cambodia, El Salvador, Laos, and Vietnam.

Guatemala: Roads of Silence
Length: 59 min.
Date: 1988
Source: Cinema Guild
1697 Broadway, Suite 802
New York, NY 10019
(212) 246-5522

This video gives an idea of what life is like for rural indigenous peoples in Guatemala who choose not to become refugees. They refuse to live under the thumb of the military and develop their own mobile communities in which they carry on their lives as normally as possible.

The Holocaust As Seen through the Eyes of a Survivor
Length: 30 min.
Date: 1989
Source: AIMS Media
6901 Woodley Avenue
Van Nuys, CA 91406

This video is aimed at junior high and high school students. It gives a general historical background and attempts to show the horrors of the Holocaust through the story of one man who survived it. It involves the audience through questions and activities.

I Miss the Sun
Length: 22 min.
Date: 1984
Source: Mary Halawani
151 Joralemon
Brooklyn, NY 11201

This is a personal account of life in exile told around family celebrations of Passover. The person at the center of the story is an Egyptian-Jewish woman living in Brooklyn, New York. Like many other exiles, she took her culture with her when she resettled.

In Prison for Freedom

Length: 15 min.
Date: 1989
Source: Refugee Voices
3041 34th Street, NE
Washington, DC 20017

This video shows what life is like for Vietnamese boat people who have been incarcerated in detention centers in Hong Kong.

Legacy of Tears

Length: 54 min.
Date: 1987
Source: University Film and Video
University of Minnesota
1313 Fifth Street, SE, Suite 108
Minneapolis, MN 55414

This video offers a comprehensive history of how the Hmong gave the Americans valuable assistance during the Vietnam War. It goes on to look at the problems the Hmong faced when they fled to the United States.

Let Us Tell You

Length: 30 min.
Date: 1988
Source: UNHCR
Liaison Office to UN Headquarters
UN Plaza
New York, NY 10017
(212) 963-6200

This video relates the plights of victims of conflicts in Southern Africa. It looks at the economic problems faced by the area's frontline states and the urgent need for international assistance. There is also a consideration of the prospects for long-term solutions to the region's humanitarian crisis.

Make a Little Difference

Length: 15 min.
Date: 1991
Source: UNHCR
Liaison Office to UN Headquarters
UN Plaza
New York, NY 10017
(212) 963-6200

This short video allows children from four continents to tell of their experiences as refugees and to give their advice on how to end the world's refugee problems.

Moving Mountains: The Story of the Yiu Mien
Length: 58 min.
Date: 1989
Source: Filmmakers Library, Inc.
124 East 40th Street, No. 901
New York, NY 10016
(212) 808-4980
Fax: (212) 808-4983

This video looks at the lives of Laotian Yiu Mien, who were refugees from Laos after the Vietnam War, and discusses the problems they faced when they were resettled in the United States.

Mozambique—An Uprooted People
Length: 30 min.
Date: 1991
Source: Refugee Voices
3041 Fourth Street, NE
Washington, DC 20017

This video looks at the civil war in Mozambique and discusses the refugee flows into the neighboring countries of South Africa and Zambia.

Namibia: The Challenge To Come
Length: 27 min.
Date: 1990
Source: UNHCR
Liaison Office to UN Headquarters
UN Plaza
New York, NY 10017
(212) 963-6200

This half-hour film gives a graphic and moving account of Namibian refugees' return to their homeland. It describes the challenges confronting them as they settle into a new life in an independent Namibia.

New Americans
Length: 25 min.
Date: 1980
Source: Coordinator of Information Services and Special Projects
Bureau of Refugee Services
1200 University Avenue, Suite D
Des Moines, IA 50314-2330

Though somewhat dated, this video is useful because it looks at the major cultural groups of Southeast Asia and the particular problems children from these groups have in adjusting to life in the United States, especially at school.

New Underground Railroad
Length: 30 min.
Date: 1983
Source: Indiana University
Audio-Visual Center
Bloomington, IN 47405

This video follows a Salvadoran family as they travel secretly along the new underground railroad to a place of safety in Madison, Wisconsin. A group of dedicated church people consider whether or not to break the law by offering sanctuary to illegal immigrants who are refugees from persecution.

Nobody Listened
Length: 117 min.
Date: 1989
Source: Direct Cinema
P.O. Box 69589
Los Angeles, CA 90069

This video looks at political oppression in Cuba through interviews with refugees.

El Norte
Length: 130 min.
Date: 1983
Source: Cinecom Films
7 West 36th Street
New York, NY 10018

This feature-length film is suitable for high school students as well as adults. It tells the story of a sister and brother who escape political violence in Guatemala, travel through Mexico, and enter the United States as illegal aliens. It vividly illustrates the dangers and disappointments such refugees face.

One Year Later
Length: 11 min.
Date: 1989
Source: UNRWA
UN Building, Room DC2-0550
New York, NY 10017
(212) 963-2255

This video looks at the difficult lives led by refugees in Jerusalem one year after the *intifada* uprising.

Open Window: Cambodian Refugee Family
Length: 46 min.
Date: 1990
Source: Georgia Mutual Assistance Association Consortium
535 Central Avenue, Suite 103
Hapeville, GA 30354

This video invites the viewer into the home of a Cambodian refugee family living in the United States. Through interviews, they tell about their experiences.

Pieces of Dreams
Length: 15 min.
Date: 1991
Source: UNHCR
Liaison Office to UN Headquarters
UN Plaza
New York, NY 10017
(212) 963-6200

This video was made as a training film by UNHCR for people doing fieldwork. It is the case study of a Mozambican family that fled to safety in Zambia.

A Promise To Keep
Length: 9 min.
Date: 1991
Source: UNHCR
Liaison Office to UN Headquarters
UN Plaza
New York, NY 10017
(212) 963-6200

A training film for people working with refugee children, this short video looks at the particular needs of refugee children. It also shows them to be like children the world over.

Que se callen las armas
Length: 46 min.
Date: 1989
Source: UNHCR
Liaison Office to UN Headquarters
UN Plaza
New York, NY 10017
(212) 963-6200

This video focuses on the problems faced by Central American countries resulting from massive refugee movements there in recent years. It looks at the various government and UNHCR programs working for refugees who have chosen to return home.

Refugees

Length: 25 min., 28 min., 15 min., 40 min.
Date: 1987
Source: UNHCR
Liaison Office to UN Headquarters
UN Plaza
New York, NY 10017
(212) 963-6200

This is a series of four films, each of which focuses on individual lives that are representative of those of refugees from their countries. *Africa,* a 25-minute film, tells the stories of two people—Seife, an Eritrean, and Lister, from South Africa. They recount their lives as refugees. *Asia,* a 28-minute film, focuses on the lives of refugees from Kampuchea and Afghanistan. Kol-som is a Kampuchean refugee living in a camp in Thailand; Afriday is an Afghan refugee living in a camp near Peshawar, Pakistan. *Central America* is a 15-minute film that follows Rufina, a Salvadoran, as she tells of her experiences as a refugee and of life at the Colomoncagua refugee camp in Honduras. *Refugee Children,* a 40-minute film, follows the lives of three young refugees. It listens to the hopes of Fatima from Chad, living in a camp in western Sudan; of Antonio and Maria, orphans from Guatemala who managed to escape to Mexico; and of Nhue, a Vietnamese girl who lives with her mother and sisters in a camp in Hong Kong.

Refugees in Our Backyard

Length: 58 min.
Date: 1990
Source: First Run/Icarus Films
123 West 93rd Street, No. 5B
New York, NY 10025
(212) 674-3375

This film deals with the migration of Central Americans to the United States. It looks at the causes of migration and means of entering the United States illegally. It considers recent legislation regarding the problem and the legal and humanitarian efforts to help migrants.

A Religion in Retreat

Length: 13 min.
Date: 1986

Source: University Film and Video
University of Minnesota
1313 Fifth Street, SE, Suite 108
Minneapolis, MN 55414

Though somewhat dated, this video gives a good background for understanding the persecution faced by Asian Buddhists, which caused so many of them to flee countries such as Cambodia in the 1970s and 1980s.

Samsara
Length: 28 min.
Date: 1989
Source: University Film and Video
University of Minnesota
1313 Fifth Street, SE, Suite 108
Minneapolis, MN 55414

This film is suitable for older high school students and adults. It explores the culture of Cambodia, looking at the effect of protracted war on the lives of the Khmer people.

Serving with a Purpose
Length: 25 min.
Date: 1990
Source: UNRWA
UN Building, Room DC2-0550
New York, NY 10017
(212) 963-2255

This video vividly presents a chronological account of the Palestinian experience from 1948 to 1990.

Since 1951
Length: 27 min.
Date: 1987
Source: UNHCR
Liaison Office to UN Headquarters
UN Plaza
New York, NY 10017
(212) 963-6200

This film tells the story of the UNHCR. It looks at its role, its work, and the causes of the evolution of the current refugee situation in the world, along with different ways of resolving it.

The Sun and the Night
Length: 26 min.

Date: 1990
Source: Indiana University
Audio-Visual Center
Bloomington, IN 47405

This video looks at the work of the UNHCR through daily operations at refugee camps in Thailand and eastern Sudan.

A Time To Weep
Length: 56 min.
Date: 1989
Source: Indiana University
Audio-Visual Center
Bloomington, IN 47405

This video looks at the plight of Ethiopians who have been displaced by the protracted civil war and drought in their own country and who seek refuge in eastern Sudan.

To Be an American
Length: 50 min.
Date: 1989
Source: MTI Film & Video
108 Wilmot Road
Deerfield, IL 60015
(800) 621-2131; (708) 940-1260

Tom Brokaw hosts this video of a television program, originally broadcast 15 August 1989, about the lives of Cambodian refugees successfully resettled in New England after fleeing repression and torture under the Khmer Rouge.

UNHCR: A Global View
Length: 16 min.
Date: 1992
Source: UNHCR
Liaison Office to UN Headquarters
UN Plaza
New York, NY 10017
(212) 963-6200

This video looks at UNHCR operations around the world and the ways in which it is dealing with the growing refugee crisis. It includes a look at recent successful repatriation programs.

Voyage of Dreams
Length: 30 min.

Date: 1983
Source: Cinema Guild
1697 Broadway, Suite 802
New York, NY 10019
(212) 246-5522

This video focuses on the Haitian boat people and their reasons for fleeing the regime in Haiti and attempting to enter the United States. It looks at U.S. policy toward Haiti and at life in that impoverished country. It was made jointly by Haitian and American film artists.

Voyage of the Damned
Length: 137 min.
Date: 1992
Source: LIVE Home Video, Inc.
25935 Detroit Road, Suite 294
Westlake, OH 44145
(216) 892-6826
Fax: (216) 835-9201

This is a feature film made in 1976, starring Faye Dunaway, Max von Sydow, Orson Welles, James Mason, Katharine Ross, and Ben Gazzara, among others. It tells the story of a shipload of refugees from Nazi Germany who are refused permission to land in Cuba.

Waiting for Cambodia
Length: 58 min.
Date: 1988
Source: PBS Video
1320 Braddock Place
Alexandria, VA 22314-1698.
(800) 424-7963; (703) 739-5380
Fax: (703) 739-8938

This video documents the work of the United Nations Border Relief Organization (UNBRO) at a refugee camp on the Thai-Cambodian border. It shows the living conditions of the inhabitants and looks at the prospects for their future. It also looks at the historical background of the refugee problems in the area.

Wall and Bridge
Length: 18 min.
Date: 1988
Source: Rhode Island Office of Refugee Resettlement
275 Westminster Mall
Providence, RI 02903

This video was made particularly for use in schools to help promote understanding between Americans and people from other ethnic and cultural backgrounds.

Women at Risk
Length: 56 min.
Date: 1990
Source: Filmmakers Library, Inc.
124 East 40th Street, No. 901
New York, NY 10016
(212) 808-4980
Fax: (212) 808-4983

This video was produced in collaboration with UNHCR and the Canadian International Development Agency (CIDA). It looks at the cases of three women living in refugee camps in different parts of the world and the hardships they must endure.

Yellow Tale Blues: Two American Families
Length: 30 min.
Date: 1990
Source: Filmmakers Library, Inc.
124 East 40th Street, No. 901
New York, NY 10016
(212) 808-4980
Fax: (212) 808-4983

This video is useful for multicultural curriculum at the high school and college levels. It looks at elements of prejudice against Asians in the United States through interviews with members of two Asian-American families and through clips from Hollywood films.

Glossary

assimilation Total acceptance of immigrants by a host society and their absorption into that society.

asylum The protection given by one country to refugees from another. First-country asylum refers to a country granting a refugee first or temporary asylum. Third-country asylum refers to a country granting permanent asylum to a refugee transferring or resettling from a first country of asylum.

asylum-seeker Someone who has fled from his or her home country and is seeking refugee status in another country.

B-status Used in Scandinavian and some other European countries to grant a form of temporary asylum.

boat people Haitians, Vietnamese, Somalis, Albanians, or others relying on ocean voyages in small boats to emigrate. Frequently such people are denied asylum.

border camp A refugee camp or settlement situated along the borders between a host country and country of origin.

brain drain Emigration of highly qualified persons, also known as reverse transfer of technology and transfer of talent.

burden-sharing Sharing of responsibilities by states in funding refugee programs or admitting refugees for resettlement.

carrier sanctions Fines or other sanctions inflicted on airlines or other transport firms for knowingly carrying international passengers lacking visas or other documentation.

citizenship Legal granted status as a member of a particular nationality, obtained through birth and registration or through a procedure of nationalization prescribed by national authorities.

deportation Act of sending people back home or to another country against their will.

durable solution Permanent settlement of refugees, whether through repatriation to their homeland, resettlement in a third country, or settlement in the first country of asylum. The term is used by the United Nations High Commissioner for Refugees.

early warning Attempts and methods to detect a possible refugee exodus and to take appropriate measures to avoid or minimize it.

economic migrant Someone who has left his or her home to look for better work and a higher standard of living in another place.

emigration Act of leaving one country or region to settle in another.

environmental refugee Person displaced by natural disaster, such as drought, deforestation, or other environmental degradation.

ethnic cleansing Forcible expulsion of one ethnic group from an area and their replacement by another ethnic group.

ethnic minority A group of people who share a distinctive culture, usually different from the culture of the majority of people in a region.

expatriate Person who leaves his or her homeland and establishes temporary residence in another country. Also known as professional transient.

expulsion Forced removal of legal and undocumented foreigners.

externally displaced person Someone who is displaced from his or her residence and forced to seek refuge across national borders.

family reunification Highest preference in many countries for legal immigration of divided spouses, siblings, or other family members.

feet-people Term used for emigrants from Central America headed north by foot and bus to Mexico and the United States.

forced migration Compelling refugees or other persons to migrate by massive coercion. May also refer to internally displaced persons moving as a result of political violence or natural disasters. Also referred to as involuntary migration.

freedom of movement The right to leave and return to one's country as well as to enter another country.

genocide The deliberate and systematic murder of one ethnic or religious group.

illegal immigrant A person who has entered a country without the proper legal documentation or permission.

immigration The act of entering a country with the intention of settling there.

immigration preferences Criteria used to select immigrants by host countries, e.g. family reunification, skills.

integration policy Policy to provide immigrants with equal status as citizens without their having to relinquish previous ethnic or other identities.

interagency cooperation Actions taken by international agencies like UNHCR and UNDP to work more closely together.

interdiction The act of intercepting boatloads of refugees and returning them to their homeland. One example is the U.S. Coast Guard program against Haitian boat people in the 1990s.

intergovernmental organization An international organization containing representatives of national governments.

internal conflict A war or dispute that takes place within the borders of a country.

internal migration The movement of people from one part of a country to another, usually for economic reasons.

internally displaced person Someone who is forcibly displaced from his or her place of residence but remains within the country.

international conflict A war that takes place between two or more countries.

international humanitarian law The laws and conventions that regulate the conduct of parties at war, including the treatment of prisoners of war and noncombatants or civilians. Also known as the Geneva Conventions, international humanitarian law is implemented by the International Committee of the Red Cross.

international migration The movement of people across national borders, usually for economic reasons.

international refugee law The laws and conventions that regulate the treatment and protection of refugees. They are implemented by the office of the United Nations High Commissioner for Refugees.

irregular migration A population movement, not regulated by agreements between governments, that occurs outside of the normal state-to-state migration.

local settlement The integration of refugees in the societies and economies of host countries.

manifestly unfounded asylum application An application for political asylum in which there is no credible evidence of persecution against the applicant. Sometimes referred to as abusive applications.

man-made disaster A disaster that occurs as a result of the actions of man, such as war, persecution, human rights abuses, and sometimes famines.

mass expulsion The sudden forced displacement of large numbers of people across borders, usually as a result of war or persecution. Sometimes referred to as mass exodus.

migrant worker A person, sometimes recruited, who is seeking employment for temporary periods in another country. Known also as guestworkers, contract workers, temporary workers, and *braceros* (the Spanish term for unskilled workers).

migration The permanent movement of people from one place to another.

minority group People of the same ethnic, religious, or racial background whose numbers are not large enough to form a majority in a country or region.

mojado Spanish term for wetback, a person who illegally enters the United States by crossing the Rio Grande River.

natural disaster A disaster that occurs as a result of natural causes, such as hurricanes, earthquakes, floods, and typhoons.

naturalization Procedure whereby the foreign-born can acquire the nationality and citizenship of another country.

nongovernmental organization (NGO) A private rather than governmental organization. A number of NGOs, such as the International Committee of the Red Cross and Oxfam, work with refugees.

nonrefoulement From the French *refouler,* this is a policy of the 1951 UN Convention Relating to the Status of Refugees that commits contracting states to not expel or return a refugee whose life or freedom would be threatened due to race, religion, membership of a social group, or political opinion. It does not protect persons denied asylum who are regularly deported.

orderly departure Official procedure for resettling refugees directly from a country of origin to a third country of permanent resettlement, e.g., Vietnamese from Vietnam to the United States. May also refer to a fixed departure schedule for legal emigrants.

persecution Unjust harassment, including threats of death or imprisonment, usually used for political, religious, or racial reasons.

prejudice Negative and unfavorable feelings about a group of people that are not based on knowledge or fact.

pull factors Forces in a country of destination, such as a higher standard of living, jobs, or freer communities, that attract people to the country. Pull factors are sometimes regarded as the variables that explain international voluntary migration.

push factors Negative forces, such as conflict, political instability, social inequalities, or poor economic opportunities, that compel people to leave their countries.

quota Number of immigrants, refugees, or asylum-seekers allowed in by a receiving state under their immigration policies. Usually decided on such terms as ethnic background, race, or nationality.

racism A belief that people of a certain race or ethnic group are generally inferior or superior.

receiving country A country that receives incoming refugees.

reception policy State policy regarding the admission and integration of incoming refugees.

refugee Person who has left his or her country of origin and has a well-founded fear of persecution if they return (according to the 1951 UN Convention Relating to the Status of Refugees and the 1967 Protocol Relating to the Status of Refugees).

refugee camp A temporary settlement established to receive and house refugees, frequently along the borders of the state from which they have fled.

refugee impact The economic and social effects in local communities of receiving countries that come from accepting an influx of refugees.

refugee in transit Refugee who is still in the process of flight from a home country to a country of asylum.

refugee participation The roles that refugees themselves might play in determining programs directed at them or in determining their own futures.

refugee-warrior Armed guerrilla who lives in or close to a refugee camp, e.g. Afghans in Pakistan, Cambodians in Thailand.

rehabilitation The reconstruction or rebuilding of a country's economy and social infrastructure after a war.

remittance Money sent home from abroad, generally by a migrant worker or other international migrant.

repatriation Returning a person to his or her home country. People can be forced to go against their will (forcible repatriation) or they can go voluntarily.

resettlement The transfer of refugees from a first country of asylum to a third country of permanent resettlement, e.g. Laotians from Thailand to the United States.

return migration The voluntary return of immigrants, migrant workers, or other persons to their country of origin.

root causes The underlying causes of refugee flight, such as political persecution or conflict.

rural/urban migration The internal migration of people from the countryside to cities, usually for economic reasons.

safe haven Temporary asylum subject to restrictions, e.g., Temporary Protected Status in the United States. Safe haven asylum may or may not allow persons to seek employment, housing, and welfare benefits.

sovereignty The right of a state to exist and to make its own decisions without external interference or intervention.

stateless persons Individuals who have been denied national identity documents or have had them removed. After World War I, the League of Nations created special passports, called Nansen passports, for such persons.

self-determination The act of a national group deciding its own political future.

temporary protected status Legal status used in the United States to give asylum-seekers of certain nationalities permission to temporarily reside in the country and to seek employment.

Third World The developing countries of Africa, Asia, and Latin America.

travel documents Passports and visas.

undocumented alien Person whose status does not meet a host country's legal conditions for immigration. Undocumented aliens are also known as illegal aliens, illegals, and irregular migrants.

unrecognized refugee A person rejected by a government as a refugee on the grounds that the primary motive for migration is economic. The term often refers to Haitian and Vietnamese boat people. The UNHCR at times screens the decisions of national immigration officials to determine whether or not applicant motives are primarily economic.

visa A stamp on a passport that allows a person to enter a particular country.

voluntary/involuntary migration The distinction between forced migration and all other types of international migration, including migration for economic reasons.

Acronyms of Organizations and Programs

ACNS American Council for Nationalities Service

AFSC American Friends Service Committee

AI Amnesty International

ARC American Refugee Committee

ARLP Alien Rights Law Project, Washington Lawyers' Committee for Civil Rights under Law

ASEAN Association of South East Asian Nations

BRP Department of State, Bureau for Refugee Programs

CDC Department of Health and Human Services, Centers for Disease Control and Prevention

CDR Centre for Documentation of Refugees

CIPRA Georgetown University Center for Immigration Policy and Refugee Assistance

CIS Commonwealth of Independent States

CMS Center for Migration Services

CPA Comprehensive Plan of Action for Indochinese Refugees

CRS Catholic Relief Services

CSCE Conference on Security and Cooperation in Europe

DHA Department of Humanitarian Affairs of the United Nations

EC European Community

ECOSOC Economic and Social Council of the United Nations

ECOWAS Economic Community of West African States

ECRE European Council on Refugees and Exiles

EU European Union

HIAS Hebrew Immigrant Aid Society

ICMC International Catholic Migration Commission

ICRC International Committee of the Red Cross

ICVA International Council of Voluntary Agencies

ILO International Labor Organization

INS Department of Justice, Immigration and Naturalization Service

IOM International Organization for Migration

IRC International Rescue Committee

JDC American Jewish Joint Distribution Committee

JRS Jesuit Refugee Service

LCHR Lawyers Committee for Human Rights

LIRS Lutheran Immigration and Refugee Service

NATO North Atlantic Treaty Organization

NCC National Council of Churches

NCHR National Coalition for Haitian Refugees

NGO Nongovernmental organization

OAS Organization of American States

OAU Organization of African Unity

ODP Orderly Departure Program

OECD Organization for Economic Cooperation and Development

ORR Department of Health and Human Services, Office of Refugee Resettlement

RPG Refugee Policy Group

RSP Refugee Studies Programme

RefWID Refugee Women in Development

SARRED International Conference on the Plight of Refugees, Returnees and Displaced Persons in Southern Africa

SEARAC South East Asia Resource Action Center

SAWSO The Salvation Army World Service Office

UN United Nations

UNDP United Nations Development Program

UNHCR United Nations High Commissioner for Refugees

UNICEF United Nations Children's Fund

UNOSAL United Nations Observer Mission in El Salvador

UNPROFOR United Nations Protection Force

UNRWA United Nations Relief and Works Agency for Palestine Refugees in the Near East

UNTAC United Nations Transitional Authority in Cambodia

USCC/MRS United States Catholic Conference/Migration and Refugee Service

USCR United States Committee for Refugees

WCC World Council of Churches

WEU Western European Union

WFP World Food Program of the United Nations

WHO World Health Organization of the United Nations

Index

Gil Loescher is a professor of international relations at the University of Notre Dame. He is an international authority on refugees and the author and editor of several books on the subject, including *Beyond Charity: International Cooperation and the Global Refugee Crisis.* He is the chairman of the Committee of International Experts for the United Nations High Commissioner for Refugees biennial report, *The State of the World's Refugees.* Ann Loescher has taught primary and secondary school and is the author of several books for children and young adults, some of which were written with her husband. She and Gil have two teenaged daughters and live in Oxford, England, and South Bend, Indiana.